No matter where or how we live, we face enormous challenges today: inequalities continue to deepen, democratic institutions are attacked and undermined, destruction of the environment increases apace and climate change is bringing us to a point where our very survival as a species is at stake. What does the tradition of critical theory have to say about the great challenges confronting us?

In *Transformations in Critical Theory*, Maeve Cooke seeks to renew and revitalize Frankfurt School critical theory in ways that will help it engage with key contemporary issues and challenges, while at the same time remaining true to its mission of identifying ways to create a better world for everyone. She seeks to foster communication between critical theory and other intellectual traditions, pushing it beyond pernicious forms of Eurocentrism and anthropocentrism and enabling it to expand and enrich its critical methodology and emancipatory visions. She urges critical theory to look outwards, beyond the epistemological and ontological contexts of Western modernity, and to investigate possibilities for better futures opened by this outwards movement. She also urges critical theory to move beyond certain kinds of anthropocentrism and adopt a more ecologically attuned perspective that acknowledges the importance of human relations to other-than-human beings and the ecosystems that sustain all life. Revitalized in this way, the mode of critical social theorizing developed by Cooke re-envisions individual freedom as ethically oriented, self-determining, self-transforming, ecologically entangled human agency, always opening outwards and towards the future. Such agency is constituted in interrelation with other-than-human entities, attentive to others, human and other-than-human, receptive to new and possibly unsettling experiences, and politically as well as ethically always on the move.

This bold work demonstrates that critical theory in the Frankfurt School tradition is not merely a static repository of texts that belong to the early twentieth century, now only of historic interest. Rather it is a living tradition ready to learn from other traditions, open to the future and capable of being renewed in ways that can help us address some of the great challenges of the twenty-first century.

MAEVE COOKE is Professor of Philosophy at University College Dublin.

Transformations in Critical Theory

For Niamh and María Pía

Transformations in Critical Theory

Decentrings, Openings, Futures

Maeve Cooke

polity

First published in 2026 by Polity Press Ltd.

Polity Press Ltd.
65 Bridge Street
Cambridge CB2 1UR, UK

Polity Press Ltd.
111 River Street
Hoboken, NJ 07030, USA

ISBN-13: 978-1-5095-7300-4
ISBN-13: 978-1-5095-7301-1(pb)

A catalogue record for this book is available from the British Library.

Library of Congress Control Number: 2025946888

Typeset in 10.5 on 12 pt Times New Roman by
Cheshire Typesetting Ltd, Cuddington, Cheshire
Printed and bound in Great Britain by CPI Group (UK) Ltd, Croydon

The publisher has used its best endeavours to ensure that the URLs for external websites referred to in this book are correct and active at the time of going to press. However, the publisher has no responsibility for the websites and can make no guarantee that a site will remain live or that the content is or will remain appropriate.

Every effort has been made to trace all copyright holders, but if any have been overlooked the publisher will be pleased to include any necessary credits in any subsequent reprint or edition.

For further information on Polity, visit our website:
politybooks.com

Contents

Thinking thought usually amounts to withdrawing into a dimensionless space in which the idea of thought alone persists. But thought in reality spaces itself out into the world. It informs the imaginary of peoples, their varied poetics, which it then transforms, meaning, in them its risk becomes realized.

(Édouard Glissant, *Poetics of Relation*)

Acknowledgements

Transformations in Critical Theory: Decentrings, Openings, Futures reflects a life spent in the orbit of Frankfurt School critical theory that began as an undergraduate student in the Department of Ethics and Politics at University College Dublin, Ireland, and gained form and shape at the University of Konstanz, Germany as a PhD student mentored by Albrecht Wellmer. The book has been twenty years in gestation, a long time by any standards. The lengthy process of generation (as it turned out to be) was enabled among other things by periods of research leave spent at Yale University and the University of California, Berkeley, by participation at the annual Philosophy and Social Science colloquium in Prague, by the critical interrogation and creative impetus I received through presenting my work to audiences at numerous academic institutions and conferences and by multiple contingent turns of event. More individuals than I can name contributed to the development of the thoughts that have found their way into this book. I am grateful to them all.

Its eventual emergence in material form was accelerated by two book manuscript workshops held at University College Dublin in 2024. Without my colleague John McGuire, co-host of the workshops, they would not have been possible. They compelled me to write the chapters for discussion and contributed significantly towards my subsequent efforts to clarify and sharpen my ideas. As well as to John, special thanks are due to the workshop participants: Ranier Abengana, Kelly Agra, Albena Azmanova, Lillian Cicerchia, Roddy Condon, Killian Favier, Sam Ferns, Sophie Foley, Iseult Honohan, James Ingram, Haikyung Kwon, María Pía Lara, Daniel Loick, Cillian McBride, Fionn McGrath, John McGuire, Lois McNay, Brian Milstein, Laura Jane Nanni, Brian O'Connor, Pat O'Mahony, Danielle Petherbridge, Roxane Pret Theodore, Clémence Saintemarie,

Martin Sauter, Jennifer Todd, Guilel Treiber, Camil Ungureanu, Philipp Wagenhals and others. Carmen Dege and Peter Dews were unable to participate due to illness but were there in spirit. During this period, several colleagues working in critical theory read and commented on drafts of various chapters. Special thanks are due to them too: Carmen Dege, Regina Kreide, Christoph Menke, Peter Niesen, Martin Saar and Ruth Sonderegger. In addition, Martin Sauter, as always, uncomplainingly read my drafts and criticized them helpfully.

As the book took shape it had a fairy godmother: María Pía Lara. Without her unfailing, tireless encouragement, careful reading and constructive feedback, writing it could easily have taken me another twenty years. In the final stages of revising and refining the manuscript, I have been helped generously and constructively by Kelly Agra, Laura Jane Nanni, Niamh Sauter-Cooke and Martin Sauter. I thank Gordon Finlayson for his swift assistance with a bibliographic reference.

I thank the two anonymous reviewers for their encouraging feedback. I thank John Thompson, editor of Polity Press, for his graciousness, attentiveness and patience. My gratitude is due, too, to Lindsey Wimpenny who played a central role in the production process, along with her other colleagues at Polity, especially Sarah Dancy.

I gratefully acknowledge the support of the National University of Ireland for a grant towards scholarly publication.

I dedicate the book to its fairy godmother, my faithful, generous friend and colleague María Pía, and to my beloved and lovingly supportive daughter Niamh.

My final thanks are to Martin Sauter, my life-partner and intellectual interlocutor, whose love sustains me and who continues to inspire and challenge my ideas.

Introduction

No matter where or how they live, humans today face ecological challenges of enormous magnitude and complexity. Environmental depredation through ruthless extraction of the planet's resources by humans for human purposes, extended and intensified over the course of industrialized modernity, has brought humankind to a point where its very existence is at stake. The anthropogenic dimension of these ecological challenges is particularly alarming.

This book explores ways in which critical social theories can help to address the challenges through tackling some troubling kinds of Eurocentrism and anthropocentrism. Doing so calls upon contemporary theories to look outwards, beyond the epistemological and ontological contexts of Western modernity, backwards towards the past of this modernity and forwards and upwards, investigating possibilities for better futures opened by this outwards movement. In other words, it calls for decentrings, openings and explorations of better futures in response to the anthropogenic destruction of our planet that has intensified, expanded and accelerated over the course of industrialized modernity and, as things stand, continues apace.

Traditionally, critical theories have defined themselves as emancipatory projects, concerned with realizing better lives for all humans, in corresponding better societies, by overcoming the prevailing socially produced obstacles to freedom and happiness (Cooke 2006a). As such they are ethical-existential endeavours that are politically engaged.

By 'ethical-existential', I mean human efforts to live a good life in an ethical sense together with others, human and other-than-human. The ethical-existential dimension is indispensable in critical social theorizing, although contemporary critical theories are sometimes disingenuous in this respect. However, those hostile to foregrounding the ethical-existential aspect of their theories inevitably rely on *tacit* assumptions about what it means to live a good life in a good society, whereby 'good' has an ethical-existential connotation. Hidden from view, the ethical-existential components of their theories are effectively protected against critical challenges by rival interpretations of the good, insulating them from the pressures of uncongenial ethical-existential arguments, which may be based on experiences unfamiliar, uncongenial or completely alien to them (Cooke 2006a).

This book addresses all humans on the planet, encouraging all of us to become agents of fundamental social transformation and inviting us to expand and enrich our perceptions of what change of this kind entails. Its interlocutors are primarily theorists in the Frankfurt School tradition of critical theory (including myself). My main concern is to decentre, expand, open and ultimately renew this tradition of critical social theorizing, which drew its initial impetus from the writings of Karl Marx.

Established in 1923 as an independently funded research institute, *Das Institut für Sozialforschung* (the Institute for Social Research) provided a base for a group of intellectuals inspired by Marxist ideas. In the footsteps of the early Marx, they sought to use a materialist version of Hegel's dialectical philosophy to identify and overcome through human action the obstacles to the free development of human agency generated by the capitalist system. Although, for the first cohort of theorists, many of Marx's early writings were not yet in the public domain,[1] like György Lukács before them they anticipated important elements of these early works, such as Marx's idea of alienated labour and emphasis on social transformation through theoretically informed collective action or *praxis* (Lukács 1972).

I am confident that critical social theories have something important to contribute to efforts to imagine and achieve a better future for all humans on the planet. To do so, however, they must reimagine and rearticulate their core normative concepts, above all their conceptions of ethical agency and, specifically, human freedom. I take issue with two aspects of the conceptions of ethical agency now dominant in critical theories, at least within the Frankfurt School tradition.

In Frankfurt School theories, ethical agency is typically conceptualized in terms of the free development of human agents in interactions with other human agents through participation in public ethical life.[2] The slogan made famous by Marx and Engels in *The Communist Manifesto* expresses this vision of ethical agency. They envisage a political association, beyond the antagonisms of the old bourgeois society, 'in which the free development of each is the condition for the free development of all' (Marx and Engels 1967, 105). My objection is not to their privileging of the free development of ethical agency as the emancipatory goal driving critical theorizing – indeed, I share Marx and Engels' view that universal freedom in this sense is its primary motivation. My objection, rather, is to two interconnected features of freedom as it is conceptualized in most contemporary variants of Frankfurt School critical theory. These features are not peculiar to the conceptualization of freedom as free human development in interrelationship with others; rather, they are characteristic of conceptualizations of freedom in modern Western moral and political philosophy in general. My book seeks to reconfigure the idea of human freedom in a way that eliminates the two troubling features I identify and, beyond this, to renew the project of a critical theory of society in the face of anthropogenic planetary destruction.

The first troubling feature is an instrumentalist approach, often coupled with a functionalist one, to the interrelationships between ethical agency and the material environments that sustain it. With few exceptions, contemporary critical theories agree that protecting or sustaining the material environments of human life on the planet Earth is an indispensable condition for meeting the goal of the free development of ethical agency. My objection is that protecting or sustaining material environments is held to be important primarily for instrumental and/or functional reasons. This leads to denial of, or disregard for, the ethical-existential significance of the particular normativity of other-than-human agencies and insufficient concern for the spheres of life that sustain all agencies. In this conception, 'sustainability' – or 'environmental stewardship' – is deemed necessary merely to ensure the material conditions necessary for ethical agency. This dismissal or neglect of the normative significance of the multiple, complex entanglements between human agencies and other-than-human agencies leaves no room for ethical learning through exploration of these entanglements. I argue, against this, that ethical agency in general, and freedom in particular, requires attentiveness to, and exploration of, the interrelationship between human and other-than-human agencies, *in which there is normativity on both sides*. I contend, further, that the relationships of humans with their material environments are important primarily for normative reasons: such relationships are not – or not just – a precondition for ethical agency but, rather, a constitutive component of ethical agency itself.

The second troubling feature I discern in the dominant conceptualizations of freedom is a reduction of the *source* of ethical validity to *human determinations* of 'the good', 'the just' or 'the true'. The result is a celebration of humans as normatively self-sufficient agents – as sovereign authorities in ethical-existential matters. I argue that this leaves no room for ethical-existential learning through relationships between human agents and other-than-human agencies and through human experiences of what is other-than-human.

Connecting both troubling features is a failure to acknowledge the ethical significance for human agency and, specifically for human freedom, of the complex entanglements between human agents and other-than-human entities and powers.

* * *

In 1931, Max Horkheimer was inaugurated as second Director of the Institute for Social Research in Frankfurt. Over the course of the 1930s, in a series of publications in the institute's official journal, he set out the elements of an interdisciplinary research programme for a Marxist social philosophy. In an influential essay that appeared in the journal in 1937, he named this 'critical theory', as distinct from 'traditional theory' (1972, 188–243). One of the hallmarks of critical theory as Horkheimer characterizes it is that it makes an 'existential judgment' on the capitalist societies of its time, identifying the obstacles they pose to human freedom and happiness (ibid., 239). In doing so, it draws on the results of empirical findings in the specialized natural and social sciences (ibid., 233). However, Horkheimer and his colleagues advocated a mode of critical reflection on society that aims not just to understand reality through theoretical, empirically based, insights; it also seeks to change it materially for the better with the help of these insights. In other words, to combine critical philosophizing with *praxis*. Reacting to deterministic tendencies within Marxism, especially from the 1880s onwards, which downplayed the role of theoretically guided transformative action, the theorists at the Frankfurt Institute endorsed the view, particularly prominent in Marx's earlier writings, that critical social philosophy in the form of dialectical materialism is itself an agent of social transformation. The early Marx describes critical philosophy as an intellectual weapon that becomes a material force when it grips the masses (2000d, 77). Its force is material not just in the sense that it helps to change the material circumstances of the lives of humans under capitalism; it is material also in the further sense that it arises from actual social struggles and articulates the needs and wishes of actual humans (1975, 209).

Horkheimer and his colleagues, while emphasizing a *praxis*-oriented understanding of dialectical materialism, also perceived the need for a renewal of Marxist theory in light of historical developments since Marx had first published his thoughts on the diagnostic and emancipatory capacities of critical philosophy. Above all, the confidence expressed by Marx in the revolutionary potential of the proletarian movement had turned out to be unfounded, necessitating exploration of alternative paths for bringing about fundamental social change for the better (Marx 2000d, 81–2). Furthermore, the validity of Marxist theory in general had been called into question by the troubling version that had become social reality in the recently constituted Soviet Union, serving as the ideological underpinning of a totalitarian regime.[3] Nonetheless, Horkheimer and his colleagues remained faithful to the general method of dialectical materialism and continued to endorse its emancipatory aims.

Much has happened since Horkheimer and his colleagues initiated their empirically supported, *praxis*-oriented programme for social critique in the 1930s. In the decades since then, Frankfurt School critical theory has moved in new directions. The linguistic turn carried out by Jürgen Habermas in the 1970s, culminating in his two-volume *Theory of Communicative Action* (1984/1987), has been paradigm-shifting, provoking further important developments, such as Axel Honneth's theory of recognition (1995). But despite significant shifts within the tradition, for the most part Frankfurt School theory has remained firmly within the Hegelian-Kantian framework of German Idealism from which Marx's thinking emerged. Recently, however, in the face of challenges from multiple alternative bodies of critical theorizing, such as feminist theory, literary theory, queer theory, decolonial theory, critical disability theory, critical phenomenology and ecological theory, Frankfurt School critical theory has begun to acknowledge the importance of lines of critique emerging from various other historical legacies. This has pushed it beyond its Kantian-Hegelian-Marxist origins, requiring it to confront its intellectual and cultural biases, including its gender and ableist ones. In my own case, it has made me aware of anthropocentric prejudices in my approach to self-determining human agency (Cooke 2023a, 119). In addition, Frankfurt School critical theory has been obliged to acknowledge its implication in colonialism and slavery (Baum 2015; Bhambra 2021) and to scrutinize the ways in which it has been complicit in the subordination of human and other-than-human agencies who do not fit its categories of a human subject.

* * *

Horkheimer contributes to the project of renewing critical theory by calling for the dialectical permeation and evolution of critical theories through collaboration with the empirically based natural and social sciences. The feedback loop he envisages between philosophical theory and empirical reality helps not only to avoid dogmatism and rigidity; it could also broaden and enrich the theory's visions of alternative, better societies. Furthermore, the feedback loop could fruitfully be expanded to include, on the empirical side, experiences of unfreedom, unhappiness and injustice by human agents in existing social realities. However, Horkheimer's programmatic writings delineate a critical social theory that remains closed in certain respects, inhibiting the unconstrained openness to unanticipated challenges and new impulses required for the reconfigured mode of theorizing I propose.

* * *

As the title indicates – *Transformations in Critical Theory: Decentrings, Openings, Futures* – this book envisages a self-transforming, forward-facing mode of critical social theorizing that is both decentred and open, in the sense of context-*expanding* and human- (as well as other-than-human-) transcending.

What do I mean by 'decentred'? My main concern in this respect is to decentre critical theory's normative perspective so that it overcomes certain pernicious kinds of anthropocentrism, which I distinguish from kinds that are relatively benign. The former are encapsulated in the 'exclusive humanist' worldview, a term I borrow from Charles Taylor (2007). Countering these pernicious kinds of anthropocentrism requires critical theories to engage critically with the European legacy they have inherited and with the Western culture within which they are presently situated. This raises questions about their relationship to their past and invites reconsideration of the Hegelian-Marxist philosophy of history, which initially provided a secure normative framework for Horkheimer's interdisciplinary research programme at the Institute for Social Research in the 1930s.

In the Frankfurt School tradition, the interrelations between past, present and future have been construed by theorists in different ways. Initially embracing a Hegelian-Marxist philosophy of history, Frankfurt School theorists subsequently revised and rearticulated it, while never repudiating it entirely. For, at its core is an idea that critical theories can never completely renounce: that the past and present harbour potentials for a better future. This means that critical theory's utopian projections of a future better human life for everyone, human and other-than-human, in a corresponding future better society, are not *abstractly* utopian; instead, they are anchored in potentials already contained within existing sociocultural practices, considered in all their planetary multiplicity and diversity. However, from the 1940s onwards, most critical theorists have been troubled by *teleological* interpretations of the movement of history, worrying that this leads to closure of the historical process. The openness of theorizing that I advocate in this book entails a non-teleological view of the historical process.

Just as some forms of anthropocentrism are relatively benign, some forms of Eurocentrism are relatively harmless. Rather than jettisoning their European legacy completely, this book invites critical theories to view their European intellectual history as a tradition that calls for reimagining and rearticulating in ways that are attentive to its 'poetry' (Glissant 1997, 9). By this, I mean the moments of poetry within history that transcend the prevailing interpretations of the past. This is how I understand Walter Benjamin's idea of the counter-historian: the writer of history who takes 'control of a memory as it flashes [*aufblitzt*] in a moment of danger', as opposed to holding fast to a picture of the past (Benjamin 2005). Thus, decentring does not mean that Frankfurt School critical theory must renounce its distinctive philosophical heritage or the Enlightenment values of freedom, equality and solidarity, which have motivated and oriented it from the outset. Rather, decentring should be understood as a demand for attentiveness to modes of knowing and being-in-the-world that are other-than-Western as well as other-than-human. This calls upon theories in the Frankfurt School tradition to be unsparingly self-reflexive, to engage with actual subjective experiences in their planetary multiplicity and richness and to be attentive to the 'citable' moments of their particular historical legacy (ibid.).

'Openings' refers to a critical-theoretical perspective that is at once context-transcending and context-expanding. What do I mean by 'context-transcending'? One of the distinguishing features of Frankfurt School critical theorizing is that the prevailing human perceptions of needs, interests and desires are not taken at face value. Instead, it allows for the possibility that its addressees may interpret their needs, interests and desires in ways that have been manipulated by social power interests, or otherwise distorted, for purposes that serve the maintenance and reproduction of the capitalist economic and social system. This means that subjective interpretations of reality are epistemically unreliable from the point of view of the critical theory's normative perspective. In Frankfurt School critical theories, furthermore, the context-transcending moment is set in dialectical relation to a context-immanent moment, which anchors the normativity of the theory's critical diagnoses and emancipatory perspective within existing social reality; sometimes they are anchored in actual subjective experiences and in the interpretations of needs, interests and desires that arise from such experiences (Marx 1975), sometimes in communicative competences and practices that are embedded as rational potentials within every human society (Habermas 1998, 21–104). This creates a tension with the theory's context-transcending moment, which it has not proved easy to navigate (Cooke 2006a). Chapter 3 proposes an alternative way of negotiating the tension that involves reconfiguration of the context-transcending component as *human*-transcending (and other-than-human-transcending), calling for a dual perspective on ethical normativity ('the good', 'the just' or 'the true'). It is important to note that 'dual' is understood not statically but dialectically; it designates a continuous movement between two separate yet interconnected moments. In this dual perspective, normativity is at once transcending of and immanent to human activity. It is experienced by humans as a human-transcending ethical power and is constituted 'in its reality' by human agents in existing societies. This ethical power is not generated by human activity, and it does not belong to any specific human agent or group of agents, past, present or future; nor is it generated by, and it does not belong to, any specific other-than-human agency. Incorporating this human-transcending (and other-than-human-transcending) moment into ethical agency, my book proposes an alternative conception of human freedom as self-determining, self-transforming and ecologically entangled ethical agency – a conception that breaks with the troubling anthropocentrism and Eurocentrism of the dominant pictures that assume or applaud the sovereign ethical will.

Context-transcendence is a diachronic movement backwards or forwards, retrieving what has been historically or projecting what is yet to come. By contrast, context-expansion is a synchronic movement outwards, towards what already exists in the present. In the reconfigured mode of critical theorizing envisaged in this book, 'context-expanding' means theorizing that endeavours to learn in ethical-existential-political matters through communicative engagements with the inhabitants of alien worldviews and cosmologies.

Learning in ethical-existential-political matters is *not* the content-neutral and non-normative mode of learning promoted by educational policies and practices in many places today (Stojanov 2017). Instead, it is an educative learning that contributes to the free development of human agency in relationships with others. Education in this sense, and the kind of learning that contributes to it, is a normative concept. Understood in this way, learning, like the project of free human development, is an ethical-existential-political enterprise. Given our contemporary situation of anthropogenic ecological depredation, this book emphasizes the importance of learning through communicative engagements with the inhabitants of worldviews and cosmologies in which human relationality is understood in ways radically different from the modern Western understanding – in particular, worldviews and cosmologies with very different understandings of the significance of the multiple, complex entanglements between human and other-than-human agencies. Learning through communicative engagements with radically different worldviews and cosmologies does not only expand and enrich Frankfurt School critical theory's ethical and political imagination; it also helps to decentre pernicious kinds of anthropocentrism and Eurocentrism within such critical theorizing.

'Futures' is plural in order to convey a theoretical openness to multiple imaginings of better human lives in better societies that could be realized by self-transforming, self-determining and ecologically entangled ethical agents. In their essay 'What is Critique? An Essay on Foucault's Virtue', Judith Butler endorses a view of critique as 'a means for a future or a truth that it will not know or happen to be' (2003; citing Foucault 1997). They contrast it favourably with views of critique that provide us with sure and already established standards for judging the ethical quality of any future world. My position in this book lies somewhere in between. It agrees that critical theories provide no secure standards for judging the future worlds they project; but it adds that they are not indifferent to the quality of these worlds: they envisage them as *better* worlds in an ethical-existential-political sense. This implies that they inevitably make judgements about ethical quality. However, in keeping with their self-understanding, they acknowledge these judgements as always open to revisions and developments. Moreover, they are receptive towards change through communicative encounters with others, human and other-than-human, and engage reflectively with the exigencies of changing historical circumstances and with the findings of empirically based research.

In sum, the envisaged mode of critical social theorizing involves openness in a double sense. On the one side, openness as receptivity to what is unfamiliar, unsettling or perhaps even barely intelligible, especially receptivity to radically different ways of understanding the significance of the multiple, complex entanglements between human and other-than-human agencies. On the other side, openness as disclosure of new, hitherto unimagined possibilities. Put differently, this book's call for decentrings and openings in critical social theorizing urges critical theories to be alert to the risk of biases and other limitations in their emancipatory projections and to alter their ethical-existential-political perspectives as they become aware of these limitations. In addition, the book alerts critical theories to the risks that they may be insufficiently cognizant of the relevant empirical facts, that they may be insufficiently attentive to concrete human experiences of unhappiness and happiness, unfreedom and freedom, injustice and justice; that they may be insufficiently attuned to the normativity of other-than-human agencies and that they may lack concern for the biospheres that sustain all agencies, human and other-than-human.

The decentrings and openings proposed in what follows may also be described as a concern to avoid ideological closures in critical social theorizing. The term 'ideology' is used in a modified sense of the concept of ideology operative in early Frankfurt School writings. In their analyses of socially produced unfreedom, unhappiness and injustice in the capitalist societies of their time, the early Frankfurt School critical theorists diagnosed a widespread lack of cognition by their inhabitants of the real facts of the situation. Theorists such as Horkheimer, Theodor W. Adorno and Herbert Marcuse use the concept of ideology as systemically generated 'false consciousness' to explain this (Horkheimer 1972; Adorno 1972; Marcuse 1991). However, Frankfurt School theorists have been less concerned with the question of ideology in their own practices of critical theorizing. The decentrings and openings advocated in this book foreground the importance of this question.

Transformations in Critical Theory seeks to renew and revitalize Frankfurt School critical theory in ways that foster communication with other intellectual traditions, enabling it to move beyond troubling forms of Eurocentrism and anthropocentrism and to expand and enrich its critical methodology and its emancipatory imaginings. From the beginning, critical theory's task was to identify ways in which humans could achieve a better world for everyone. This book seeks to show that contemporary critical theories can contribute to fundamental social transformation through disclosive critiques, which, in illuminating ways, reveal what is wrong with established social orders, enabling a perspective that things could be otherwise through their emancipatory imaginings of realizable alternatives. Concretely, they can point to cracks in the omnivorous capitalism system, which, as Marx and Engels perspicuously observed in their 1848 manifesto, demands constantly expanding markets for its products, chasing the bourgeoisie over the entire surface of the planet (Marx and Engels 1967). By pointing to chinks and fissures, apertures and interstices, contemporary critical theories can help to provide partial answers so that humans everywhere can imagine a better life for every human agent on the planet in their complex entanglements with other-than-human agencies, and work together to achieve it. It maintains that they can do this only through communicative engagements with other epistemologies and ontologies, based in other worldviews and cosmologies, seeking to learn from them in matters relating to a better life in a better society for everyone everywhere.

It will become evident as the book develops that decentring and opening critical theory is no easy task. There are tensions between the very idea of a critical theory as a socially transformative ethical-existential-political endeavour and the decentring and context-expanding movements it advocates. Among other things, critical theory's in-built context-transcending moment is difficult to reconcile with a concern to guard against ideological closures in its own critical practices. Moreover, its context-transcending moment makes critical theory tendentially epistemologically and ethically authoritarian, threatening its commitment to the free development of ethical agency. While the argumentative approach to philosophical criticism of society that I propose in what follows seeks to mitigate the risk of such authoritarianism, it may lead to epistemic imperialism, compromising its efforts to move beyond troubling forms of Eurocentrism and anthropocentrism. *Transformations in Critical Theory* does not claim to navigate all these tensions successfully; it claims merely to open some new paths that contemporary critical theories concerned with decentrings, openings and futures may wish to follow.

1

Frankfurt School Critical Theory: Openings and Closures

Critical theories aim to transform societies in ways that will enable everyone on earth to live a life that is good in an ethical-existential sense.[1] In the Frankfurt School tradition, such a good life is one of freedom and happiness.[2] Freedom entails equality and solidarity, two other central values within European modernity. Their interdependence is evoked by the famous lines from *The Communist Manifesto*, cited in the Introduction, where Marx and Engels envisage a political association 'in which the free development of each is the condition for the free development of all' (1967, 105). In our present situation of anthropogenic planetary devastation, such transformations will have to be radical, fundamentally altering the ways humans relate to themselves, to other agencies (human and other-than-human) and to the biospheres that sustain all agencies. I seek to show that Frankfurt School critical theory can contribute to the fundamental transformation of society, and to the fundamental transformations in self-understandings and behaviour this entails, provided it is open to fundamental transformations in its methods, normative concepts and own self-understandings. The transformations in question involve decentrings, openings and explorations of new possible futures for every human on the planet, in relationship with all other human and other-than-human agencies. These three motifs are intimately entwined. Nonetheless, in some of the chapters that follow one of them tends to be foregrounded. In the present chapter and the next, the motif 'openings' is to the fore. By this, I mean opening critical theorizing to learning through reflective engagements with empirically based research as well as with the subjective experiences of human agents in existing social realities. It also means learning from mistaken philosophical paths pursued within the Frankfurt tradition of critical theory, which have blocked learning, and exploring alternative ones. As explained in the Introduction, the learning in question is educative in a broadly Hegelian sense of *Bildung*, contributing to the free development of human agency in interactions with others. As such, learning of this kind is *ethical* learning – learning concerned with 'the good' or 'the just' or 'the true'. Moreover, it is always potentially self-transformative, involving reflective communicative engagements between human agents in which every agent may be changed because of it. It is expanded and enriched by epistemically and ethically significant encounters between human agents and other human agents, and between human agents and other-than-human agencies.

In the following, I show how the critical theory project developed by Max Horkheimer and his colleagues at the Frankfurt Institute for Social Research in the 1930s opened up possibilities for self-transformative ethical learning *by* philosophical criticism of society, especially in relation to empirical reality. Such learning had no place within the theoretical framework of the Hegelian-Marxist philosophy of history they had inherited. However, I also show how, towards the end of the 1930s, historical circumstances led Horkheimer to retreat to the theoretical safety net of the Hegelian-Marxist philosophy of history and the epistemic and ethical closures this entails. Since, for reasons I will explain, epistemic and epistemological forms of authoritarianism, and the ideological closures that typically accompany them, are a serious risk in critical theorizing, I propose an argument-based model of philosophical critique in response to it, which I elaborate in Chapter 2.

Horkheimer's research programme

In 1931 Max Horkheimer was inaugurated as second director of the Frankfurt Institute for Social Research. Over the course of the 1930s, in a series of publications in the institute's official organ of publication, *Die Zeitschrift für Sozialforschung*,[3] he laid out a research program for a Marxist critique of society. In a famous essay published in the journal in 1937, he calls the proposed mode of critique 'critical theory', distinguishing it from 'traditional theory' (1972, 188–243).[4] Traditional theory, as he characterizes it, refers to theorizing in the natural sciences, the social sciences and the humanities. In the account he offers, these disciplines, and the subdisciplines within them, have come to share a structurally identical conception of theory. In this conception, theory is self-referential: the relationship between theory and facts is viewed as a purely intra-scientific process, disconnected from 'the social life-process in its totality' (ibid., 8). Critical theory, by contrast, brings to light the connections between ideas and the totality of social life with a view to changing it for the better. Its goal is human emancipation from enslaving circumstances.[5]

Horkheimer does not dismiss the value of traditional theory. In his 1937 essay he cautions that indiscriminate hostility to (traditional) theory is a hindrance for those concerned with a rationally organized future society, by which he means a social condition that would make universal human freedom possible. For Horkheimer, such a society is impossible so long as human activity is determined not by human will and consciousness, but by the capitalist economic system. If there is to be any prospect of universal human freedom, critical theory must enlist the aid of traditional theory, especially the results of empirical findings in the specialized natural and social sciences (1972, 233). When doing so, it must recognize that traditional theories have their own legitimate criteria for truth, which are internal to each particular scientific discipline (ibid., 3). Nonetheless, although traditional theories can be good theories according to their own internal criteria of fruitfulness, they are ignorant of the real social function of science and disinterested in what theory means 'in human life' (ibid., 197). Only critical theory contributes directly to what Horkheimer calls the rational development of society. It does so by way of its distinctive combination of explanatory and utopian power. In a double movement, it both explains the course of history as the necessary product of economic mechanisms, and protests against the resulting order of things in the name of a better social order (ibid., 229).

Horkheimer attributes to critical theory a number of specific features. Taken together, they constitute a new kind of social theory that in his view addresses the inadequacies of traditional theory. For present purposes, this new kind of theory has three salient features.[6]

The first salient feature is a concern with fundamental questions about human existence – questions about the relationship of the individual to society, the meaning of culture, the formation of communities and the overall status of social life (Horkheimer 2018, 113). In his 1931 inaugural address Horkheimer refers to these as questions about the 'fate of humans' or 'the great principal questions' (ibid., 113, amended translation[7]). He implies that traditional theories are impoverished by their unwillingness to take a stance on such questions. By contrast, critical theory makes an 'existential judgment with a historical dimension' (1972, 239). By this, I take him to mean that it subjects human existence under conditions of capitalism to a thoroughgoing (Marxist) critique. Following Marx, it charts the development of capitalism from its initial emancipatory stages to its subsequent reversal into new forms of brutality and oppression. Critical theory's evaluative approach is, in the first instance, negative: it exposes the iniquities of capitalism and says little directly about the shape and content of an emancipated social condition. This does not mean that it lacks an ethical-existential *utopian* moment, although Horkheimer does not use this term.

In earlier writings I argue that critical social theorizing, however negatively articulated, presupposes a concern for alternative social arrangements that would foster ethical-existential values such as freedom and happiness (Cooke 2006a). In the Frankfurt School tradition, extrapolation of the concrete shape of the projected better alternative arrangements is typically left to the theory's addressees. Nonetheless, such theories have an inbuilt utopian dimension.

This utopian dimension is evident in Horkheimer's 1937 essay, most obviously in its postscript, where he invites imagination of a future society, consciously shaped by concrete human activity, that would enable the development of the potentialities of all humans (1972, 244–6). Although he identifies certain core elements of such a society, he avoids what I call 'bad utopianism' by doing so in a sufficiently indeterminate way to permit subsequent critical theories to rearticulate them imaginatively, tailored to the exigencies of particular historical contexts.[8]

The second salient feature of this new kind of social theory is a dialectically materialist perspective. In his 'Theses on Feuerbach' (2000e), Marx criticizes the undialectical character of all previous versions of materialism for failing to conceive of reality as the product of human activity and praises Hegelian idealism for conceiving of reality as humanly produced. Nonetheless he ultimately rejects Hegelian idealism because it conceives of productive activity abstractly, disregarding its sensuous character. Similarly, the early Horkheimer applauds Hegelian idealism for insisting on the interactive moment in the relationship between humans and material reality (1972, 245) and welcomes its efforts to develop human intellectual capabilities (ibid., 9). Like Marx, however, Horkheimer ultimately rejects Hegel's idealism for holding that the salient mode of activity exercised by humans on material reality is purely intellectual, taking place only in the realm of thought (ibid., 245). He emphasizes that critical theory follows Marx by adopting, instead, a dialectically *materialist* approach, taking as its object humans as producers of their own way of life in its totality (ibid., 244). This means that it views the constitution of the human subject as a dynamic historical process involving the material as well as intellectual culture of humanity (Horkheimer 2018, 113; cf. Horkheimer 1972, 144–5).

There is a further sense in which it is a materialist theory. It gives voice to human experiences of freedom and unfreedom, justice and injustice, in existing social realities (Hegelian idealism could also be described as materialist in this sense). Accordingly, critical theory follows Marx (and Hegel) in endorsing the practice of immanent critique, which grounds the normativity of the theory's critical diagnoses and emancipatory perspective in the needs, interests and aspirations of concrete human subjects in actual historical contexts. This context-immanent moment has a context-transcending counterpart: critical theory offers a utopian perspective that goes beyond the prevailing perceptions of needs, interests and aspirations, revealing them to be impaired by the structural and institutional features of the given historical context.

The 'bottom-up' method characteristic of immanent critique is important for at least two reasons. It reduces the risk of bad utopianism, especially utopian projections too detached from actual reality to have motivating power, and it allows for a critical approach that inhibits epistemological and ethical authoritarianism.

Authoritarianism in critical theorizing has an epistemological and ethical aspect; usually the two are entwined. The epistemological aspect refers to ways in which the theory denies or conceals the contestability of its view of what it means to know the truth or of the contestability of the specific truth claims it makes. The ethical aspect refers to ways in which the theory disallows challenges to its conceptualizations of 'the good' or to its specific arguments about what it means for humans to live a good life in a good society. In other words, authoritarian modes of theorizing categorically deny the possibility of educative learning *from* those they address. Since authoritarian modes of theorizing violate the normative idea of the free development of human agency and the educative, self-transformative learning this presupposes, they have no place in critical theorizing (Cooke 2005).

When a critical theory *conceals* the inherent contestability of its validity claims – claims to know what is wrong with existing social reality, how to address the problems it diagnoses or what a good life in an emancipated society would look like – it not only succumbs to epistemological and ethical authoritarianism; it is also guilty of ideological closure. Its concealment may be unintentional or deliberate. Irrespective of this, it results in a theoretical rigidity and dogmatism that is troubling epistemically and has unwelcome ethical-existential-political consequences. This too is a pitfall for critical social theorizing. I come back to the problem of ideological closure later in this chapter.

A further advantage, especially relevant for present purposes, is that 'bottom-up' approaches tend to focus on subjective experiences of unfreedom and unhappiness in existing social reality. When their critical perspective is expanded to include all subjective experiences in their planetary multiplicity and richness, approaches of this kind expand and enrich the emancipatory imaginations of critical theories and foster a reflexive, self-interrogating stance towards the normative assumptions underlying their critical diagnoses and emancipatory projections.

The third salient feature of Horkheimer's conception of critical theory is an empirically based, interdisciplinary methodology. It has been argued that Horkheimer's greatest intellectual achievement was not a single text or even series of texts, but his implementation of an undogmatic, non-positivist version of Marxism as a programme of social research (Brunkhorst 1985).[9] In his programmatic writings in the 1930s, Horkheimer calls for a critical theory that is based on collective inquiry in multiple areas, especially in scientific disciplines that have an empirical component. This means that it must organize investigations in which it collaborates with sociologists, economists, historians and psychologists, among others. He describes science as a storehouse of information about humans and the world that is 'one of man's productive powers' (1972, 3). In the same vein, he writes: 'every step [of critical theory] rests on knowledge of man and nature, which is stored up in the sciences and in historical experience' (ibid., 226). The scientific storehouse contains empirical facts that are building blocks for Marxist – and by extension – critical theory (ibid., 224–30).[10] Employing the most precise scientific methods, these empirically based inquiries not only supply critical theory with fundamental facts; they also provide the basis for revision of the theory and may help critical theory to develop new methods of inquiry (Horkheimer 2018, 118). Thus, cooperation with scientists in the empirically based disciplines helps to guard against dogmatism and rigidity (ibid., 119). Horkheimer emphasizes that critical theory must remain in constant connection with the material world (with 'the social life-process in its totality') and avoid advancing theses that are fundamentally immune from external scrutiny. He emphasizes that verification procedures are indispensable for any theory, and he is critical of theories that dispense with scientific, empirical support when they claim to present the truth, tendencies he discerns in the writings of Spinoza, Hegel and even the later Marx (ibid.). On the other hand, he is equally critical of any hypostatization of the empirical facts, insisting that the empirically based sciences do not have the final word. Rejecting the modern positivist fact–value distinction, he argues that, in critical theory, facts are not extrinsic to the human mind; rather, 'they emerge from the work of society' and are 'products which in principle should be under human control' (Horkheimer 1972, 209).

In these writings, a picture of critical theory emerges in which its hypotheses and theses are set in motion through engagement with empirically based inquiries. Indeed, Horkheimer states this explicitly, describing the research programme he envisages as the 'ongoing dialectical permeation and evolution of philosophical theory and empirical-scientific praxis' (1972, 118). In this way, in line with its dialectically materialist self-understanding, critical theory's questions about 'the fate of humans' become part of a feedback loop, in which they are drawn into the empirical scientific process; this may require it to modify its values and, accordingly, its substantive content. On the other side, the ethical-existential questions driving its concern for social transformation impact the empirical-scientific process of inquiry.[11]

This is one picture that can be extrapolated from Horkheimer's writings in the 1930s.[12] However, the matter is more complicated. On closer consideration, a different picture emerges in which the feedback loop is less open than it may initially appear. In this other picture, philosophical learning from empirically based research is constrained in at least two ways. The first, relatively benign, form of closure arises from its 'dogmatic' core. The second, more serious, form of closure arises from its allegiance to a Hegelian-Marxist philosophy of history.

Horkheimer's 'dogmatism'

The account of critical theory Horkheimer offers in the 1930s has a dogmatic residue that it owes to its Marxist underpinnings. On closer inspection, his programme is vulnerable to an objection similar to the one he raises against the hypostatization of the truth of empirical facts and the related tendencies he discerns in the writings of Spinoza, Hegel and the later Marx: it likewise advances theses that are fundamentally immune from external scrutiny. Some facts, it turns out, are not 'in principle . . . under human control' but are, rather, natural facts about the human species that have a foundational, unquestionable status (Cooke 2017, 62–4).

This ambivalent stance towards facts is also evident in the writings of the early Marx. On the one hand, Marx emphasizes that the human essence is a historically contingent product of social relations within a particular economic system. In his 'Theses on Feuerbach', he states: the 'human essence [is] in its reality . . . the ensemble of the social relations' (2000e, Thesis VI, 171). As such, facts about humans and their experiences are historically variant. On the other hand, he maintains that there are natural facts about humans, which define their 'species-being'. For example, in his fragment 'Alienated Labour' (2000c), he distinguishes the human animal from other animals on the basis of the human interest in free creative activity. Humans are distinctive among other animals due to their interest in production independently of physical need: 'Man produces freely from physical need and only truly produces when he is thus free' (ibid., 90). Marx elaborates this idea of freedom as the production of objects 'according to the laws of beauty' (ibid., 91). These natural facts appear to be historically invariant. On my reading, accordingly, the emphasis in his sixth thesis on Feuerbach must be placed on 'in its reality': the human essence may be defined in a general way in terms of natural facts such as a primordial interest in free creative activity or happiness, but *in its reality* it is the ensemble of social relations within the given historical context.

As discussed, for Horkheimer, as for Marx, human activity in the world is driven by an interest not just in physical survival but also in freedom and happiness. Both theorists appear to understand these interests as primordial, natural facts, with their origins in the human species as such. This explains why Marx identifies free creative activity as a natural fact about humans that is integral to their 'species being'. Horkheimer attributes to humans an interest in happiness, which he likewise characterizes as a natural fact: 'materialists [have always recognized] man's striving for happiness as a natural fact requiring no justification' (1972, 44). This implies that for Horkheimer, as for Marx, human nature is not *entirely* socially produced, but rather socially produced within the limits of certain natural facts about humans as a species. Paraphrasing Marx, its reality is socially produced, but its essence is a fact of nature.

Horkheimer's 'natural facts' constitute what might be called the 'dogmatic core' of his conception of critical theory. I take the view that this is not necessarily cause for concern.[13] Many critical theories rely on foundational claims about human nature and human sociality that are resistant to conclusive empirical testing. This is not to say that they cannot be tested and contested empirically, for example by ethnographic studies. But neither such studies nor theoretical speculation nor empirically based scientific research could ever finally establish the truth of such foundational claims. Rather than requiring critical theories to avoid dogma *tout court*, I recommend instead making explicit their reliance on ultimately unprovable assumptions about humans and human sociality, opening them to the 'soft' testing of the full range of natural, social and human sciences. Jürgen Habermas is an example of a theorist who does so. In *Between Facts and Norms* (1996), his critical theory of law and politics, he makes explicit the dogmatic core of the new legal paradigm he proposes: the idea of autonomy as collective self-legislation by human subjects according to insights they have gained intersubjectively. He maintains that his position is dogmatic only in 'a harmless sense', for it recognizes the historical contingency of the idea of autonomy on which the paradigm depends (ibid., 445–6). His remark reminds readers that critical theorizing relies on foundational ideas about what is important ethically and existentially. At the same time, it reassures them that such 'dogmatism' is relatively harmless when it is acknowledged self-reflexively and modestly, as Habermas does in this instance. From this perspective, the 'dogmatic' core of Horkheimer's account is worrying only if it is concealed from view, and if in this way (or in some other way) his Marxist view of natural facts is presented as the indisputable truth about the essence of humans, forever removed from the domain of questioning and contestation.

Horkheimer and the philosophy of history

There is a second, related, but more worrying respect in which critical theory is insulated against critical challenge in Horkheimer's programmatic account. Although he calls for the dialectical permeation of critical theory and empirical-scientific praxis, a closer reading shows that he sets limits to the ways in which critical theory can learn from empirically based scientific research (or, with the supplementation I propose, subjective human experiences in existing social realities). It turns out that, for Horkheimer, empirical findings in the 'traditional' sciences can never fundamentally challenge the epistemic validity of critical theory's ethical-existential evaluations of existing social reality. This is because these evaluations are grounded in the truth of Marx's theory and the Hegelian-Marxist philosophy of history on which it depends.

On this closer reading of Horkheimer's early writings, the dialectical permeation of critical theory and empirical-scientific praxis is weighted epistemically in favour of critical theory, whose methods of inquiry and information about reality can be enhanced by scientific research, but whose grasp of the rationality implicit in the contradictions of actual social life is, in the end, indisputable. This is because for Marx, as for Hegel, the validity of their critical diagnoses of existing social reality, and of the emancipatory message accompanying them, is underwritten by the movement of history, to which the critical philosopher has privileged epistemic access. In other words, Horkheimer grants Marxist critical philosophers an epistemically privileged position when identifying rational potentials for emancipation within existing social realities. By doing so, he blocks possibilities for self-transformative ethical learning on the part of critical theories that his feedback loop model in principle opens up. This is a regression, since, as I now explain, by opening possibilities for such learning, Horkheimer's research programme initiated an important development of Hegel's and Marx's respective views of critical philosophy.

Reason in history: Hegel

The core thesis in Hegel's philosophy is that reason is at work within human history. The *telos* of human history is individual freedom in association with others. Underlying this view of history is his philosophy of Mind or Spirit [*Geist*]. Reason is held to be sedimented in social practices and in deep-seated normative intuitions and expectations, which manifest in subjective experiences in the real world; it is released progressively over the course of human history through a dialectical process of productively overcoming contradictions, called sublation [*Aufhebung*]. Thus, both the contradictions and their sublation are necessary steps towards the actualization of reason in the world, which is interpreted as the progressive full realization of freedom. I take this to be what Hegel means when he proclaims in his Preface to *Philosophy of Right*: 'What is rational is real. And what is real is rational' (2005, xix).

In Frankfurt School critical theory, Hegel's thesis of the progressive self-realization of Spirit is frequently criticized for closing the process of history. Theodor W. Adorno's final chapter of *Negative Dialectics* draws attention to several unwelcome consequences of this closure (1973, 361–408). The nub of Adorno's objection is that Hegel imagines history as 'a space of pure immanence without alternatives' (Gordon 2023, 47). In consequence, the promise of the future is predetermined by the *telos* of history, which is the full development of human freedom; in addition, the evils of the past are vindicated as necessary steps towards this predetermined future. As Hegel famously writes: 'The wounds of the spirit heal and leave no scars behind' (2018, 387, #669).[14]

There is a further, less often noticed, respect in which the Hegelian philosophy of history effects a closure. Many commentators (including Adorno) notice that, for Hegel, the dialectical movement of reason in history operates independently of the work of the philosopher. Philosophy does not function to educate or to motivate. Its task is not 'to teach the world what it ought to be' (Hegel 2005, xxi). For such a purpose it always comes too late. Instead, it retrospectively sheds light on the process through which reality is formed. Philosophy is 'the thought of the world' – but a thought after the fact (ibid.). However, commentators tend to focus on just one aspect of this: the inability of the critical philosopher to change the world. Less frequently noticed is a further aspect: Hegel not only denies the power of philosophy to transform reality; he also denies *reality the power to transform philosophy*. He immunizes philosophical critique against epistemic pressures arising on the side of empirical reality that would oblige it to significantly modify or even abandon its ethical-existential premises. Horkheimer's call for the 'dialectical permeation and evolution' of philosophical critique, on the one side, and empirical reality, on the other, could overcome this limitation of the Hegelian view of philosophical critique. It could also overcome a similar limitation in the early Marx's view. In both cases, it allows for self-transformative ethical learning *by* critical philosophy through engaging with empirical reality.[15]

Reason in history: Marx

The early Marx subscribes to a materialist version of Hegel's philosophy of history. Like Hegel, he locates a rational potential within actual historical reality – a potential for the realization of a rationally ordered society in which the free development of every human would be possible. Moreover, like Hegel he asserts that realization of this potential is guaranteed by the dialectical process of history. And, as for Hegel, the theorist merely uncovers this rationality, bringing to light a potentiality that is already present. By contrast with Hegel, however, Marx views philosophy's interpretation of the development of history as forward-looking rather than backward-looking. His well-known eleventh thesis on Feuerbach expresses this succinctly: 'The philosophers have only interpreted the world, in various ways; the point is to change it' (2000e, Thesis XI, 173). For Marx, changing the world changes the role of philosophy, which is now tasked with offering enlightening explanations of the prevailing socially produced impediments to the free development of human agency and pointing towards the means of overcoming them; in addition, it is tasked with connecting its insights with actual experiences of unfreedom, unhappiness and injustice resulting from these impediments, thereby motivating transformative action. Unlike Hegel, therefore, Marx attributes to critical philosophy the power to change empirical reality.

However, for Marx as for Hegel, epistemic pressures from the side of empirical reality cannot change the fundamental premises of critical philosophy. At first glance, his 'bottom-up' approach opens critical philosophy to self-transformative ethical learning through engagement with the subjective experiences of actual human agents in the real world. He insists that 'critical philosophy' (later, 'dialectical materialism' or 'communist theory') is not a top-down mode of theorizing; rather, it is attentive to the subjective experiences of human agents in existing social realities. In the famous phrase used in his 1843 letter to Arnold Ruge, critical philosophy is the 'self-clarification . . . of the struggles and wishes of the age' (1975, 209). As Marx writes in the same letter, it does not 'confront the world with new doctrinaire principles and proclaim: Here is the truth, on your knees before it!' (ibid., 208). Instead, it develops new principles for the world from the existing principles of the world. In the same vein, Marx and Engels emphasize that communist theory is not based on ideas or principles that have been invented or discovered by some universal reformer; rather, it expresses in general terms 'actual relations springing from an existing class struggle' (Marx and Engels 1967, 95–6).

However, a closer reading shows that this is not Marx's position. The subjective experiences of human agents in concrete social reality can be mobilized by critical philosophy to change the world, but they have no *philosophically* transformative power. This is because the truth of critical philosophy is underwritten by a philosophy of history that guarantees the validity of its critical diagnoses and emancipatory projections. In other words, there is no feedback loop between philosophical critique and empirical reality, which I identified as a strength of the research programme sketched by Horkheimer in the 1930s. For Marx, philosophical critique, at least in principle, has the power to change empirical reality through enlightening the masses as to the real causes of their experiences of unhappiness, unfreedom and injustice. By contrast, subjective experiences are merely the 'raw data' for its critique. They do not have the power to challenge philosophical critique epistemically, not even in principle. Instead, critique proves its truth through the movement of history.

Horkheimer's retreat

When faced with the (genuine) problem of propaganda machines deployed by authoritarian political regimes in Europe and the Soviet Union in the 1930s, Horkheimer arrests the movement of the continuous feedback loop and retreats to a view of the truth of critical theory that mirrors Marx's view in the 1840s. It is noteworthy to begin with that, in his programmatic essay of 1937, Horkheimer does not *uncritically* take over the Hegelian-Marxist perspective on history, although he still subscribes to core elements of it. Thus, for example, he does not dispute the Hegelian-Marxist thesis that history is a process of sublating contradictions. Nor does he dispute the Hegelian-Marxist view that the end goal of history is a rationally ordered society in which all humans would experience happiness and freedom. However, over the course of the 1930s he loses confidence in Marx's view of the working classes as the agents of revolutionary change. By the time of writing his 1937 essay, he no longer believes that the proletariat's experiences of unhappiness, unfreedom and injustice under conditions of capitalism could be mobilized by critical theory to bring about the required revolution. He holds that, in the given historical circumstances, the experiences of the working classes provide no epistemic foothold for critical theory and cannot readily be marshalled for revolutionary transformation of society. The consciousness of the working class is epistemically impaired, in part due to propaganda machines wielded by authoritarian regimes and in part due to the increased availability of material goods, which are experienced by the proletariat as compensating for their negative experiences in existing social reality. Thus, Horkheimer writes: 'Even to the proletariat the world superficially seems quite different than it really is'; 'even the situation of the proletariat . . . is no guarantee of correct knowledge' (1972, 214, 213). Compounding this is the corruption of Marxist theory by power interests under communism in the political regime of the recently established Soviet Union, who distort it ideologically and use their propaganda machines to manipulate people's perceptions of their experiences. Perhaps for prudential reasons, Horkheimer makes this point obliquely: '[A] version of the theory which has the propaganda apparatus and a majority on its side is not therefore the better one' (ibid., 241). However, taken together, the epistemic unreliability of the working classes' understanding of their own situation and the ideological distortion of Marxist theory by the propaganda machines of the Soviet Union leads him to arrest the dynamic movement between philosophical critique and empirical reality he envisaged in his earlier writings. This is an evident tension in the essay, most noticeable towards the end of it. On the one hand, Horkheimer seems still to affirm the 'dialectical permeation' of critique and empirical reality, writing that the concern for revolutionary change 'will necessarily be aroused ever anew by prevailing injustice, but it must be shaped and guided by the theory itself and in turn react upon the theory' (ibid.). On the other hand, in the continuation of the passage his pessimism about the manipulative effects of authoritarian propaganda machines seems to gain the upper hand. Apparently retracting this possibility, he now appears to understand critical theory's role as a 'critical promotive factor in the development of the masses' (ibid., 214) quite differently. He writes: 'In the general historical upheaval the truth may reside with numerically small groups of men. History teaches us that such groups, hardly noticed even by those opposed to the status quo . . . may at the decisive moment become the leaders because of their deeper insight' (ibid., 241).

Here, Horkheimer seems to deny possibilities for critical theory to learn from the side of empirical reality, in this instance from the subjective experiences of agents in existing social reality. If this is so, it would put a halt to the feedback loop he envisaged. Not only that: he appears also to grant critical theorists privileged insight into empirical reality, at least in the given historical conjuncture, opening his view of critique to the objection of epistemological and ethical authoritarianism. It is hard to avoid the conclusion that when faced with 'the general upheaval' of political life in the 1930s, Horkheimer retreats to the epistemic safety net of the Marxist view of critical philosophy. On this view, as discussed, critical philosophy (later, communist theory) has an epistemic authority that cannot be contested by its addressees. Accordingly, by falling back to this Marxist position, Horkheimer responds to the (real) problem of ideology with an ideological closure of the new, more open and flexible, model of critical theorizing he had earlier proposed. However understandable, this is not a good path for the decentred, expansive and exploratory mode of critical theorizing that I advocate. At the same time, there is something to learn from Horkheimer's retreat. It is a response to a genuine problem that faces all critical theories. This is the problem of ideology in the sense of an epistemically impaired consciousness that is generated and reinforced by the prevailing social structures and institutions and dominant power interests.

Ideology

In critical theorizing, openness to learning from the subjective experiences of human agents in existing social realities is in tension with its practices of ideology critique. The reason for this is its concern for fundamental social transformation, entailing a context-transcending ethical-existential perspective that cannot rely on the prevailing perceptions of needs, interests and aspirations. As explained in the Introduction, all critical theories have a context-transcending moment in this sense. Rather than taking the prevailing perceptions of needs, interests and aspirations at face value, they question their epistemic – and by extension also their ethical – reliability. Indeed, they allow for the possibility or even likelihood that the humans concerned interpret their needs, interests and aspirations in ways that reproduce the social structures and institutions that currently prevent their free development as ethical agents in relationships with others.

The all-pervasiveness and entrenched nature of this kind of epistemically and ethically impaired cognition was a central concern for the early Frankfurt School theorists from the mid-1930s onwards. Alongside Horkheimer, theorists such as Adorno and Marcuse diagnosed a society-wide inability to perceive the 'real facts' of the situation due to the closed system that capitalism had now become (Adorno 1972; Marcuse 1968; 1991). Thus, Adorno argued that, under conditions of twentieth-century capitalism, the 'false consciousness' characteristic of bourgeois liberalism has been replaced by a closed system of illusion that left no room for any moment of transcendence or criticism (Adorno 1972). In *Dialectic of Enlightenment* (2002), Horkheimer and Adorno describe this kind of closed system in terms of immanence: the elimination of any kind of 'outside', claiming that the immanence of enlightenment mirrors the immanence of the mythic world.

The early Frankfurt School theorists used the concept of ideology to describe this all-pervasive, systemically generated, illusory perception of reality. Their basic thesis was that the capitalist system ensures its own reproduction through generating false perceptions. In Adorno's words: ideology is 'objectively necessary and yet false consciousness'.[16] In their view, the inhabitants of industrialized societies fail to perceive that the economic system, and the social relations that arise from it, create obstacles to the realization of human happiness and freedom; they also lack awareness that the obstacles include false perceptions of needs, interests and aspirations.[17] This explains the phenomenon of 'voluntary servitude', to use de la Boétie's famous phrase (2012), adopted by Michael Rosen in his examination of the early Frankfurt School theory of false consciousness (1996).

In earlier discussions of ideology as impaired cognition, I emphasized a further characteristic, particularly relevant for present purposes: ideologies *hide* their connection with socially generated impediments to universal happiness and freedom; they *conceal* their own closures (Cooke 2006a, 99–104; 2006b).[18]

Following the 'linguistic turn' initiated by Habermas in the 1970s and culminating in his two-volume book *Theory of Communicative*

Action (1984/1987), the concept of ideology fell out of favour among theorists in the Frankfurt School tradition. Habermas maintained that the process of desacralization characteristic of modernity entails subjection of ever more areas of social life to critical scrutiny. As a result, 'global' interpretations that bestow meaning on society as a whole are no longer sustainable; fragmentation of consciousness has replaced 'false consciousness' as a functional equivalent (Habermas 1987, 354). Further objections to ideology critique have been raised over the years. One is that it lends itself to authoritarianism, granting critical theorists insight into the evils of capitalism that is not available to those who do not embrace their particular emancipatory perspective. Another is a variant of Habermas' objection: ideology critique pictures the socioeconomic system as a self-interested, self-maintaining organism. In this picture, the socioeconomic system itself is held responsible for bringing about a condition of general false consciousness and is accused of doing so for the sake of its own interests as opposed to the interests of the human beings it is supposed to serve. The socioeconomic system is thus equipped with the attributes of a rational agent with interests of its own and an ethical agent responsible for its actions, against whom moral claims can be made. This kind of personification of the socioeconomic system has become increasingly implausible in modern societies, which are not only internally complex, but connected with a multitude of other societies in complicated ways.

In the meantime, some critical theorists have sought to address the objections of Habermas, while retaining and revitalizing the concept of ideology critique.[19] They have done so, for example, by recommending a less totalizing view of the epistemically impaired consciousnesses that is criticized. Cristina Lafont (2023) points out that, for many scholars working in traditions such as black liberation, feminism, critical race theory or de-colonial theory, the primary aim of ideology critique is not theoretical but practical. The point is not to articulate a causal explanation but to contribute towards emancipation. Accordingly, ideology critique is taken to be a practice that is equally accessible to all participants. This means that it is unwarranted (as well as outrageously paternalistic) to assume that the oppressed are generally unaware of their oppression and must therefore be 'enlightened' by the social critic.[20] 'Instead, the dissonant experiences and emotions of the oppressed are themselves an essential source of knowledge that can be used to articulate alternative frameworks to undermine the power of prevalent ideologies' (ibid., 391).

In my terms, this kind of less totalizing view enables critical theories to uncover the ways in which, in a specific historical context, social structures and institutions block self-transformative ethical learning, and to disclose new epistemic and ethical-existential-political resources for such learning. It also avoids the authoritarian moment – what Lafont terms 'paternalist' – in the early Frankfurt School view of ideology, which ascribes true knowledge of the facts of the situation to epistemically privileged people – usually to critical theorists themselves.[21]

Relevant in this respect is a sociological study by Jennifer Todd, which shows how the authority of epistemically and ethically closed structures may be questioned following subjective identity changes resulting from a confluence of factors that magnify over successive iterations. In her empirically based critical study of 'groupness', Todd shows how 'everyday identity change erodes the moral authority of "groupness", promoting new modes of reasoning and interrelations' (2024, 592). Groupness, as she describes it, is a complex multilevelled configuration with considerable inertia that hinders efforts to achieve and sustain a social order that would be better in (what I call) an ethical-existential sense. Its principal features are closed group boundaries, particularist group perspectives and constraining group identities.[22] Todd's concern is with changes in groupness and corresponding identity changes that contribute to substantive changes in the social order, while taking diverse, individualized forms. Her examples of everyday identity changes include breaching and blurring group boundaries socially and symbolically; challenging group norms and authority in friendships, partnerships and modes of childrearing; transversal identification and intermittent activism; new modes of everyday reasoning that lead to more universalist values; and everyday acts of kindness across boundaries (ibid., 572).

Todd draws on empirical data to demonstrate that these changes in groupness, though often triggered by conflicts, are a product of a confluence of factors, including everyday agency, that 'magnify over successive generations and in the end cascade' (2024, 583).[23] Highlighting the role played by everyday agency in furthering such changes, she shows how uncoordinated and dispersed practices combine to reconfigure social relations and create new pathways of understanding and moral interpretation (ibid., 576). Indeed, in her account, everyday agency is key to dispelling the repressive moral authority of groupness. It impacts by magnifying with successive generations, feeding into ongoing institutional change and creating a new moral common sense that leads to the collapse of group authority.[24]

The key point is that, on the surface, insignificant, banal identity changes *can happen* and, due to an accumulation of undramatic, perhaps at the time unnoticed, everyday intersubjective interactions, they may contribute to an erosion or even dismantling of ideologically closed structures.

In earlier writings, I too recommend a modification of the early Frankfurt School concept of ideology as 'objectively necessary and yet false consciousness'. I propose a shift in focus from *false* consciousness, which suggests that the theory has superior insight into true consciousness, to *closures* of consciousness and concealment of this closure (Cooke 2006a; 2006b). According to my proposal, closures are troubling when they remove contents from the realm of critical interrogation, leading to conceptual rigidity and petrification.[25] By doing so, they generate and reinforce static conceptions of the good life and good society that refuse to acknowledge their dependency on particular, context-specific values, fail to respond to their own constitutive exclusions and block attempts to rearticulate them in more expansive ways (Cooke 2006a, 78; cf. Butler 2000b, 268–9). I emphasize, however, that a concept of ideology focused only on closures is too weak for the purposes of critical theory. The ethical normativity of critical theorizing requires, beyond this, a concept of ideology that explains its negative impact on human freedom. Accordingly, critique of ideological closures cannot be a plea for conceptual openness, mobility, flexibility and creativity *for its own sake*.[26] Rather, it must consider these conceptual qualities necessary for human endeavours to live good lives in corresponding good societies, achievable only through fundamental social change. In other words, there is an epistemic-ethical dimension to ideology critique: it targets epistemic and ethical closures that are hostile to the free development of ethical agency.

Contemporary critical theories can learn in at least two respects from Horkheimer's apparent retreat to the early Marxist conception of philosophical critique, effectively abandoning a theoretical approach to critical theorizing based on an open and dynamic feedback loop between theory and empirical reality. They can learn, first, that ideology critique must itself avoid ideological closures: the validity of critique cannot rest on the indisputable truth of the diagnoses of society made by any critical theory, even if the theorist is Marx himself. For the same reason, it cannot rely on the security of the Hegelian-Marxist philosophy of history.

They can learn, in addition, that ideology must be confronted rather than simply ignored or dismissed. Horkheimer's retreat is a response to a real problem that arose in certain societies during the 1930s and impacted significantly on the emancipatory power of critical theory. Moreover, they can learn that the problem is perennial. Horkheimer responds to a problem of ideological closure that is just as relevant for the critical analyses of many societies in the twenty-first century as it was in the 1930s. Today, new kinds of authoritarian regimes, together with new kinds of information dissemination, manipulate everyday consciousness in ways not so different from Horkheimer's propaganda machines, although it may be harder to discern their manipulations and harder to resist and combat them. In recent decades, for example, there has been a proliferation of epistemically and ethically closed social structures often described as 'echo chambers' that impede or block any kind of educative, transformative learning. How should critical theories respond? While their responses must always be sensitive to the specific sociocultural and political context in question, my recommended less totalizing account of ideology in terms of epistemic and ethical closure may help to address the problem.

For example, taking a less totalizing view of the ideological effects of epistemically and ethically closed social structures may help contemporary critical theories to discern chinks and fissures that over time lead to the collapse of a particular structure, as suggested by Todd's study cited above. Moreover, it enables them to differentiate between degrees and kinds of ideological closure, helping them to identify cases where dismantling the structure is highly unlikely without fundamental structural and institutional change and cases where everyday agency is more likely to contribute to their collapse.

C. Thi Nguyen (2020) proposes a distinction between echo chambers and what he calls 'epistemic bubbles' that may also prove useful to critical theories in this respect. He considers both to be problematic social structures that impair cognition and reinforce ideological separation. He argues, however, that they are different in their origins, mechanisms for operation and avenues for treatment.

An epistemic bubble is a social epistemic structure in which some relevant voices have been excluded through omission. Epistemic bubbles can form with no ill intent, through ordinary processes of social selection and community formation. People seek to stay in touch with their friends, who tend to have similar political views. But when they also use those same social networks as sources of news, they impose on themselves a narrowed and self-reinforcing epistemic filter, which leaves out contrary views and illegitimately inflates their epistemic self-confidence. Nguyen argues that epistemic bubbles are quite ramshackle – they go up easily, but they are easy to take down.

By contrast, echo chambers are not easy to dismantle. They are social epistemic structures in which other relevant voices have been actively discredited. An echo chamber's members share beliefs that include reasons to distrust those outside the echo chamber. Echo chambers work by systematically isolating their members from all outside epistemic sources. They do so through a manipulation of trust, leading to epistemic inoculation. Their members are not just cut off; they are actively alienated from sources of counter-argument.

Both are structures of exclusion. However, epistemic bubbles exclude through omission, while echo chambers exclude by manipulating trust and credence. Nguyen's distinction helps critical theories to recognize that, even within the same sociocultural and political context, ideological closures can take different forms, for which different responses are appropriate. For example, while arguments (in an expansive sense) may help to dismantle epistemic bubbles, they are unlikely to have purchase in the case of echo chambers. However, even in the case of echo chambers, where dismantling may require fundamental changes to the existing social structures and institutions, individual members may succeed in escaping from them. As an empirical example, Ngyuen offers the case of a person who was raised by a neo-Nazi father in the USA, who was groomed from childhood to be a neo-Nazi leader and who, as a teenager, had a sudden rise to fame on white nationalist talk radio. In other words, they became an active and prominent member of an echo chamber. When they eventually broke away from it, they went through a lengthy process of self-transformation, in which they abandoned their belief system and rebuilt a worldview of their own. As Nguyen interprets this identity-change, the key factor was everyday agency in the form of acts of generosity, kindness and friendship shown to the person while at college by a fellow undergraduate. Such acts, as Todd's study shows, may cascade over time, leading to collapse of the given epistemically and ethically closed ideological structure.

In sum, a less totalizing and more differentiated view of ideological structures encourages critical theories not to give up when confronted with the problem of widespread ideologically impaired cognition, for not all the structures in question are completely impermeable. It also calls on them to distinguish between kinds of ideological structures and, in each case, to identify ways in which they can be countered or dismantled.

Ideological closures within critical theorizing

A less totalizing and more differentiated view of ideological structures may also help critical theories to lessen the risk of ideological closures in their own theorizing.

The main reason for this risk is their integral concern for better lives for everyone in better societies through fundamental transformation of the existing social structures and institutions. As emancipatory projects concerned with profound and far-reaching social change for the better, they are ethical-existential-political endeavours, conceptually committed to taking a position on the meaning of a good life for human agents in a good society. This emancipatory dimension inevitably involves more or less determinate projections of a better life, in a corresponding better society, than is deemed to be possible under the prevailing social conditions (Cooke 2006a). Committed to taking a specific ethical-existential position on the meaning of a good life, whether in formal or substantive terms, they inevitably exclude other such positions. In earlier writings, in my critical discussions of Ernesto Laclau's radical politics and theory of ideology, I describe this as 'metaphysical closure'. This kind of closure, while relatively harmless per se, leads easily to ideological closure. It makes critical theories prone to theoretical rigidity and inflexibility and, with this, epistemological and ethical authoritarianism. Since such authoritarianism is at odds with their emancipatory self-understanding, generally accompanied by an emphasis on individual human freedom, critical theories tend to conceal any authoritarian moment in their own theorizing. In this respect, the danger of ideological closure is endemic to critical theorizing.

In the Frankfurt School tradition, there is an additional reason why there is a high risk of epistemological and ethical authoritarianism and, alongside this, ideological closure. The risk is due to the immanent approach to criticism of society that Marx takes over from Hegel. As discussed earlier in this chapter, the immanent approach anchors the normativity of critique in rational potentials already existing within social reality that manifest in subjective experiences. This is why Marx insists that critical philosophy is not a top-down mode of theorizing; it merely articulates in an illuminating way the subjective experiences of human agents in the real world, which are in turn expressions of the movement of reason in history. As he puts it, it develops new principles for the world from the existing principles of the world. Evidently, from the point of view of the decentring, expansive and exploratory mode of critical theorizing that I advocate, such a 'bottom-up' approach is congenial, for it potentially opens critical theories to self-transformative ethical learning *from* the subjective experiences of their addressees. In addition, by grounding their ethical-existential-political dimension in the subjective experiences of human agents in existing social realities, critical theories are better able to lessen the risk of simply imposing their idiosyncratic ideas about the good life and good society on those they address (and, hence, lessen the risk of epistemic and ethical authoritarianism). They are also better able to avoid 'bad utopianism' in the form of abstract projections of the good life and good society that lack motivating power due to their failure to connect with the needs, interests and aspirations of the human agents they address.

However, the discussion so far has shown that openness to self-transformative ethical learning by critical theories does not automatically follow from a theoretical approach that starts with subjective experiences in existing social realities. Marx's view of critical philosophy served as my example. In Marx's view, as discussed, such experiences can be *mobilized* by critical philosophy to change the world, but they have no *philosophically* transformative power. The truth of critical philosophy is guaranteed in advance, immunized against epistemic pressures on the side of empirical reality, by a philosophy of history that guarantees the validity of its critical diagnoses and emancipatory projections. This means effectively that critical philosophy cannot learn in an ethical-existential-political sense from empirical observations and findings. I concluded, accordingly, that Marx's theorizing fails to make good the promise of self-transformative ethical learning on the side of critical philosophy that is implicit in his experience-based approach. I showed Horkheimer's theory, as presented in the final pages of his 1937 essay, to be open to the same objection.

But critical theories must also be alert to the risks involved in overreliance on empirical findings, including subjective experiences of unfreedom, unhappiness and injustice in actual social reality. *Unmediated* appeal to empirical data or phenomena gives rise to the same kind of risk of authoritarianism and ideological closure, for it denies or obscures the interpretative role of critical theories.

Critical theories *interpret* actual subjective experiences; they do not – and in my view cannot – access them directly. Moreover, their interpretations are always at least two steps removed from the experiences in question. This complex mediation of experience through interpretation takes various forms. Some theorists interpret subjective experiences that the human subjects concerned have communicated to them directly. For example, Angela Davis' critical-theoretical writings on the US prison system (2003) are based on research that includes interviews with incarcerated women. In this case, the incarcerated women communicate their interpretations of their experiences to the critical theorist (i.e. Davis), who then interprets them. Other critical theorists interpret subjective experiences based on empirical research in the social sciences. In the early 1990s, Axel Honneth endorsed this kind of 'bottom-up' approach when he called for a mode of critical theorizing that is normatively anchored in existing social reality in subjective interests or moral experiences that serve as a pre-theoretical court of appeal [*vorwissenschaftliche Instanz*] (1994, 255).[27] Todd's empirically based critical study of the moral authority of 'groupness', discussed earlier, could also be described in these terms. In this case, group members communicate their experiences to the researcher (i.e. Todd), who undertakes a qualitative analysis of them, interpreting their moral and political implications. A further variant is critical-theoretical interpretations of already interpreted experiences in films, novels, paintings and other aesthetic media. For example, in her critical reflections on the public sphere, María Pía Lara (2020) draws on a wide range of films, dissecting cinematic images of women's struggles and their oppression in order to develop a concept of the feminist social imaginary as a space for thinking through possibilities for emancipatory social transformation. In this case, the film-makers interpret women's experiences, and the theorist (i.e. Lara) interprets the films' interpretations. I myself, in later chapters, reflect theoretically on empirically based ethnographic studies of subjective experiences among indigenous peoples in Peru. In this case, the anthropologist who conducts the study interprets the experiences of indigenous human agents (often on the basis of the indigenous agents' own interpretations of their experiences) and I interpret the anthropologists' interpretations. The key point in all these examples is that critical theories do not re-present subjective experiences in an unmediated way; instead, they always interpret experiences and, in many cases, they interpret interpretations of experiences. At issue, therefore, is not the epistemic significance, or even reliability, of the subjective experiences of human agents within existing reality but, rather, the validity of the theorist's interpretations of (interpretations of) these experiences. The two questions are separate, although closely connected. For, even if subjective experiences are held to be epistemically reliable, which I dispute, it does not follow that the theory's interpretations of the (interpretations of the) experiences are epistemically reliable.[28] In other words, it is one thing to consider subjective experiences to be reliable forms of knowledge (although I do not take this view); it is another to hold that critical theories can rely on them as justification for the validity of the critiques of society they make on the basis of them. Put differently again, knowledge acquired experientially in particular situations may be epistemically significant for the agents concerned; indeed, it may even be considered reliable by some critical theories. Nonetheless, it cannot guarantee the epistemic validity of the ethical-existential-political claims the theories make on the basis of it.

The inherently interpretative character of critical theory's analyses of empirical reality means that these analyses are always contestable by other interpretations. This is why I maintain that critical theories cannot dispense with an *argumentative* approach to their criticisms of society. However, I also hold that argumentation must be understood in a decentring, expansive, exploratory sense. In the next chapter, I consider some ways in which Frankfurt School critical theories could develop a conception of argumentation along these lines.

2

Philosophical Criticism of Society: Closures and Openings

In critical theorizing, the risk of epistemological and ethical authoritarianism is high – and with it the pitfalls of ideological closure. This became evident in Chapter 1. The lesson I draw is that decentring, expansive and exploratory critical theories must take an argumentative approach to their philosophical criticism of society. However, they should do so in an expansive sense of argumentation that involves ongoing renewal of their conceptual and methodological toolkits. A potential difficulty here is that critical theories that are conceptually and methodologically innovative often downplay the importance of reasoned argumentation – in some cases they even disparage it.

On occasion, Adorno leans in this direction. At times, he seems to ground morality in a preconceptual, nonlinguistic knowledge of inhumanity and evil. As Gordon Finlayson writes, in certain places he 'appears to think that we can *reliably know* that the world is false or radically evil' (Finlayson 2002, 8; my emphasis). Textual evidence to support this reading includes passages where Adorno claims that morality has its basis in 'the practical abhorrence of the unbearable physical agony to which individuals are exposed' (1973, 365). Or again, where he insists that we know very well what the inhuman is (2000a, 175). The knowledge to which he refers here is not in the first instance linguistic, nor can it ever be fully expressed linguistically, or at least not in propositional language; it is, rather, a bodily sensation. Moreover, it is not something that requires justification by moral philosophers. Indeed, he holds that in some cases it would be immoral to demand such justification. He writes: 'No man should be tortured; there should be no concentration camps . . . The lines are true as an impulse, as a reaction to the news that torture is going on somewhere. They must not be rationalized; as an abstract principle they would fall promptly into the bad infinities of derivation and validity' (1973, 285). Similarly, he maintains that it would be an outrage [*Frevel*] to demand philosophical justification of the 'new categorical imperative' imposed by Hitler: that Auschwitz should never be repeated (ibid., 365).[1]

Finlayson observes further that this preconceptual, intuitive knowledge of the world may take the form of a mood of despair at the horror of the world or a shudder, a kind of involuntary fright at the awfulness of reality. He characterizes these moral reactions as 'ineffable insights'. According to Finlayson, their value resides in the experience of being shown something that is more than can be put into words, a surplus that Adorno takes as the promise that the realm of the possible outstrips the real. On Finlayson's reading of Adorno's writings, actual human experiences within existing reality are shot through with fragments of normativity that point beyond the landscape of our current suffering.

Peter Gordon (2023) makes a similar point in his discussion of Adorno's idea of 'emphatic' experiences, to which he attributes the quality of 'material epiphanies'. Experiences that qualify as true or emphatic offer a glimpse of things in their singularity. In such experiences, we 'really come to know something . . . our thinking is fulfilled, instead of simply feeding off the already given and socially approved view of the object'. Experiences of this kind are a kind of collision or explosion. The 'sudden and illuminating character of what is called intuition' springs from them (ibid., 116; citing Adorno 2017b, 98). In Gordon's words: 'In such moments of emphatic experience we are afforded a glimpse of the non-identical' (ibid.). They provide a normative standard against which we can measure the distortion of our experience in the everyday sense (ibid., 117).

In these passages Adorno can be read as casting doubt on the 'linguistic turn' of twentieth-century Western philosophy (Rorty 1992), suggesting that it leads to a privileging of language and reason over the body and affect that impoverishes philosophical criticism of society. He points in the direction of a more encompassing conception of philosophical knowledge that includes prelinguistic and non-propositional modes of knowing and also, potentially, other-than-human modes.

I share the view that Adorno's writings contribute towards developing more open and richer conceptions of philosophical knowledge and social criticism. I contend, nonetheless, that for the decentring, expansive, exploratory mode of critical theorizing I advocate, his appeal to prelinguistic and non-propositional knowledge, together with his emphasis on the body and affect, must be integrated into an approach to philosophical criticism of society that is argumentation-based. Otherwise, his approach is vulnerable to objections of epistemological and ethical authoritarianism and, alongside this, ideological closure – the very objections I raised against Horkheimer in Chapter 1. There, I pointed out that it is one thing to consider subjective experiences to be reliable forms of knowledge (although I do not); it is another to hold that critical theories can rely on them as justification for the validity of the criticisms of society they make on the basis of them.

The pitfalls of an affect-based approach that bypasses philosophical argumentation are evident in Adorno's reading of Kafka's stories. In his essay 'Notes on Kafka' (1982), he offers an illuminating reading of Kafka's stories, but one that effectively blocks the possibility of counter-readings (Cooke 2014a).

Adorno's reading is commendable for insightfully drawing attention to the ways in which Kafka's prose writings speak to their readers on a bodily level, how they evoke a sense of horror, making them *feel* the desolate condition of humankind as capitalism becomes increasingly instrumentalizing and reifying. Adorno writes: 'He over whom Kafka's wheels have passed, has lost forever both any peace with the world and any chance of consoling himself with the judgment that the way of the world is bad' (1977, 191). In other words, he shows how Kafka's stories *perform* criticism of society. Insightfully, too, against facile attempts to extract ethical-existential or ethical-political meanings from them, Adorno shows how their readers are at once invited to interpret their 'message' and prevented from doing so; as he puts it, in Kafka, every sentence 'says "interpret me", and none will permit it' (1982, 246). In other words, he notices astutely that Kafka's stories collapse aesthetic distance – they draw their readers into their imaginary worlds – while at the same time frustrating their efforts to make rational sense of what they find there. However, alongside his illuminating interpretation of Kafka's stories, Adorno tacitly seems to make a further, stronger, claim. He appears to claim that the affectively charged, somatic power of Kafka's stories is *undermined* by attempts by readers to reflect on their meaning. In consequence, he inhibits readers of his analyses of these stories from offering alternative readings that run counter to his own. For example, he discounts from the outset readings in which Kafka's stories at once invite *and permit* their readers to engage in ethical-existential-political interpretations (as I mentioned, he insists that they invite and *prevent* such interpretations). This leads him to categorically deny the validity of ethical-existential-political interpretations offered by readers in response to their experiences of Kafka's stories (Cooke 2014a, 636). A philosophical analysis that makes itself the sole judge of what counts as a valid analysis (in this case of a literary text) is not only epistemologically authoritarian; it testifies to a view of philosophical criticism that is closed to learning through communicative engagement with interpretations that might not accord with its own.

I maintain, therefore, that critical theorizing of the kind I envisage should *not* follow Adorno on those occasions when he distances himself from philosophical argumentation, for this easily leads to authoritarianism and ideological closure.[2] Instead, it should embrace an argumentative approach to its criticisms of society – in a decentring, expansive, exploratory sense of argumentation.

An argumentative approach is necessary not only to guard against dangers to which critical theories are prone; it is necessary in addition for the transformative dimension of critical theorizing as I understand it. I conceive of the educative learning required for self-transformations of human agents, social institutions and critical theorizing as a reciprocal intersubjective process of communicative exchange. In analogy to the model suggested by Horkheimer's research programme, discussed in the previous chapter, I view it as a perpetual feedback loop, in which all participants in the communicative exchange are engaged in a continuous dialectical process. In this dialectical movement, each agency may be changed for the better and, in being so changed, may contribute to changing the other agencies for the better. This is one part of what I mean by argumentation in an expansive sense. I say more about this reciprocally transformative process in Chapter 7. The other part of what I mean is the importance for critical theories of constantly expanding and renewing their conceptual and methodological toolkits. This is my main concern in the present chapter.

Drawing for inspiration on resources both within the Frankfurt School tradition and outside it, I give examples of interventions that creatively challenge orthodox views of philosophical argumentation. My aim here is to encourage further exploration of possibilities for conceptual and methodological transformations that could expand and renew philosophical criticism of society. Some of these interventions *perform* or *stage* criticism of society as opposed to presenting a reasoned argument, articulated in propositional language. Others use argumentative reasoning to draw attention to the socially critical power of performances and stagings in the aesthetic domain (broadly understood). Others again challenge prevailing conceptions of the practice of argumentation as an agonistic exchange of reasoned arguments. Alongside these I offer examples of approaches to critical theorizing that employ methods not traditionally part of the Frankfurt School lexicon, such as braiding, translating, figuring and phenomenological attentiveness. I view these as regenerative impulses that could open up and revitalize critical theorizing. At the same time, I emphasize that they must find a place within an *argumentative* approach to philosophical criticism of society that fosters reciprocal learning of an ethically educative, self-transformative kind – moreover, learning by all parties involved in the communicative exchange. Learning by all parties requires critical theorists to clarify the meaning of their critical analyses and utopian projections, when called upon to do so, and give reasons for them to their interlocutors. This also holds for criticisms of society that are performed or staged rather than presented as reasoned arguments. Here too, critical theories must be willing to elucidate in propositional language the ethical-existential-political import of their performances or stagings and to do so in communicative engagement with their interlocutors.

The indispensability of arguments formulated in propositional language explains why learning, as I construe it, is ultimately an inter*subjective* process: only human agents can argue, since (as far as we know) only human agents can reason with each other in propositional language. In consequence, my argumentative approach is anthropocentric but, as I explain in Chapter 4, in a relatively benign sense.

In sum, I maintain that mitigating the risks of authoritarianism and ideological closure requires, at a minimum, efforts to render intelligible to one's interlocutors the reasons why one makes certain claims, in ways that permit disagreement and, if necessary, further questioning. I hold, furthermore, that this calls upon those involved to articulate their arguments in linguistic form, at least partly and at least at some point. However, it is not always easy to meet this demand. At any given time, in any given place, the vocabularies human agents have at their disposal may prove inadequate for articulating their experiences in ways that are linguistically intelligible to other humans, especially if they inhabit a very different worldview or cosmology. It will become evident in the following chapters that the challenge of avoiding authoritarianism and ideological closure is increased considerably when communicative engagements involve either relationships with other-than-human agencies or experiences of human-transcending powers. In consequence, critical theories must be alert to the permanent need to expand their argumentative vocabularies and engage in processes of semantic renewal. Nonetheless, in any given situation, articulating the ethical-existential-political significance of such relationships and experiences in the form of reasoned arguments may pose what appear to be insurmountable difficulties. The difficulties are compounded by the risk of epistemic imperialism. Epistemic imperialism occurs when the ethical-existential-political vocabulary of more powerful political agencies is imposed (usually tacitly) on less powerful ones. This poses a dilemma for critical theories of the kind I advocate. On the one hand, reasoned argument is necessary to avoid authoritarianism; on the other, reasoned argument may be experienced as epistemically imperialistic.

The problem may be described as how to devise an integral framework that takes multiple voices into account – in particular, voices that articulate ontologies and epistemologies that are radically different from Western ones – without simply imposing a Western vocabulary on these other voices. It has received little attention from contemporary writers, even from those who share my concern to explore the implications for contemporary ethical and political theory of engagement with radically different perspectives on relationality. The argumentative dimension is strikingly absent in the writings of many prominent contributors to these discussions, such as Donna Haraway (2016) and Jane Bennett (2020), with the result that they neglect the problem of nonimperialist discursivity. However, in his writings shortly before his death, Bruno Latour shows awareness of the problem. Arguing that the 'New Climatic Regime' requires an alternative set of values and meanings upon which the societies of the future must be built, Latour (2018) calls for a form of politics in which overlapping dynamics and attachments between humans and other-than-human beings and their environments are at the forefront. However, he offers little concrete help when it comes to meeting the challenges of authoritarianism, ideological closure and epistemic imperialism. Towards the end of this chapter, I draw attention to a more promising approach, which I find in the writings of Isabelle Stengers. But even here, the difficulties do not disappear. My response to them, further elaborated in the following chapters, is to conceive of argumentation not in terms of achieving full intelligibility or complete understanding; rather, I envisage it as a process of making partial epistemic connections between apparently incompatible worldviews (de la Cadena 2017; 2021), together with ontological openings that could enable playful 'world-travelling', along the lines proposed by María Lugones (1987). I return to this in Chapter 5.

Bearing in mind my proviso about the importance of argumentation in philosophical criticism of society, I turn now to alternative methodologies and conceptual innovations that may help to expand and revitalize the concept and practice of philosophical social criticism. Since I insist on the importance of an argumentative frame to any such expansion and revitalization, my point of departure is the argumentative model of communicative rationality developed by Jürgen Habermas.

Habermas' communicative model of argumentation

Intersubjective learning through the argumentative exchange of reasons is the core element of Habermas' critical theory of communicative action and rationality (Habermas 1984/1987). He develops this theory by way of a 'paradigm shift' made in response to troubling closures that he discerned in the critical theories of his Frankfurt School predecessors, in particular in Horkheimer and Adorno's *Dialectic of Enlightenment* (2002). The shift entailed a move from the subject-object model of cognition and action, the operative paradigm in the writings of Horkheimer, Adorno and most other early Frankfurt School theorists, to an intersubjective framework of linguistic communication. It enabled him to develop a normative account of cognition and action in terms of intersubjective processes of reaching understanding [*Verständigung*]. This is the basis for his account of communicative reason, which is the rational potential contained in everyday practices of communicative exchange that involve the reciprocal evaluation of validity claims (Cooke 1994). Communicative rationality results from formalized argumentative practices ('discourses') in which participants seek to reach an understanding with one another about the validity of the claims they make concerning the questions under discussion. Discourses must satisfy certain procedural conditions. These include the requirements that no relevant argument is excluded from the discussion, that the exchange of arguments is conducted in an even-handed and hermeneutically open manner, that no force apart from that of the better argument is deployed and that participants are concerned to find the right answer to the questions that brings them together in discussion.

For present purposes, a strength of Habermas' argumentative model is that it is processual, procedural and epistemic (Cooke 2000). The processual aspect means that argumentation takes place over time and is in principle open-ended. The exchange of reasons may have to be curtailed for pragmatic reasons – a decision may have to be made – but in principle it continues until it achieves its epistemic objective of determining the 'right answer' to the questions under discussion.[3] Habermas' model of argumentation leaves open the question of the 'right answer' to the questions under discussion, but it is not epistemically indifferent to it. It specifies epistemic principles for determining the validity of outcomes in certain kinds of argumentations, primarily discourses concerning moral validity claims and discourses concerning empirically based theoretical truth claims. The salient principle, specified somewhat differently in the case of truth than in moral rightness, is a consensus achieved among all participants as to the validity of the claim in question (Habermas 2003b, 237–76; Cooke 1994, 156–7; 2006a, 109–12).[4] By contrast, in purely procedural approaches, the validity of the outcome is determined solely according to procedural criteria such as inclusivity and fairness.[5]

For reasons I elaborate in the next chapter, a context-transcending epistemic dimension is an indispensable component of critical theorizing. Habermas' model of argumentation interprets this epistemic dimension in a way congenial for the mode of theorizing I advocate by tying it conceptually to the (in principle) never-ending, unconstrained exchange of reasons in intersubjective processes of reciprocal learning. However, his model requires decentring and opening in several respects. First and foremost, for reasons that will become clearer in the following chapters, it must relinquish its perniciously anthropocentric, intramundane ('this-worldly') perspective on context-transcending validity and embrace, instead, a human-transcending (and other-than-human-transcending[6]) conception of 'the good'. This decentring move also opens up the model, permitting its reconfiguration to include practices of argumentation in which the epistemic quality not just of moral validity claims but also of ethical validity claims is evaluated, which Habermas' model disallows.[7]

There is an empirically based and a conceptually based reason for Habermas' exclusion of the epistemic quality of ethical claims from processes of argumentation. His empirically based argument is that, under conditions of modern value-pluralism, it is virtually impossible for participants in argumentation to reach agreement in ethical-existential or ethical-political matters and, hence, to determine the epistemic quality of ethical validity claims. His philosophical argument is that the concept of context-transcending *ethical* validity cannot be rendered intelligible within the conceptual frame of the philosophical thinking he considers appropriate for European modernity. Habermas' name for this is 'postmetaphysical thinking' (1992).

Postmetaphysical thinking is the result of the linguistification and desacralization of the world characteristic of European modernity (Habermas 1984; 2017; Cooke 2019b). It de-transcendentalizes reason, bringing it down from the 'transcendental heaven to the earth of the [human] lifeworld' (Habermas 1996, 19) and 'permits a deflationary interpretation of the "Wholly Other"' (Habermas 2003b, 10). Habermas describes his deflationary understanding of the transcending power of reason as an 'intramundane' or 'this-worldly' one (1991, 127–56; Mendieta 2002, 237–76). On his postmetaphysical understanding of rationality, the only ideas of context-transcending validity that can claim to hold universally with an unconditionally binding force are truth and moral rightness. This is because only such claims can be validated by human reasoning without appealing to an idea of normativity whose origins are not within the human world. However, the unwelcome consequence is that the inhabitants of modernity have no way of rationally assessing the claims to validity raised (implicitly or explicitly) for ethical arguments. Accordingly, Habermas' 'this-worldly' argumentative model excludes the epistemic component of ethical validity claims from the process of discursive evaluation.[8] In the Introduction, I characterized critical theories as emancipatory projects, concerned with realizing better lives for all humans than is possible under the prevailing social conditions, pointing out that, as such, they are ethical-existential-political endeavours. In the present chapter, building on the discussion in Chapter 1, one of my main concerns is to explain why mitigating the risks of epistemological and ethical authoritarianism (and the ideological closures that often follow from them) requires critical theories to make the validity of their critical diagnoses and emancipatory projects a matter for processes of self-transformative ethical learning in argumentation. Assessing the validity of the emancipatory claims made by critical theories is not a matter to which Habermas gives much attention. Indeed, he is remarkably silent concerning the normativity of such claims (Cooke 2017, 68–76). Nonetheless, it seems safe to say that his postmetaphysical account of context-transcending normativity prevents argumentative assessment of their validity. This is one reason for decentring his argumentative approach by releasing it from its intramundane, 'this-worldly' perspective and opening it to allow for the epistemic evaluation of ethical claims.

Expanding critical theory's conceptual lexicon

Philosophical argumentation can be a hostile and inward-looking activity, unreceptive towards unfamiliar ideas, experiences and practices: it may block or obscure alternative ethical-existential-political interpretations of reality; the exchange of reasons may involve asymmetric power relations and the participants' understandings of what constitutes a good reason may be exclusionary, parochial and rigid.

Some of the first generation of Frankfurt School critical theorists were acutely aware of this. They creatively expanded traditional views of philosophical argumentation and, with this, the concept of philosophical criticism of society. Such expansions are welcome contributions towards developing the kind of argumentation that I envisage. In the envisaged conception, philosophical criticism of society may include critical interventions that are not articulated propositionally. For instance, the critical theorist may convey support for, or opposition to, a particular position by way of a picture (Haraway 2016, 59; Hartmann 2019, 155) or a musical score (Gordon 2023, 168). Similarly, philosophical critique may rely on rhetorical strategies and devices. Or again, it may perform or stage its criticisms of society. While critical interventions of this kind are not themselves arguments, they contribute epistemically to the argumentative process. They are what I call 'co-arguments'.[9] They work together with propositionally articulated reasons in the service of philosophical criticism of society. In German, I characterize them as *Mitargumente* and describe their critical contribution as *mitargumentieren*.

In its first phase especially, Frankfurt School theories frequently employed unorthodox and at times innovative techniques and devices in their philosophical criticisms of society. They took the view that the fundamental social transformation required for universal freedom and happiness demanded a kind of social critique that also *performed* or *staged* its criticisms as opposed to relying on traditional methods of analysis, explication and argument. Accordingly, they often practised disclosive modes of critique. Disclosive critique works on the affects, with a directness and immediacy usually absent in argumentatively reasoned philosophical criticism.

Performing and staging philosophical criticism of society

Dialectic of Enlightenment (2002), Horkheimer and Adorno's co-authored book, demonstrates the disclosive power of performative philosophical criticism of society. In the book they enact a critique that makes use of multiple rhetorical devices such as exaggeration and hyperbole and in which narratives play an important role. Qua enactment, their criticism is performative in the sense used by J. L. Austin in his speech act theory (1962). As for Austin, who argues that the speaker does something by saying something, Horkheimer and Adorno's text both conveys epistemic content and performs an action. Through its performance, it establishes a particular kind of relationship with the reader. Like Nietzsche's writings (and many writings by Foucault), their book addresses its readers *directly*. It establishes a relationship of immediacy between text and readers that impacts on them affectively as well as rationally (Saar 2007), provokes critical reflection and generates imaginative energy. One of its specific aims, it has been argued, is to undermine its readers' affective investment in the alleged achievements of European modernity, thereby eroding their confidence in its claim to constitute historical progress and prompting them to think about historical progress in alternative ways (Andreev 2023).

Adorno's model of thinking in constellations is likewise a practice of disclosive philosophical criticism of society that engages his readers affectively, prompting reflection and stimulating their imagination (1973, 16–66).[10] Its specific intention is to render fluid ideologically congealed concepts. Adorno describes such thinking as a way of setting the conceptual in relation to the nonconceptual, without assimilating the one to the other but rather maintaining the distinctiveness of each. It is a way of indicating the limits of what in any given historical context can be captured conceptually – of setting a concept in relation to the 'more' than the concept, which the concept in question has cast out of itself (ibid., 162): 'As a constellation, theoretical thought circles the concept it would like to unseal, hoping that it might fly open like the lock of a well-guarded safe-deposit box: in response, not to a single key or a single number but to a combination of numbers' (ibid., 163). In sum, thinking in constellations is a way of making the tensions and inconsistencies generated by the attempt to say the unsayable philosophically fruitful, by indicating the limits of representational thinking (Finlayson 2002, 15).

Adorno's model of thinking in constellations could be described as a *staging* of philosophical criticism of society in a sense analogous to the aesthetic curation of contents in art exhibitions. In both cases, objects are carefully set in relation to one another to dramatic effect. In the domain of philosophy, Fred Moten may have something similar in mind when he encourages rearranging familiar concepts into new relations with each other. Provocatively substituting the term 'conceptual toybox' for 'toolbox', Moten invites a view of philosophical concepts as props or toys: 'If you pick them up you can move into some new thinking and into a new set of relations, a new way of being together and thinking together' (Harney and Moten 2013, 41).

Adorno's thinking in constellations draws on Walter Benjamin's use of 'dialectical images', which are a methodological cornerstone of his unfinished 'Arcades Project' (1999). Dialectical images are both performances and stagings (the line between the two is fluid). They *perform* disruptive, disclosive philosophical criticism of society through *staging* relationships between opposing elements or ideas in ways that highlight their contradictions and tensions, crystallizing them within a particular historical moment or context (Pensky 2004). Benjamin describes them as sudden emergences in the 'Now' of what has been: they are moments in history, where the past and present come together in a flash to form a constellation. Their power is at once disruptive and disclosive, challenging the dominant narratives of historical progress, while at the same time revealing the hidden truth of historical experiences.

Alongside the dialectical image, Benjamin performs social critique through his use of quotations. In her introduction to *Illuminations*, a collection of Benjamin's essays, Hannah Arendt observes that he quotes the past as a means of disrupting the present and revealing obscured or forgotten elements that have an emancipatory potential. She cites his remark: 'Quotations in my works are like robbers by the roadside who make an armed attack and relieve an idler of his convictions' (Benjamin 1968, 38). Arendt takes them to have the double task of interrupting the flow of a given presentation with, as Benjamin puts it, 'transcendent force' and at the same time of concentrating within themselves that which is presented (ibid., 39).

The social critiques performed and staged in *Dialectic of Enlightenment*, thinking in constellations and dialectical images and quotations, are disruptive, disclosive practices of social criticism that impact upon their addressees affectively, provoking critical reflection and awakening their imaginations. But not only that: through their use of unorthodox philosophical techniques and devices, they also help to expand further and enrich the very concept of philosophical criticism of society. Accordingly, these performances and stagings may be said to have a double function: regenerative criticism of society and regenerative criticism of philosophical criticism of society.

The critical power of aesthetic performances

Horkheimer and Adorno's, Adorno's and Benjamin's critical interventions perform and stage alternative ways of engaging in philosophical criticism of society, thereby expanding and renewing critical theories' perceptions of what such criticism means. Critical interventions that demonstrate the critical power of literature, music, film or artworks may likewise expand and renew its meaning. Earlier in this chapter, I took Adorno to task for offering an interpretation of Kafka's stories that blocks the possibility of counter-readings. I nonetheless acknowledged the disclosive power of his illuminating textual analyses, which showed Kafka's stories to be performances of social critique. By doing so, Adorno – like Benjamin and Herbert Marcuse (1979) – calls on critical theories to recognize the power of the aesthetic dimension for critique of society and, in general, to be open to unfamiliar or new practices of social criticism.

Among contemporary writers, Fred Moten does something similar. Like Adorno he invites consideration of the ways in which disclosive, subversive, but also regenerative, criticism of society is performed in the aesthetic domain (broadly understood). Like Adorno, too, he offers insightful analyses of how a particular work or performance succeeds in doing so, paying close attention to its aesthetic form.[11] An example is his commentary on what he describes as the subversive yet redemptive power of Amiri Baraka's poem/song 'nation time' as performed by the saxophonist and composer Joe McPhee in 1970.[12] In Moten's interpretation, McPhee echoes, riffs off and reconfigures Baraka's own, previous, performance of it. The poem/song is often heard as a celebration of the emerging unified Black resistance movement and, in this sense, as a 'call to order'. Moten hears it instead as a regenerative *disruption* of order – as a 'call to *dis*order', a breaking up of the unity of 'the one', by setting the one in relation to the many who have come before and the many who are here now. This is 'the generative informality out of which his form emerges . . . that combination of question and answer, that gathering in the break of all those already broken voices, is when music becomes a demand' (Harney and Moten 2013, 52–3). Moten does not tell us explicitly what the demand is, but suggests that it is at once a demand for the destruction of the existing social order and something that would be radically alternative to it. The demand is spoken in a 'crazy language' (ibid.) and hence not generally intelligible. It works primarily on the affects of those who hear it and engages them directly. In addition, the *bodily performance* of the song is an act of protest, moreover one that establishes an affectively charged, immediate relationship with its audience.

Another contemporary example is Fumi Okiji in her writings on jazz music as a performance of disclosive, at once subversive and regenerative, social criticism. Countering Adorno's dismissive view of jazz as merely a commodity in the culture industry and the 'false liquidation of art' (Adorno 1983), Okjii draws on his aesthetic theory, which claims that the contradictions, fissures, falsehoods and other structuring conditions of contemporary life can be read from a work of art (Adorno 1997). Thus, using Adorno against Adorno, she argues that jazz music is a socio-musical practice that gives access to the conflicted form of subjectivity that is blackness in North America (Okiji 2018). As others too have observed, blackness is a subjectivity compelled ceaselessly to reflect on itself and its conflicted position in the social world.[13] Through this self-reflection, it is forced constantly to regenerate itself, in the process inhabiting modes of individuality and sociality that are invisible through the lens of the culturally and politically dominant majority. In this context, as part of her own philosophical criticism of racialized capitalism, Okiji shows that jazz performs a socio-musical, sociocultural critique that is disclosive, subversive and regenerative.

Argumentative criticism of society: counter-concepts

Stefano Harney and Fred Moten, and Moten in his subsequent writings, do the same for the 'undercommons', a marginal space of protest and resistance to the prevailing orders of political and sociocultural recognition. On my reading, it is also a space of protest and resistance to the dominant *intellectual* culture, its framings and its vocabularies (Harney and Moten 2013).

They describe the undercommons as a 'submerged space' on 'the outskirts of town', where imagination and improvisation play with normativity in ways of being together that are at once critical and generative (Moten 2018, x). Resistance to the prevailing orders of recognition emerges from everyday practices of sociality among those who have been radically excluded from these orders (ibid., 183; cf. Harney and Moten 2013, 44). It is a space for everyday experimental engagement in criticism through sociality.

Generative protest and resistance, as I understand it, means the creation of something new through engagement with others in activities and practices that obliquely subvert the prevailing frames of recognition and vocabularies. Most evidently in Moten's writings, generative protest and resistance in the undercommons also subvert the intellectual culture of capitalist modernity, creatively calling into question the structuring principles of the 'Anglo-American intellectual identity'. As an example, Moten offers the use of the term 'the grasp' in this intellectual tradition, with its connotations of mastery and control – presumably as in the phrase 'grasping a fact'. In the same vein, the subversive power of the undercommons upsets the tradition's preoccupation with sovereign human agency, which has similar connotations (Moten 2018, 185). Or again, generative protest and resistance disrupts the widespread 'reduction of intellectual life to critique' in the contemporary world, as well as its 'really, really horrific reduction of critique to debunking . . . where people are tied together by the bad feeling they compete over' (Harney and Moten 2013, 46). In the undercommons, by contrast, criticism is the capacity 'to see things in their branching and unfolding and generative differentiation' (Moten 2018, 184). Unlike 'critique', which they hold is deployed in the normative human sciences to *police and regulate* generation, criticism in the undercommons *attends* to generation (ibid.). It is a 'more-than-critical' criticism that's like 'seeing things' (ibid., 183).

Harney and Moten introduce 'study' as a counter-concept to practices of critique that serve to police and regulate (re)generation. Study evinces the inherent intellectuality of activities in the undercommons and is understood as a mode of sociality, of being with others: '"Study" is about what you do with other people . . . It's talking and walking around with other people, working, dancing, suffering, some irreducible convergence of all three, held under the name of speculative practice' (2013, 43). As mentioned, it also designates an experimental space for engaging in criticism (ibid.). Their concept of study destabilizes any sharp distinction between philosophical criticism of society and everyday criticism of society. They emphasize that there is no way of being in the undercommons that is not intellectual and, by extension critical, and there is no way of being intellectual (and by extension critical) that is not social (ibid.). In this way, 'study' further unsettles traditional understandings of philosophical social criticism. However, I reiterate my cautionary note. With the concept of study, Harney and Moten critically interrogate the dominant understandings of philosophical criticism of society, both in contemporary Frankfurt School theorizing and in moral and political philosophy more widely. But, like Adorno on occasion, they seem to lean too far in the direction of hostility to philosophical argumentation, disregarding the importance of the exchange of reasoned arguments for educative, self-transformative learning processes. They show little awareness either of the dangers of epistemological and ethical authoritarianism that arise when social critics block counter criticisms, whether deliberately or inadvertently, or of the risk of ideological closures.

By contrast, an argumentative practice described by Isabelle Stengers unsettles dominant understandings of argumentation as the agonistic exchange of reasons, while at the same time inviting further exploration of how argumentation itself could be reconfigured and integrated within a regenerated conception of philosophical social criticism. Stengers' work is concerned with 'slowing down' reasoning in ways that provoke thought and create an opportunity to create a different understanding of the problems and situations mobilizing deliberation (Stengers 2005a, 994; 2018). As she puts it, the idea is to slow down 'common sense', to create a space for hesitation regarding what it means to say 'good' (2005a, 995). One of her specific concerns is to slow down politics in ways that would allow a 'cosmos' to emerge, by which she means 'the unknown constituted by multiple divergent worlds and the articulations of which they could eventually be capable' (ibid.). Referencing François Jullien's book *The Propensity of Things* (1999), Stengers offers the example of the palaver system. As Stengers relates it, palavers are ritual assemblages that assume the existence of a transcendent world-order, but in which the participants do not have final authority concerning it; they are authorized merely to attest to the fact that the world has an order. In the palaver, people gather together who are recognized as knowing something about the world-order but are unclear how it applies to the issue at hand. Stengers emphasizes that they are not 'owners' of their opinions, for these are a product of the palaver. Each participant acknowledges that their knowledge is insufficient. The issue around which they are gathered has the power to activate thinking, but it is a thinking that belongs to no one, in which no one is right. Nor does it belong to the group of humans who constitute the palaver. Stengers writes that the 'palaver proceeds "in the presence of" the world-order and what emerges is recognized as its unfolding' (ibid., 1001).

In this picture, the emergence of agreement in a slow process of deliberation is the arrival of something as yet unknown but which all involved might be capable of recognizing and accepting – what Stengers calls a 'cosmos'. Deliberation is activated by a specific political issue and includes all those affected by that issue. It is a generative, self-transforming mode of collective political agency in which the participants attest to a human-transcending world-order and act authoritatively in its presence (in this respect, the palaver is clearly not an intramundane, 'this-worldly' mode of argumentation). The participants seek to become clearer about what this transcendent world-order means for the political issue in question and to develop their views on it, while acknowledging that the participants, either individually or collectively, do not 'own' the views they express.

Unlike Harney and Moten's concept of study, Stengers' account of the palaver provides an *argumentative* counter-concept to traditional agonistic understandings of argumentation. However, it harmonizes with 'study' in their account. The palaver is a generative mode of argumentation out of which something initially unknown emerges, which impacts educatively on all involved, potentially changing them more or less profoundly. Understood in this way, it is a practice that the undercommons could readily embrace. Furthermore, it is an argumentative practice that may fit better than 'study' in cases of communicative exchanges between the inhabitants of fundamentally divergent worldviews or cosmologies, helping to address the challenge of mutual intelligibility, and facilitating the 'world-travelling' that Lugones and others call for.[14] In sum, Stengers' account of the palaver is a provocative starting point for conceptualizing self-transformative ethical learning processes by critical theories from their various interlocutors, helping to decentre and expand the concept of argumentation in ways congruent with the decentring, expansive, exploratory mode of critical theorizing that I develop.

Philosophical critique as braiding, figuring, translating, attending

Moten and Harney evoke a picture of 'study' as a counter-concept to 'critique'. A different, but complementary, way to renew the concept of philosophical criticism of society is to think of it as a process that 'braids' arguments, and approaches to argument, as opposed to assessing them epistemically, sorting them qualitatively and synthesizing those deemed rationally acceptable into a coherent whole. 'Braiding' is a suggestive metaphor that has gained currency among indigenous political theorists in North America to characterize a non-foundationalist and non-reductivist mode of engaging with what Stengers calls 'multiple divergent worlds and their articulations. For present purposes, it refers to a method for engaging with disparate arguments and approaches to argument ' (Borrows et al., 2019; Allard-Tremblay 2022). The practice of braiding reveals each strand as unique and important without merging or erasing any of the distinct strands; it also shows how the intertwining of the strands creates a stronger and more complete whole.[15] Braiding does not assess the conformity of the arguments, or approaches to argument, with some already held norm; nor does it seek to produce a single coherent discourse from the activity. Its aim, instead, is a complex synthetic outlook that reveals overlaps and disagreements without merging the discourses, and acknowledges the possibility of irresolvable contradictions. Although it remains a form of critical inquiry that can point to problematic or wrong aspects of one or another of the discourses – when braiding, there are strands that go under the other ones or that are left out because they do not fit the pattern being woven – it ultimately favours diversity and the (temporary) incommensurability of contrasting perspectives (Allard-Tremblay 2022, 262).

There are resonances between braiding and what Maria Popova calls 'figuring' in her book of the same name (2019). I understand figuring, as used by Popova, to describe a concern to further enhance the illuminating power of visionary historical figures by poetically weaving a tapestry of their lives, creating resonances and synchronicities between them. The main figures in the tapestry she weaves are Johannes Keppler,

Maria Mitchell, Margaret Fuller, Harriet Hosmer, Emily Dickinson and Rachel Larsen. Accordingly, she addresses questions of the good life and good society in a poetic-literary context: 'Some truths, like beauty, are best illuminated by the sideways gleam of figuring' (ibid., 4).

Popova's concept of figuring adds a further dimension to criticism as braiding. This is the epistemic dimension, which in this case is ethical-existential-political. Furthermore, she highlights the *opacity* of 'the good', in the sense of its inherent resistance to attempts to capture it in human languages. This opacity complicates philosophical criticism of society, suggesting the need for a playful, indirect approach rather than a frontal assault. Through interweaving the 'facts and figments' of the lives of certain historical figures, she demonstrates how we are perpetually figuring and reconfiguring reality and that 'facts crosshatch with other facts to shade in the nuances of a larger truth' (2019, 5). Thus, like Adorno's thinking in constellations, Benjamin's use of dialectical images and quotations, and other stagings, well characterized by Moten's 'conceptual toybox' metaphor, Popova's figuring works playfully and indirectly, arranging disparate elements to create synchronicities that have the disclosive force she calls a 'sideways gleam'.

Braiding and figuring as methods of philosophical criticism of society resonate in turn with at least three of the practices of cultural translation advocated by Judith Butler (2000a; 2000b; 2000c). In their account, practices of cultural translation serve to radically interrogate and restage ideas, concepts and norms and include working with the texts of subordinated cultures (Cooke 2006a). Using the writings of Gayatri Chakravorty Spivak (1996) as their main example, Butler shows how cultural translation brings into relief the nonconvergence of discourses in order to expose the founding violence of the culturally dominant discourse. They also discuss a second kind of practice, which seeks to expose the limits of what the dominant system of knowledge can handle through the innovative misuse of dominant terms. Here, their main example is the 'mimetic doubling' discussed by Homi Bhabha in his writings on colonialism (1996). A third kind of practice of cultural translation, which chimes with 'braiding', involves threading together competing positions, for instance concerning universality, freedom or happiness, into an 'unwieldy movement, whose "unity" will be measured by its capacity to sustain, without domesticating, internal differences that keep its own definition in flux' (Butler 2000b, 168). The aim in this case is composition of a set of competing, overlapping positions that illuminates the concept or idea at stake.

Philosophical criticism of society requires attentiveness, especially attentiveness to the subjective experiences of human agents in the real world. In this respect, theories in the Frankfurt School tradition can learn from Husserlian phenomenology and contemporary developments of it. Even in its traditional Husserlian modes, phenomenology relies on close description to investigate structures of lived experience and embodied consciousness as these emerge in intersubjective relations with others and with the world. Cheryl Mattingly (2025) highlights phenomenology's capacity to illuminate how experience can exceed or challenge our formed category assumptions. In addition, she foregrounds its attentiveness to an otherness that speaks to an irreducible singularity; to an alterity that cannot be captured by the notion of one's social identity or membership in a collective community. As she puts it, phenomenology draws attention to the perplexity that can attend a particular situation in a 'sticky' way, eluding any ready explanation or summing up. It brings into view a 'difficulty of reality' that is irresolvable within existing categories of thinking and in this sense concept-resistant (ibid., 356; citing Cora Diamond 2003). In short, phenomenology presumes that close attention to the world will surprise and perplex us, disorienting our taken-for-granted assumptions about the world.

Lisa Guenther (2021) develops a 'critical phenomenology' as an outgrowth of this original project of disorienting common sense. The form of criticism she proposes foregrounds 'quasi-transcendentals': historical realities which come to take on the quality of naturalness within particular social formations. Close investigation of experience helps to denaturalize structurally oppressive categories of social difference (ibid., 5). Thus, rather than focusing on universal features of experience, Guenther advocates philosophical practices of social criticism that fit well with the Frankfurt School concept of ideology critique. In this and other ways, critical phenomenology reveals theoretically fruitful synergies between its approach and Frankfurt School theory, providing a resource for the kind of decentring, expansive, exploratory mode of critical theorizing that I envisage.

The dominant motif in this chapter and the last has been 'openings': openings in critical theory and openings for critical theory. Its main concern was to explain why an argumentative approach to social criticism is necessary for critical theorizing and to propose an expansive, exploratory conception of philosophical argumentation congruent with the decentring, opening, future-oriented mode of theorizing that I envisage. In Chapters 3 and 4, I focus on the closely connected question of decentring.

3

Immanence and Transcendence: Decentrings, Openings

Critical theories claim that the emancipatory visions they pursue are valid for everyone. How is this compatible with the decentring, expansive, exploratory mode of theorizing that I propose? How could the theories I envisage uphold a claim to the general validity of their emancipatory perspectives, while remaining attentive to human conceptions of the good life and good society in all their planetary multiplicity and richness? The dominant motif in Chapters 1 and 2 was 'openings'. There, I emphasized the importance of learning, in an educative, self-transformative sense, by critical theories from empirical research in the natural and social sciences and through communicative engagement with multiple kinds of interpretations of experience and reality. I discussed the potential fruitfulness of the research programme developed by the early Horkheimer and his colleagues in the 1930s for learning of this kind. But I also drew attention to ways in which learning possibilities enabled by his feedback-loop model of critical theory were blocked, first by Horkheimer himself and later, in a different way, by other critical theorists such as Adorno and Habermas. Such blockages increase the risk of epistemological and ethical authoritarianism in critical theorizing and, with this, the risk of ideological closures. In response, I advocated an argumentative approach. Building on resources both within and outside the Frankfurt School tradition, I proposed an expansive conception of argumentation as part of an expanded and revitalized conception of philosophical criticism of society. In this chapter, emphasizing as before the importance of educative, self-transformative learning, I focus on questions about the ethical normativity of critical theorizing. The dominant motif here is 'decentring', whereby decentring, as is evident from the previous chapter, enables openings and involves expansions and explorations. Steering a course between immanence and transcendence, I develop an account of the normativity of 'the good' (or 'the just' or 'the true) that fits with the decentring, expansive, exploratory model of critical theorizing I envisage.[1] I adopt a dual perspective on normativity, in which subjective experiences of a human-transcending ethical power ('the good') are a source of educative learning for self-transforming, self-determining, ecologically attuned human agents, as well as for self-transforming philosophical criticism of society.

My key thesis is that critical theories require a conception of ethical-existential-political validity – 'the good' – with an integral human-transcending moment.[2] This is necessary in order to mitigate the risk of ideological closures and foster self-transformative ethical learning of an open-ended kind. At the same time, the theory's normativity must be immanent to actual social reality. As discussed in Chapter 1, Frankfurt School theories follow Marx (and Hegel) in endorsing the practice of immanent critique, which grounds the normativity of the theory's critical diagnoses and emancipatory perspective in the needs, interests and aspirations of human subjects in existing social realities. I pointed out that critical theories cannot lightly dispense with the thesis of *immanent* transcendence, since it enables them to lessen the risks of 'bad utopianism' and of epistemological and ethical authoritarianism.

But I pointed out, too, that critical theories have an integral context-*transcending* moment. This arises from their claim that the prevailing human perceptions of needs, interests and aspirations should not be taken at face value. Due to the ideological effects of the existing social structures and institutions, subjective interpretations of reality are likely to be epistemically impaired from the point of view of the theory's normative perspective on freedom and happiness. If this transcending moment, as I now propose, is construed not just as context-transcending but also as human-transcending, an additional challenge arises for critical theories concerned to anchor normativity in existing social practices. The human-transcending moment I attribute to ethical-existential-political validity makes it likely that subjective experiences of 'the good' will be difficult to articulate in propositional language, inhibiting rational assessment of their epistemic reliability; for reasons explained in the previous chapter, this takes the form of intersubjective reasoning in argumentation. I acknowledged that, at any given time, in any given place, the vocabularies human agents have at their disposal may prove inadequate for articulating their experiences in ways that are propositionally intelligible to other humans, which is a precondition for their argumentative evaluation. When the experiences in question involve encounters with human-transcending powers and relationships with other-than-human agencies, it may seem virtually impossible to render them intelligible in an argumentative process. However, this is not an option for decentring, expansive, exploratory critical theories of the kind I envisage, since it would block possibilities for self-transformative ethical learning. I made some suggestions in the previous chapter for how best to respond to the challenge; these will be developed further in Chapter 5. One was to think of argumentation as a process of making *partial* epistemic connections between apparently incompatible worldviews, as opposed to a procedure that demands full intelligibility or complete understanding. Another was to explore possibilities for ontological openings that could enable playful 'world-travelling', by which is meant epistemic movements between constructions of life in which one feels (more or less) at home and those in which one feels an outsider. In addition, I provided an example of an argumentative practice very different from the prevailing Western conceptions of the agonistic exchange of reasons: the 'palaver' as interpreted by Isabelle Stengers. I suggested that practices such as these might be better able to facilitate communicative exchanges between the inhabitants of fundamentally different worldviews or cosmologies, and their journeys from one epistemic world to another, thereby helping to address the challenge of mutual intelligibility. This challenge will never disappear for critical theories that are decentring, expansive and exploratory; their task, accordingly, is not to solve a problem, but to perpetually seek new, nonauthoritarian, nonimperialist ways of responding to a challenge. In an exploratory spirit, in the final part of the present chapter, I show the potential fruitfulness for this endeavour of Karl Jaspers' concept of 'cipher' and my own concept of 'fictions' in critical theorizing.

To begin with, I consider how decentring, expansive, exploratory critical theories could navigate the tensions between transcendence and immanence in ways that lessen the risks of authoritarianism and ideological closure and foster self-transformative ethical learning. This entails reconfiguring the dialectics of immanence and transcendence as it has played out so far in Frankfurt School critical theories.

Reconfiguring the dialectics of immanence and transcendence

Navigating the tensions between immanence and transcendence has not proved easy for theories in the Frankfurt School tradition (Cooke 2006a). Some end up weakening their claims to context-transcending validity; elsewhere, I raise this objection against Axel Honneth's account of the social foundations of democratic life (Honneth 2014; Cooke

2022). Others disconnect the normativity of their theories from subjective experiences of (un-)happiness and (un-)freedom in existing social realities; Honneth raises this objection against Habermas' account of the colonization of the communicatively structured domains of social life by the functionalist rationality of the economic and administrative systems (Habermas 1987; Honneth 1994). In each case, in different ways, the result is diminished critical power.

In *The Gender of Critical Theory* (2022), Lois McNay takes contemporary Frankfurt School critical theories to task for weakening the *immanent* moment of social critique. She accuses some of its currently prominent exponents of abandoning critical theory's original emphasis on the connection between social criticism and subjective human experiences in favour of a paradigm-led mode of critical social theorizing. She claims that, from Habermas onwards, an obsession with justifying the theory's context-transcending normative foundations has distracted theorists in this tradition from what was once its main concern: unmasking oppression and revealing the structural forces that produce and perpetuate relations of violence and subjugation. In her view, this justificatory obsession has too often resulted in stylized grand theories, closed to external challenges and impulses, that have lost sight of critical theory's commitment to an experientially grounded critique of power. Offering critical analyses of six contemporary theories, McNay exposes what she calls their abstract formalism and disregard for the multiplicity and complexity of actual subjective experiences resulting from this.[3] She contends that these formalist tendencies are motivated by an overinflated sense of the importance of context-transcendence; the theories in question, concerned to ensure the context-transcending validity of their critical diagnoses and emancipatory projects while respecting value pluralism, pursue justificatory strategies that appeal to highly abstract norms and principles. She urges contemporary critical theory to embrace instead a problem-led process of abductive reasoning from experience and suggests that it has much to learn in this respect from the work of radical thinkers, especially feminist ones. The critical theory of Angela Davis is a case in point.[4] McNay draws attention to how Davis, in her critical account of the USA prison system, weaves back and forth between the micro and macro levels, between concrete life-worlds and underlying structural forces, building up a nuanced and far-reaching analysis of the way in which contemporary democracy is underpinned and enabled by a pervasive system of racialized carceral power.

Nancy Fraser – ironically one of the six theorists targeted by McNay – makes a similar point when discussing the limitations of 'freestanding' normative critique (Fraser and Jaeggi 2018, 123–4). By 'freestanding', she means theorizing in which a crucial aspect of critique's immanent moment is underplayed. The theory fails to engage with the standpoint of situated agents as potential participants in social struggles aimed at transforming the system, offering instead policy prescriptions from a position outside and above the terrain of social struggle. What is missing, according to Fraser, is an account of how differently situated agents understand themselves, what they consider their due, what they expect from their bosses and rulers, and what spurs them to act politically. In this respect, she endorses a remark by Thomas McCarthy: critical theory doesn't give participants in social struggles the last word, but it does give them the *first* word (McCarthy 1994, 248).

At the same time, McNay – like Fraser – acknowledges that a context-transcending perspective is an integral component of critical social theorizing.[5] As mentioned, however, she favours a non-foundationalist, abductive approach in which the theory's normativity is generated through the *interplay* of interpretations of experiences that emerge within multiple different sociocultural contexts. Viewed in this way, the context-transcending validity claimed by critical theory is based on learning and insight arising from a dialogical process that brings unfamiliar worldviews to bear on each other, enriching and expanding the existing immanent horizons of understanding.

From a social-epistemological perspective, Kelly Agra (2023) advocates a similar approach, which she describes as knowledge or experience sharing. Here, Agra builds on José Mendina's (2012) argument for a pluralistic, resistant imagination as a shared social sensibility based on differences rather than at their expense. She draws attention to ways in which interpretations of experiences traverse and circulate across members of an epistemic community, showing how experientially based knowledges may expand and transcend their original contexts. Accordingly, she prefers the term 'context-expanding' to context-transcending'. Observing that, even though some members of a given epistemic community may not have personally gained knowledge of particular experiences shared by others in the same community, and indeed may never do so, they may nonetheless gain epistemic access to them if their epistemic faculties and social sensibilities are sufficiently receptive and responsive; in such cases, this can lead to new learning and insight.

McNay's and Agra's context-expanding perspectives on normativity fit well with the expansiveness that is a core component of the mode of critical theorizing I propose. In this context-expanding perspective, normativity is permanently in a process of constitution and reconstitution.

It is a process in which epistemic and ethical-existential-political horizons are stretched and developed through interactions between human
agents with very different experiences and interpretations of them.[6]
However, neither McNay nor Agra goes far enough along the path they
advocate. Each assumes that the learning and insight resulting from
context-expansion is an epistemic-ethical-political gain, resulting in a
critical perspective that is normatively better in a context-transcending
sense. But neither of them explains the basis for this assumption.
Given their concern with human emancipation, critical theories can
view an expanded perspective as a positive development only if it is
in the service of context-transcending ideas such as freedom, happiness, justice and truth. Accordingly, the dialogical process that brings
unfamiliar worldviews to bear on each other must be oriented by a
concern to achieve better lives for all humans – that is, better in a
context-transcending sense. Neither McNay nor Agra explains what
'better' could mean in this instance. Moreover, neither explains the
source of the normativity of the expanded perspective. Evidently, it can
neither originate in, nor belong to, any *particular* sociocultural context
for this would compromise its ever-expanding movement. I conclude,
therefore, that context-expansion is a welcome additional aspect of the
context-transcending moment as it has traditionally been construed in
Frankfurt School critical theories, but insufficient for present purposes.
What is missing is an idea of ethical-existential-political normativity as
radically transcending all particular contexts and all particular agencies, human and other-than-human.

I contend that critical theories require a view of normativity that
is at once context-expanding, context-transcending and *human-
transcending*, while nonetheless immanent to the actual social order.
By human-transcending, I mean that it is neither generated by any
kind of human activity nor owned by the inhabitants of any specific
normative context.[7] Nor is it generated or owned by any particular
other-than-human agency or power. For this reason, it is more accurately characterized as 'human-transcending and other-than-human-
transcending'. However, since this formulation is cumbersome, in what
follows I usually abbreviate it to 'human-transcending' because this is
the key point for my critique of 'exclusive humanism', a central concern
in these chapters.

Due to its human-transcending moment, 'the good' (like 'the just' and
'the true') resists every attempt by humans to capture their experiences
of it in propositional language or, indeed, through the use of figurative
language or nonverbal – 're-presentational' – modes of expression.[8]
Although the meaning of 'the good' cannot be captured by human

representations, linguistic and nonlinguistic articulations of human experiences of 'the good' help to gain closer access to it. A similar thought is expressed by Albrecht Wellmer concerning 'the absolute' in Adorno's writings on art and philosophy. As Wellmer reads Adorno's view of the absolute, it is always 'veiled in black' (1985b, 155, 161).[9] In the context of Adorno's negative dialectics with its often hypothesized hostility to images of the good (Jay 2020; cf. Gordon 2020), this means, on the one side, that the absolute is not fully accessible to humans (it is 'veiled'), and, on the other, that the absolute, after Auschwitz, has to be thought of negatively ('blackly').[10] Wellmer draws the conclusion that the absolute must be approached indirectly. In the following, I address the question of the human-transcending moment of the normativity of 'the good' indirectly, through the 'sideways gleam' (Popova 2019) of the figure of the gift. I elucidate this thought with the help of Christoph Menke's theory of liberation (2022).

A dual perspective on normativity

Menke's theory of liberation seeks to liberate liberation from the thought of *self*-liberation. This is the thought that liberation must be achieved by human subjects themselves, whether individually or collectively. It is a thought at the core of the European Enlightenment, famously expressed by Immanuel Kant (1798), when he calls for the courage and resolution to use one's own reason without direction from another. Viewed in this way liberation is the self-reflexive appropriation of the practical ability to act, which is gained by human subjects when they wrest their freedom from their masters. It is intimately connected with the Kantian idea of autonomy as giving oneself the law, and corresponds to the modern idea of democratic political authority as collective self-authorization. Menke rejects the democratic view that freedom is a human achievement (2022, 30).[11] He argues that liberation, when thought of as *self*-liberation, traps the emancipatory goal of freedom in a never-ending cycle of liberation and domination: every new attempt at (self-)liberation produces new conditions of domination, against which new attempts at liberation are directed. He proposes a different path in which liberation is transformed radically on the basis of an alternative account of its genealogy and constitution.

Menke's theory of liberation helps to illuminate an idea of normativity that is human-transcending and yet immanent to practices in the human world. In other words, it enables a dual perspective on normativity.[12] However, it will become clear in the course of this chapter and the following ones that the transcending moment in Menke's 'dual perspective' is entirely materialist, whereas in the perspective I propose it is partly ethical.

Menke's central insight for present purposes is that the process of subjectivation, which in his account is the precondition for human freedom, does not begin with an act by individuals but originates outside of them. Freedom is the freedom to begin anew or to act spontaneously and it is given to human individuals by a force that is external to them in an existentially momentous experience. Prior to this experience they are not human subjects in Menke's sense: they are individuals characterized by a drive [*Trieb*] to become something other than they are. The concept of 'drive', which he also articulates as 'energy' or 'force' [*Kraft*] designates the distinctive form of naturalness that distinguishes humans from other animals and allows them alone to become subjects (2017; 2022, 548–9).[13] Menke's two principal examples of a liberating experience are: Moses in the Hebrew Bible, to whom the Angel of God appears in the burning bush; and Walter White, the central character in the US TV drama series *Breaking Bad*, who is liberated by a combination of two experiences, one a vision of economic plenitude, the other of his own mortality.[14]

In these momentous experiences the individuals affected are passive: they hear a command [*Gebot*] and they respond to it. The command cannot be obeyed without being heard and cannot be heard without an experience of fascination, which makes the experience an aesthetic one for Menke (2022, 570).[15] The individuals 'suffering' the momentous experience [*erleiden*] are rendered utterly indeterminate. But this condition of utter indeterminacy means that they become (self-)determin*able*, capable of bringing about new (self-)determinations that are not generated by the conventions and norms of the existing social arrangements. The command they hear, accordingly, is to become human subjects, to begin anew and to act spontaneously, disregarding the prevailing regulatory codes. Thus, the passive moment of the liberating experience is twinned with an active moment, for the individuals affected are called upon to act creatively in a perpetual, infinite movement of self-renewal and determination.

Menke writes that the act in which the affected individuals are normatively addressed is not yet normative (2022, 557). Instead, the command *instigates* normativity. The command calls the affected individuals into a normative order within which the substance or content of normativity is humanly determined (ibid., 554–7).

In doing so, to reiterate, it also instigates subjectivation: Menke describes the command as a call to the individuals affected to become human subjects. Since the normative substance of the command is indeterminate, it is a command to individuals to become subjects who determine normativity for themselves rather than in accordance with the prevailing norms and conventions. However, he adds an important qualification: becoming a subject entails *reflectively remembering* the momentous experience that called the individual into the normative order in the first place. What do they remember? As I read Menke, they remember not just the fascination of the experience, but also that it was something that *happened to them*, not caused by their agency. In other words, part of what they remember is the aesthetic power of the experience as human-transcending in origin.[16] Reflective remembering keeps alive their awareness that the human process of determining normativity is set in motion by a force that is human-transcending and, hence, that only the *concrete meaning* of normativity is humanly determined. This liberates normativity from the trope of self-authorization and allows it to take on a new shape as 'an infinite, unconditional, transcendent command' (Menke 2022, 566; my translation). But, as explained, the command is also a call to action – it calls upon the affected individuals to determine the content of normativity for themselves. Accordingly, normativity is a dual movement: it is received by human individuals who *passively* hear the command and who must then *act* in thoughtful recollection of their experience of it. In a perpetual, infinite movement of subjectivation they must hold on to the memory of the fascinating experience, reflect on its implications and endeavour to redirect their whole existence from it (ibid., 541–2, 554–5). On this view, accordingly, normativity is at once human-transcending and human-dependent (and in this sense immanent to the human world). The figure of the gift helps to elucidate this dual perspective further.

Normativity as a gift

It is noteworthy that Menke on several occasions uses the figure of the gift to illustrate his thesis that liberation, and the freedom resulting from it, is something *given* to humans as opposed to a purely human achievement. For instance, he refers repeatedly to Moses' conviction, when experiencing the angel in the burning bush, that the angel's appearance and the command it issues are a gift from God (2022, 142, 148, 150, 431). However, as I have emphasized, freedom in Menke's account is not only passively received by humans, given to them by a power external to them; it is also an activity by humans in which they affirm the gift of freedom and embark on an open-ended, infinite voyage of self-determining subjectivation in reflective recollection of the aesthetic experiences in which they received the gift (ibid., 574–6).[17]

Menke's liberation of liberation from the thought of *self*-liberation chimes with a discussion by the social anthropologist Joel Robbins of how his discipline might learn from theology with regard to 'the gift', a topic that, since Marcel Mauss, has been close to the hearts of many anthropologists (Robbins 2020; Mauss 2016). Mauss famously wrote that the gift is constituted by three obligations: to give, to receive, to return (2016, 73). For Mauss, the act of giving constitutes an obligation. According to the view widely accepted in contemporary anthropology, he held that the act of receiving constitutes a further obligation: this is the obligation to return the gift. For the Lutheran theologians discussed by Robbins, this is a misapprehension – there is no obligation to return the gift. From their perspective, a gift does not become a gift when someone acts to receive it. Rather, it becomes a gift when one agent makes another agent into a (passive) receiver (Robbins 2020, 135). Receivers do not decide whether to become receivers. As in the case of Menke's 'command', receiving is entirely passive and no obligation arises from the act of receiving. The affected agents passively receive something of fundamental importance from outside themselves, but they incur no obligation – receiving is not an obligation but 'a fate' (ibid.). Again, as for Menke, only when they have received the gift are they called upon to respond appropriately to the new normatively generative role into which they have been cast. In other words, they are called upon to become a certain kind of normatively active agent. However, there is no obligation here either. The liberated individuals, transformed by their liberating experience, embrace their new freedom to determine for *themselves* what is right or good; the experience frees them from the very concept of obligation.[18]

Imagining 'the good' as a gift from a human-transcending power helps to elucidate my dual perspective on normativity: the thesis that decentring, expansive and exploratory critical theories, and likewise self-transforming, self-determining, ecologically entangled ethical agents, must construe normativity as human-transcending and yet immanent to human activity in existing social realities. In analogy to the gift, human agents who passively experience the human-transcending power of 'the good' are not *obliged* to obey ethical-existential commands. Instead, they are called upon to *become* ethical agents: to explore what it means to lead a good life as a human. The normativity of 'the good' – a complex, multifaceted set of self-imposed determinations concerning 'the good life' and 'the good society' – comes into play only once it has been involuntarily received. In other words, receiving the gift is the beginning of efforts by human agents to determine how they should live a good life with others, human and other-than-human, and what the good society corresponding to such a life would look like.

With the help of Menke's theory of liberation and the figure of the gift, I have argued that normativity – the ethical impulse – does not originate with human agency, but that its concrete meaning is realized only through human agency. This dual perspective on normativity reconfigures the dialectics of immanence and transcendence in Frankfurt School critical theory. Figured as a gift from a human-transcending power, the normativity of critical theory's emancipatory aims is at once human-transcending and human-dependent, extramundane and intramundane, involving a dynamic movement between passivity and activity in which each moment is indispensable. It also reconfigures the meaning of freedom as self-authorship or self-determination. The dual perspective opens a view of self-determining agency as responsive to a human-transcending power ('the good') that motivates the ethical-existential-political activities of human agents in the human world. Their experiences of a human-transcending power propel them to act: to embark on an open-ended journey of self-transforming, self-determination, in which they endeavour to realize 'the good' in actual social reality – to make it part of that reality. For this reason, despite the asymmetry of the relationship between gift-giver and gift-receiver, and the passivity of the gift-receiver, my view of transcendence as human-transcending is readily compatible with critical theory's concern with human freedom. I return to this in the following chapters.

Is my dual perspective readily compatible with the argumentative approach to critical theorizing proposed in the previous chapter? At first glance there seems to be a conflict between the momentous experiences of a human-transcending power Menke invites us to imagine and my emphasis on articulating subjective experiences in propositional language (alongside dramatic performances and stagings and the use of rhetorical strategies and devices). Thus, the question of argumentative intelligibility arises yet again: how could such momentous experiences be the basis for reasoning together in argumentation, which presupposes at least some degree of mutual comprehension? It seems probable that some participants in the argumentative exchange will not be able to understand the reasons offered by other participants due to the experiential basis of the reasons. I now suggest that Jaspers' concept of a cipher, together with my concept of a fiction, can help to address the difficulty.

Ciphers and fictions

Momentous experiences such as those evoked by Menke merely drama-tize the problem of intelligibility – the problem is independent of their momentousness. It arises not only in the case of experiences of a nor-mative command that are extraordinary and overwhelming; it arises for *every* unsettling subjective experience. The unsettling experiences may be aesthetic (Menke refers to experiences of 'fascination'); they may be existentially destabilizing or debilitating, such as the experiences of suicide-survivors described by Jean Améry (1994; Cooke 2021b); or they may be existentially energizing or affirming – such as the epipha-nies described by Charles Taylor (1989) or the conversions narrated by William James (1935). They are not necessarily extraordinary. In his fictional 'A Letter' (2005), Hugo von Hofmannsthal depicts exis-tentially unsettling subjective experiences that are banal. He presents his readers with a fictional letter sent from Philipp Lord Chandos to Francis Bacon dated 1603. Lord Chandos is the youngest son of the Earl of Bath, a literary prodigy in his youth, who subsequently, for reasons not explained, experienced years of complete literary incapaci-tation. A turning point comes when, on his morning rides on horseback around his estate, he is profoundly affected by the everyday objects he encounters, such as an abandoned half-full watering-can, in which a beetle swims from side to side, or a crooked apple tree or a rat or a stone overgrown by moss.[19] Chandos describes these encounters as moments of happiness or fulfilment in a sense that bears an affinity with what Peter Gordon calls Adorno's emphatic conception of experience, dis-cussed in Chapter 2. Such experiences can happen anywhere, indeed in the most ordinary circumstances. In a commentary on Kafka's story 'The Castle', Adorno writes:

> When poor Frieda calls herself Klamm's beloved, the world's aura is brighter than at the most sublime moment in Balzac or Baudelaire; when . . . 'she places her little foot on his chest', and bends down and 'quickly kisses him', she finds the gesture for which one can wait an entire lifetime in vain; and the hours which the two spend lying together 'in little puddles of beer and other garbage which covered the floor' are those of fulfilment in a world so foreign that 'even the air did not have a particle of the air at home'. (1982, 263–4)

Happiness in this emphatic sense is an existentially unsettling experience that changes the affected individual's perception of reality and, even if only momentarily, makes reality appear in a new light. In these moments, in Adorno's words, the world seems so foreign that 'even the air [does] not have a particle of the air at home'. This explains why the affected individuals will generally not be able to rely on the linguistic resources already available to them to explain them (Cooke 2025c, 1039–41). Not surprisingly therefore, in his letter to Bacon, Chandos struggles to find words to express what he feels in these fleeting moments of happiness. Although he succeeds very well in conveying a sense of how he is affected by the everyday objects he encounters,[20] many people will find it difficult to convey to others what has happened to them. However, as I point out in earlier writings, the problem of intelligibility as it arises in such instances is not a shortcoming of language in general or of any specific use of language; rather, it is a difficulty that may occur at any time and in any historical context, indicating that the reservoir of reasons available to the inhabitants of that context is in need of renewal. Furthermore, from the point of view of decentring, expansive, exploratory critical theories, this is a desirable state of affairs – a lack of such difficulties is indicative of semantic stagnation (Cooke 2006a, 154–60; here p. 159). Nonetheless, in any specific argumentative context, when arguments are based on momentous (Menke) or emphatic (Adorno) experiences, lack of intelligibility may be a considerable obstacle to assessment of the quality of the arguments in question.[21] If the quality of the reasons based on momentous or emphatic experiences cannot be assessed argumentatively, critical theories seem to have only two options, neither of them congenial: an authoritarian determination by the theorist of their ethical-existential quality (this is what Adorno does on occasion, as discussed in Chapter 2) or principled exclusion of such experiences from argumentative contestation (this is what Habermas does, as also discussed in Chapter 2).

However, these are not in fact the only options. A third option is an expanded conception of argumentation that builds on my suggestions in the previous chapter. There, I proposed an understanding of argumentation that embraces non-propositional contributions alongside propositional ones – I called such contributions 'co-arguments' [*Mitargumente*] – and does not require complete intelligibility. In addition to the various expansions I proposed, I now suggest that a renewed conception of argumentation would construe it as a matter of 'reasoning in transitions' (Taylor 1989, 72–3; Cooke 2006a, 149–52). This is a mode of reasoning that is not absolutist but, rather, concerned primarily with comparative propositions and with moving beyond a particular way of thinking or behaving by showing that the transition from one position to another constitutes an epistemic gain – and, in the case of ethical-existential and ethical-political reasoning, also an ethical gain. Moreover, it is concrete, not abstract. Thus, rather than abstractly assessing the epistemic-ethical-political validity of a given contribution to the discussion, critical evaluation is a matter of exploring its implications for real-life situations and practices in communicative exchanges with others. Construed in this way, a final judgement on the validity of ethical-existential-political positions is never attainable, argumentatively or otherwise. Accordingly, the point of argumentation is not to reach a judgement that is true once and for all, but rather one that is epistemically *better*. Furthermore, in this conception, the reasons offered in the communicative exchange do not have to be fully understood by everyone (if such a thing is possible) but merely *sufficiently* intelligible for the conversation to take place.[22]

Furthermore, although intelligibility is undoubtedly a challenge for the argumentative dimension of critical theorizing, its practical implications vary from situation to situation. Intelligibility depends on multiple, contingent, subjective and contextual factors, including the psychic constitution and hermeneutic capacities of those involved in the exchange of arguments. It is impossible to say in advance of a specific situation whether or not the participants will understand each other's reasons sufficiently to be able together to consider their epistemic quality.

A renewed conception of argumentation would also entail moving beyond the inductive view of argumentation that has been predominant in Western modernity at least since Francis Bacon (1561–1626), in which reasons are contrasted with articles of faith, expressions of emotion and fantasies. On the inductive view, since subjective interpretations of ethical-existential experiences may express feelings, involve imaginative projections and refer to human-transcending powers whose reality could be considered a matter of faith, such contributions to discussion would be disqualified as reasons from the outset. However, there have always been influential counter-strands within European modernity, such as Kant's critiques, in which his 'postulates of reason' destabilize the reason versus faith dichotomy (I come back to this below). Alongside this, there has been a wealth of writings in recent years, often based on ethnographic case studies, that have called into question the reason versus emotion dualism, showing that it is by no means a cultural universal (Descola 2013; Imbert 2009); this is supported by a significant body of research in the neurosciences that has impacted on the philosophical literature (Damasio 2005). My own view of fictions in critical theorizing goes some way towards unsettling the reason versus fantasy dualism.

In an earlier work, *Re-Presenting the Good Society*, I use the figure of a 'fiction' to refer to imaginative constructions in critical social theorizing. I call these *re*-presentations of the good society (2006a, 100, 113–27). The hyphenated word is intended, on the one side, to convey the *mediated* character of all representations: their non-immediate, indirect relationship to the transcending power they incarnate. On the other side, it is intended to convey the *immediacy* for the affected human individuals of the pictures of the good society (and the good life) evoked imaginatively by critical social theories: the *presentness* of the evoked images, their vividness and imagined realness. As I emphasize, these pictures are often negative ones, from which a positive image of the good life and good society may be extrapolated, and they may be relatively inchoate, indeterminate as to the specifics of the imagined life and society. The term 'fiction' is intended to convey both the imaginative nature of the re-presentations and their human fabrication. In that book, I do not yet construe the ethically charged, transcending power that instigates the process of self-determining subjectivation as human-transcending; nonetheless, then as now, I maintain that it is never completely accessible to human knowledge: it is a 'veiled absolute', to recall Wellmer's characterization of the absolute in Adorno, as discussed earlier in this chapter. In other words, I posit an ineradicable gap between what I then referred to as the 'transcendent ethical object' and its re-presentations in critical theories of society.[23] I used the word 'object' in the sense of *object of attraction or desire*.[24] This implies, in turn, that the transcendent ethical object exerts an affective pull (Husserl refers to an 'affective allure'). Thus, while I agree with Georges Sorel that revolutionary myths such as 'the general strike' evoke warmly coloured and vivid images that motivate revolutionary agents, I attribute at least part of the affective pull or allure of the images to the transcendent ethical object that the myths *re*-present (Sorel 1975; Cooke 2006a, 87–90). I leave open the questions of whether this object is an *entity* – a being or thing – and whether it is material or immaterial (or both). Due to the ineradicable gap between object and knowledge of it, re-presentations of 'the good' (or 'the just' or 'the true') are always, at best, only approximations.[25] As I wrote then, they are 'stand-ins' for truth (and 'the good' and 'the just') operating: 'In a metonymic fashion, signalling in a partly symbolic, partly substantive, and partly imaginative way something that cannot be fully re-presented in language or rendered fully transparent to our knowledge and practices' (2006a, 115).

In *Re-Presenting the Good Society*, I advance a thesis that is especially important for present purposes. It is the thesis that discussing with others the truth-content of fictions – *re*-presentations of the good life and good society – can contribute to ethical-existential learning. Put differently, I claim that argument (in the expansive sense I advocate) can help to move us closer to the transcendent object of desire (2006a, 146–71). Notice that, in my account, the affective allure of fictions derives from their connection with the transcendent object. Fictions enable human individuals to experience its normative force more emphatically. At the same time, human articulations of such experiences can never capture the transcendent object completely. The gap between transcendent object and articulations of experiences of it makes these articulations unreliable epistemically. This is why, as I explained in Chapter 2, argumentative evaluation of their truth value is necessary. But why should we think that it moves us closer to the truth? Here, as in several other places in my account of context-transcending validity, I make assumptions that, in analogy to Kant's postulates, I hold to be 'needs of reason'.[26] In his critiques, Kant introduces God and Immortality as two assumptions – postulates – which are 'a need of reason' when thinking about human freedom. In this way, Kant destabilizes the reason versus faith dichotomy. In a similar vein, I postulate that there are human-transcending forces that can be experienced subjectively by humans and that reasoning together about the ethical-existential-political implications of such experiences can be epistemically fruitful. Like God and Immortality for Kant, these postulates are rationally necessary to make sense of a conception of 'the good' that is at once human-transcending and immanent to the human world, which in turn is a postulate rationally necessary to make sense of the decentring, expansive and exploratory critical theorizing that I propose.

There are interesting points of overlap between my account of fictions in critical social theorizing and Jaspers' critical theory of myth, in which the notion of a cipher is a central component. Jaspers maintains that the reality of transcendence is present for us objectively only in the language of code or cipher (Jaspers and Bultmann 2005, 52). The 'magnificently ambiguous language' of 'mythical figures and speculative concepts' is the medium in which the incomprehensible may show itself (ibid., 41). Jaspers emphasizes that ciphers are the *language* of transcendent reality, not transcendence itself (1967, 93). Commenting on Jaspers, Carmen Dege observes: 'Ciphers do not determine or prove something but spark a sensitivity for what is inscrutable and contradictory' (2023, 766). Ciphers are ambiguous symbols: at one and the same time they present us with a human-transcending reality and detract from its reality (ibid., 771). In my words, they *re-present* a reality that we can *feel* in its reality even when we know that ciphers are human fabrications. Moreover, as the language of transcendent reality, ciphers give voice to the '*magnetism* of Transcendence' (Jaspers 1967, 92; my emphasis). In terms I used previously, they allow us to feel the *affective allure* of the transcendent object ('the good'). Like fictions, further- more, ciphers motivate us to pursue a human-transcending truth, even though we will never succeed in capturing it. This is how I read Jaspers' lines: 'We should like to transcend all ciphers, to reach the point where they will disappear. But even for this transcending we are dependent on a cipher language – on one that includes this disappearance' (ibid., 134). In my words again: while truth (or 'the good') may lie beyond all ciphers, cipher language is necessary for us to move towards it.

Jaspers' extensive writings on ciphers offer a wealth of examples of their multiplicity and variety. He maintains that anything can be a cipher, as can anything humans make, be it real or a product of thought and imagination. Myths are ciphers, so too are concepts such as 'Truth', 'Freedom', 'God', 'Nature' and 'Beauty'. Ciphers are found in mythology, ritual, sacramental, poetic and artistic traditions as well as in philosophy (1967, 123). Helpful, too, is Jaspers' insistence that the cipher world is not a harmonious realm. It is embattled. Ciphers contradict one another. However, the battle is not for power but for original truth. Moreover, the battle is never-ending. If we end it, we either give up our concern for transcendence or leave behind the world of cipher language and enter the silence of the ineffable, giving up our concern for the world (ibid., 128).

Nonetheless, for present purposes Jaspers' account of ciphers has a serious weakness. It makes personal experience the ultimate determinant of the truth of ciphers. Put differently, he holds that subjective experiences of 'the good' are epistemically reliable. In Chapter 2, I attributed a similar position to Adorno in the case of subjective experiences of suffering and injustice. Against this, I maintain that, in general, subjective experiences are epistemically unreliable due to the ineradicable gap between the 'transcendent object' and its re-presentations. However, as I explained, I also hold that critically reflective, communicative engagement with other human agents is epistemically fruitful in pursuit of the truth content of subjective experiences (and other claims to truth).

For this reason, I tie evaluation of the truth of ciphers to intersubjective processes of reasoning, where there is always the possibility of challenge and contestation. By contrast Jaspers insists that ciphers convey an untranslatable truth that cannot be interpreted rationally. Instead, it can be interpreted only by new ciphers, by being *transformed*. This is how I understand his statement that ciphers interpret each other (Jaspers and Bultmann 2005, 31). The narrow view of rational interpretation implicit in this position may explain why Jaspers makes 'the decisive criterion' for testing the validity of ciphers subjective truthfulness: the individual's sincere belief in its validity (1967, 252). He maintains that 'the truth of ciphers . . . cannot be known, [it] can only be experienced existentially' (ibid., 135). In other words, he draws an unwarranted existentialist lesson from an assumption, which I share with him, that the *fullness* of ethical-existential-political truth can only be experienced.[27] In my account, such momentous, emphatic experiences are the *starting point* for assessing the validity of fictions; in Jaspers' account, they are also its conclusion. Dege struggles with this aspect of Jaspers' thinking (2023, 767–9); Habermas identifies it as one of the weak points (2019, 104).

In the next chapter, I elaborate my worry about existentialist and similarly solipsistic approaches to the question of ethical-existential-political truth, arguing that they reproduce a model of normatively self-sufficient human agency that has no place in decentring, expansive and exploratory critical theorizing.

4

Self-Determining Agency: Decentrings, Openings

Individual human freedom is the central aim in Frankfurt School critical theorizing. As observed in Chapter 1, it is held to entail equality and solidarity, two other important values within European modernity and, in the case of the early critical theorists, to be entwined with happiness. I have characterized the normative conception of freedom predominant in Frankfurt School theories as *Bildung*, in the broadly Hegelian sense of the free development of ethical agency in interactions with other human agents (to which I add: 'and other-than-human agencies'). In the present chapter and the next, I depict the version of this conception that fits best with the decentring, expansive, exploratory mode of theorizing that I advocate. Individual human freedom, as I picture it, is self-determining, self-transforming ecologically entangled ethical agency.

In the proposed picture, self-determination *is* self-transformation and self-transformation *is* self-determination. The difference in the terms is merely a difference in accent. The word 'self-determination' foregrounds the *directionality* of the agency; the word 'self-transformation' foregrounds its *mobility*. Self-determination, like self-transformation, has a passive, receptive moment as well as an active, critically reflective one. Self-determining, self-transforming human agents change *in response to* experiences, encounters and events that they do not control – things that happen to them – and they actively *respond to* what happens, critically and reflectively. I occasionally use just one or other of the terms for convenience, but I take them to be metonyms. As in Chapter 3, the motif guiding the discussion in these chapters is 'decentrings'. As before, decentring involves opening and exploring. In Chapter 3, decentring meant developing an account of ethical-existential-political validity – 'the good' – with an integral human-transcending (and other-than-human transcending[1]) moment.

Steering a course between immanence and transcendence, I argued that a human-transcending moment is necessary to mitigate the risk of ideological closures in critical theorizing and to foster educative, self-transformative learning on the side of theory. In this chapter and the next, I take this argument a step forward. I show that an account of 'the good' as human-transcending allows for a perspective on freedom in which the free development of ethical agency is enhanced by communicative engagement with the normativity of other-than-human agencies. Embracing this perspective calls for a decentring of humans from their position as the ultimate authority for the validity of ethical judgements – the view of normativity that is operative in most contemporary 'positive' conceptions of freedom as self-authorship, self-legislation or self-determination. Borrowing the term from Charles Taylor (2007), I refer to this as the 'exclusive humanist' perspective on human freedom. I argue that the exclusive humanist view of normatively self-sufficient human agency is anthropocentric in a pernicious sense. By construing normativity as entirely a product of human agency, it leaves no room for an account of human and other-than-human relationality in which *there is normativity on both sides.*

Ecologically entangled agencies

I target two troubling features of the exclusive humanist perspective. The first is an instrumentalist approach to the interrelationships between human freedom and the material environments that sustain it. The second is the idea of autonomy as an intramundane mode of self-authorship, a mode of freedom in which humans, individually or collectively, are the self-sufficient authors of the moral norms and principles that bind them. Linking the two is a disavowal or neglect of the *ethical* significance of the multiple, complex entanglements between human agency and other-than-human agencies.

Anna Tsing's 2015 ethnographic study of practices of matsutake mushroom foraging gives a sense of what I mean by entanglements. Tsing writes of 'histories made in concert by humans, plants, and fungi', offering an account of cross-species entanglements, specifically between humans, pine-trees and matsutake mushrooms (ibid., 172). In her multifaceted story, the lines of mushroom lives are 'life-performances', entwined with the lines of pine-tree lives and the lines of human lives. Mushroom foragers incorporate the life-performances of plants and fungi into their own life-performances. She describes these 'lines of life' as 'dances', pursued through senses, movements and orientations. As she relates it: 'The dance is a form of forest knowledge – but not that codified in reports. And, although every forager dances in this sense, not all the dances are alike. Each dance is shaped by communal histories, with their disparate aesthetics and orientations' (ibid., 241).

My claim, however, is not merely about cross-species entanglements. It is about the normative, ethical-existential-political significance of these entanglements. In the conception of freedom that I propose, the free development of ethical agency involves openness to educative, self-transforming learning in engagement with the normativity of other-than-human agencies. This entails the claim that both human and other-than-human agencies have their own normativity: there is normativity on both sides. The following quotation from Bonnie Honig's *Public Things* helps to clarify my position. Quoting Lolita Chavez of the Mayan People's Council, Honig writes:

> Corn taught us Mayan people about community life and its diversity, because when one cultivates corn one realizes that there is a variety of crops such as herbs and medical plants depending on the corn plant as well. We see that in this coexistence the corn is not selfish, the corn shows us how to resist and how to relate with the surrounding world. (2017, 4)

Honig continues: 'To say that the corn is not selfish, and that it gives us instruction, is to say that the corn . . . has agency' (ibid.).

A similar thought is expressed by Robin Wall Kimmerer in *Braiding Sweetgrass*. She relates how one day she received a gift of a small corn leaf packet from Awiakta, a Cherokee writer. Opening it in Spring, as she had been told to do, she found it to contain three seeds, a kernel of corn, a glossy bean and a pumpkin seed. Observing that 'plants teach in a universal language' (food), thereby speaking 'in a tongue that every breathing thing can understand', Kimmerer writes: 'I hold in my hand the genius of indigenous agriculture, the Three Sisters. Together these plants – corn, beans, and squash – feed the people, feed the land, and feed our imaginations, telling us how we might live' (2013, 129). Here, corn, beans and squash communicate with each other; in their communicative entwinement they have agency. They instruct ('teach'), nourishing human imaginations, inviting humans to consider ways of living corresponding to what Tsing calls their own 'dances' and 'lines of life'.

The key point for present purposes is that human engagements with other-than-human agencies may be sources of educative, self-transformative learning by humans. As Honig and Kimmerer put it, other-than-human agencies can give us 'instruction' and 'teach' us in ways that open new imaginings of new futures.

Human naturalness

My view of ecologically entangled agency may be described as a variant of Theodor W. Adorno's perspective on human naturalness [*Naturwüchsigkeit*].

In the summer of 1942, in an informal seminar with colleagues, Adorno made a characteristically pithy remark: 'Need is a social category. Nature as "drive" is contained within it' (2017a, 102).[2] For Adorno, drives are incorporations of human naturalness, connecting humans with their origins in nature. As originally and always part of nature, the human subject is driven by a bundle of archaic, untamed impulses that are objectified and synthesized by human will. Adorno holds, furthermore, that human agency – specifically, human freedom – is animated by 'nature within', comprising drives that are tendentially transgressive, destabilizing the autonomy of the will. Subsequently, in *Negative Dialectics*, he refers to a 'dawning sense of freedom [that] feeds upon the memory of the archaic impulse not yet steered by any solid "I"', describing it as 'pre-temporal freedom' (1973, 221). In his view, denial of, or disregard for, human naturalness results in a delusion characteristic of philosophical thinking within Western modernity, increasingly evident since Kant: a self-flattering, self-exalting confidence in the autarky of the human subject. By foregrounding human naturalness as incorporated in drives, Adorno sought to decouple the ideal of self-reflective, self-directing agency from this delusion. However, this did not for him mean rejection of the normative value of autonomous self-reflection. To the contrary, most frequently in his later writings, he repeatedly invokes autonomy, understood as 'the power of reflection, of self-determination, of not cooperating', as the 'single genuine power standing against the principle of Auschwitz' (2005, 195). Far from positing a contradiction between autonomous agency and human naturalness, he asserts a mutual dependency: self-conscious – 'mindful' – human subjects are liberated from bondage to both nature and society when, in their autonomous, self-reflective thinking, they tap into the will's dynamic, transgressive power. This is why genuinely autonomous agency involves self-reflection not just in the form of independent critical thinking and relentless self-examination, but also *remembrance of nature within the subject* (Horkheimer and Adorno

2002, 32). I take this to mean remembrance of nature as the transgressive drive contained within human agency.

The transgressive drive is the natural moment of need; the social moment is the constitution and interpretation of need in historically specific social contexts. Adorno emphasizes that the natural and social moments are ultimately inseparable: 'Each drive is so socially mediated that its natural side never appears immediately, but always only as socially produced. The appeal to nature in relation to this or that need is always merely the mask of denial and domination' (2017b, 2). I read this as the view that all attempts to distinguish theoretically between higher and lower needs, or genuine and false needs, stand accused of complicity with the existing power relations. By ignoring the ways in which subjugating and repressive social systems generate and manipulate needs for their own purposes, they not merely fail to challenge the power of these systems, they also reinforce their power.

My focus here is the natural as opposed to the social moment of need as Adorno understands it.[3] For Robin Celikates and colleagues in the Berlin Critical Theory Network, this natural moment lends the social category of need a certain objectivity, preventing the politics of need from sliding into voluntarism and socio-technocratic manipulation: needs can be reduced neither to purely subjective preferences nor to purely ideological constructs (Celikates et al. 2023). By 'objectivity' I take Celikates and his colleagues to mean that the category of human need refers to something *beyond* human sociality, which makes possible critical engagement with particular, socially constituted, need claims. However, they pass over Adorno's emphasis on the destabilizing force of the natural moment, which adds a transgressive power to the context-transcending one. Furthermore, not only do they neglect the destabilizing, transgressive power of the natural moment of human need, they overlook his point that this natural moment connects humans with their constitutive materiality. In my terms, it testifies to their ecologically entangled agency, entwined in multiple, complex ways with other-than-human ones.

Interpreted along the lines of transgression and entangled agency, Adorno's view of the natural moment in human need fits well with my conceptualization of human freedom in terms of self-transforming self-determination. However, I diverge from Adorno by interpreting the self-transformative power he attributes to the transgressive drive as an ethical impulse or energy. For him, by contrast, the transgressive drive has no ethical quality. In this respect, his account of the drive is similar to Christoph Menke's view of the drive characteristic of human individuals prior to the process of subjectivation. As discussed in the previous chapter, Menke imputes to humans a distinctive form of naturalness that distinguishes them from other animals: a drive to become something other than they are.[4] This drive enables them to respond to the 'command' to become (what I call) ethical agents, but it is not itself ethical.

There is a second respect in which I diverge from Adorno and Menke. Not only do I connect self-transformation with an ethical impulse that motivates educative learning; in addition, for reasons explained in the previous chapters, I tie it to communicative exchanges with other humans that are argumentative (in an expansive sense). Lacking this communicative, argumentative dimension, self-transformation becomes 'subjectivist' or 'solipsistic', terms that I used to describe Karl Jaspers' existentialist perspective on the validity of ciphers, and is prone to ideological closures. In addition, it expresses a view of human agency as normatively self-sufficient. As I now explain, I characterize such a view as perniciously anthropocentric.

Differentiating anthropocentricism

I propose a differentiated account of anthropocentrism in critical theorizing, referring to some kinds as pernicious and others as relatively benign.

All critical social theories are unavoidably anthropocentric in at least one respect. This is due to their concern, by definition, with 'the good' *for* humans, which means that they inevitably take a human-centred view of 'the good'. In other words, they view relations between human and other-than-human agencies from the ethical perspective of humans. Even critical theories that prioritize 'the good' for animals or plants over 'the good' for humans are anthropocentric in this sense: they hold that it is good for humans to privilege 'the good' for other-than-human agencies over their own. Since this kind of ethical anthropocentrism is definitional of critical social theorizing, I describe it as relatively benign.

In Chapter 2, furthermore, I acknowledged the anthropocentricism of my argumentative approach to critical theorizing, claiming that it too is relatively benign. In that chapter I restricted the possibility of educative, self-transformative learning, and, by implication, the ethical dimension of freely developing agency, to *human* agents. One reason for this is that such learning involves argumentation, which depends in turn on reasons articulated in propositional language. (I made clear, however, that non-propositional modes of expression such as gestures, performances, stagings and various rhetorical strategies and devices can be 'co-arguments' that contribute epistemically to ethical learning.) As I explained, in the case of theory the connection with argumentation is due to the risks of epistemological and ethical authoritarianism, often accompanied by ideological closures, which arise when theories do not open their critical diagnoses and utopian projections to discursive contestation. The same holds for self-determining, self-transforming agency: if human agents do not open their interpretations of their subjective experiences, and the ethical implications that they draw from these, to critical challenges from other humans in argumentation, they risk setting themselves up as ultimate authorities for the validity of their views of 'the good' and inhibiting revisions to these views that could improve their epistemic quality. In short, I claim that an argumentative approach, though inevitably anthropocentric, is indispensable both for the mode of theorizing I advocate and the conception of human freedom I place at the centre of it. For this reason, I describe its anthropocentrism as relatively benign.

Arne Vetlesen (2023) draws attention to another kind of ethical anthropocentrism that likewise may be relatively benign. He argues that human powers of reflexivity are morally significant, especially their future-oriented capacities for abstraction and imagination, because they help constitute humans as agents accountable for their actions. This is a peculiarity of human agents, as far as we know. Vetlesen makes the point that the other-than-human agencies for whom we are responsible may not exhibit the same capacities for reflexivity, while nonetheless qualifying as moral addressees. Contending that moral accountability does not imply moral superiority, he proposes an asymmetric model in which not all moral addressees are moral agents. Vetlesen's point is correct: just as focusing on the good *for* humans does not necessarily imply an ethical value pyramid with human requirements and aspirations at the pinnacle, human peculiarity does not necessarily imply human superiority. Nonetheless, caution is advisable; claims to moral distinctiveness lend themselves easily to supremacist thinking and open the door for the kind of pernicious ethical anthropocentrism that I discuss in the next section under the heading 'exclusive humanism'.

Ethical anthropocentricism has an epistemological counterpart: a human-centred view of knowledge. Here too it is helpful to distinguish between variants that are pernicious and variants that are relatively benign. My discussion in Chapter 2 suggested that the epistemological anthropocentrism characteristic of the 'linguistic turn' falls into the benign category. The 'linguistic turn' casts doubt on the view that direct, unmediated access to a nonlinguistic or prelinguistic reality is philosophically available. It could be argued that this view is reprehensibly Eurocentric and anthropocentric, privileging a conception of philosophical knowledge that is closed to the multiplicity of human ways of knowing as well as to other-than-human ones. However, in Chapter 2, while acknowledging the importance in critical theorizing of prelinguistic and non-propositional knowledge, I insisted, nonetheless, on an epistemic model of argumentation in which participants also endeavour to formulate their arguments in propositional language. This is not to say that decentring, expansive and exploratory critical theories should refrain from questioning the epistemological anthropocentrism of the 'linguistic turn', however benign they may deem it to be. Just as a claim about human peculiarity slides easily into a claim about human supremacy, the claim that philosophical knowledge of reality is always mediated linguistically, culturally and historically slides easily into the claim that human modes of knowing are inherently *superior* to other-than-human modes, opening the door for pernicious kinds of anthropocentrism.

There may well be several kinds of ethical and epistemological anthropocentrism that are relatively benign. That is a matter for further exploration. However, some kinds are emphatically cause for concern. One such is the exclusive humanist perspective on freedom.

Exclusive humanism

In *A Secular Age* (2007), Taylor discusses the secularity of the (Western) modern moral order.[5] He distinguishes between three understandings of secularity. The first is an emptying of public spaces of any reference to God or an ultimate reality. The second is the falling off of religious belief and practice. The third is the move from a society in which belief in God is obvious to one in which it is understood as one option among others. Taylor's concern is the secularity of contemporary (Western) societies in the third sense. He argues that, in the course of Western modernity, there has been a shift from a sociocultural condition 'in which it was virtually impossible not to believe in God, to one in which faith, even for the staunchest believer, is one human possibility among others' (ibid., 3). He calls this modernity's 'immanent frame', and holds that it is common to everyone in Western modernity. He contends that a proper understanding of the immanent frame allows for both closed and open interpretations. Open interpretations seek meaning outside the immanent frame, closed interpretations seek meaning within it. Although the immanent frame *permits* closure without demanding it (ibid., 544), some inhabit it in a closed way, denying that this is just one option. As I read Taylor, European secularization is characterized by the progressive dominance of a closed understanding of the immanent frame, whose salient feature for present purposes is what I call a belief in human normative self-sufficiency (Cooke 2021a).

Taylor describes the closed understanding of the immanent frame as a sociocultural condition in which we come to understand our lives as taking place within a 'self-sufficient immanent order; or better, a constellation of orders, cosmic, social and moral' (2007, 543). From this perspective, which he characterizes as a form of 'exclusive humanism', the immanent order is one 'which can be understood in its own terms, without reference to interventions from outside' (ibid., 832n7). As Taylor puts it: 'Exclusive humanism closes the transcendent window, as though there were nothing beyond' (ibid., 638). He views this belief in human self-sufficiency as a (non-necessary) consequence of an anthropocentric shift that took place around the turn of the seventeenth to eighteenth century. This shift involved four directions of change, each one reducing the role and place of the transcendent and placing human flourishing at the centre of human concerns (ibid., 221–4). In Taylor's narrative, it gives rise to multiple understandings of humans as moral agents. Some understandings, such as exclusive humanism, make humans the ultimate source of ethical meanings (ibid.). Although it is not a necessary consequence of the anthropocentric shift he describes, it gradually became widely and deeply entrenched.

Exclusive humanism is a complex phenomenon; its constitutive parts typically include a sense of self-possession (Taylor 2007, 301), a confidence that our ultimate purposes are those that arise within us, ensuring a secure inner life (ibid., 37); a rejoicing in the self-sufficient power of human reason (ibid., 8–9); and an understanding of the moral order as a self-sufficient framework within which to find the standards of our social, moral and political life (ibid., 238–9). It is intimately connected with an understanding of the modern self as 'buffered'. The buffered self is 'a new sense of self and its place in the cosmos: not open and porous and vulnerable to a world of spirits and powers' (ibid., 27). This sense of invulnerability to the superordinate power of human-transcending forces has two further important facets: a distance from everything outside the mind ('disengagement') and an ethics of instrumentalizing control of desire by reason ('discipline') (ibid., 13–17).

On my reading, Taylor's account of exclusive humanism narrates the emergence, in the course of European secularization processes, of a new self-understanding by humans of their ethical agency as normatively self-sufficient. Normatively self-sufficient agency is a close cousin of the sovereign human agency that Horkheimer and Adorno castigate in *Dialectic of Enlightenment* (2002). In their 'philosophical fragments', they present a vivid account of capitalist modernity as a closed system of instrumental rationality, in which nature is denied any distinctive, or even individual, qualities and is reduced to mere matter to be mastered and manipulated by humans at will. They show it to be driven by an ideal of freedom as self-determining agency that is likewise instrumentalizing, characterized by a need for domination and control. This ideal of freedom, exemplified for the authors by Homer's Odysseus, glorifies human sovereignty, celebrating the limitless potential of human agency, and exalts the human possession and exercise of a will that chooses and determines as it pleases. 'Nature' is treated as an instrument for human manipulation and inexhaustible resource for unconstrained human choosing and uninhibited self-expression. As Horkheimer and Adorno put it, sovereign human agency seeks to learn from nature for the purposes of dominating it and other humans (ibid., 2).

Dialectic of Enlightenment hints at a close connection between anthropogenic ecological depredation and the ideal of the sovereign human subject. However, although I find the implied connection plausible, and a strong reason to jettison conceptions of freedom that celebrate sovereign agency, my critique of the modern ideal of freedom is somewhat different to theirs. My focus in these pages is not the sovereign human will *simpliciter*, but the sovereign *ethical* will.[6] My criticisms are directed primarily at the exclusive humanist view that humans are self-sufficient authorities in matters of ethical value and, hence, the ultimate source of determinations of good and evil. In other words, my focus is the trope of self-sufficient ethical agency. This view of agency, which Taylor shows to have its roots in European modernity, is incompatible with the decentred, open, exploratory conception of human freedom I propose. This is because it blocks educative, self-transformative learning, in particular learning from worldviews or cosmologies that understand human relationality in radically different ways from its own.[7] Furthermore, by construing normativity as entirely a product of human agency, it leaves no room for an account of human and other-than-human relationality in which there is normativity *on both sides*. Chapter 3 opened an alternative perspective on normativity in a context-transcending sense. There I proposed a conception of context-transcending validity as human-transcending validity, more precisely as a power that is not a property of any specific agency, individual or collective, human or other-than-human, or generated by any specific agency. This human-transcending (and other-than-human-transcending) perspective allows for an account of ethical agency in which communicative engagements with the normativity of other-than-human agencies may contribute substantively to its development and, hence, to human freedom.

Freedom as self-will

Christoph Menke's critique of rights adds a further dimension to Taylor's account of the exclusive humanist perspective. Menke argues that European modernity institutes new forms of law and politics based on a conception of human freedom as self-will [*Eigenwille*]. In a political context, freedom as self-will is essentially indifferent to the content of the choices, decisions and actions of citizens. It grants permission to individuals to do as they please, limited only by requirements of security and stability.

Menke (2020) claims that the defining feature of politics in bourgeois modernity is its system of subjective rights. He contends that the bourgeois revolution – the revolution that establishes subjective rights as the principle of political association – fundamentally changes the *form* of law. For the ancient Greeks, law functions as an educative force that transforms natural striving or 'willing' [*Wollen*] into virtue through habitualization. For the ancient Romans, it functions as an educative force that controls natural willing, subjecting it to the laws of reason through commanding obedience.[8] In modern bourgeois society, by contrast, law has no educative, moral or rational function. Its purpose is not morality or reason, but to safeguard a social contract on the part of free and equal individuals motivated by the need for security and stability. Accordingly, the function of law is to ensure subjective rights.

Menke views the bourgeois understanding as radically changing law's relation to natural impulses. As observed previously, he attributes to humans a distinctive form of naturalness that distinguishes them from other animals, which he characterizes as a drive to become something other than what they are.[9] This is part of what I call the constitutive materiality of humans. In contrast to the ancient Athenian and Roman forms of law, which seek to educate natural impulses in order to bring them into line with morality or reason, the natural willing of individuals in the bourgeois form is not something to be changed or controlled; instead, natural willing is always permitted in principle. Although the actions resulting from natural willing may have to be controlled in the interests of social security and stability, the law is *fundamentally indifferent* to the content of an individual's willing. Anything is permitted within limits that are generally accepted as necessary for security and stability. Thus, bourgeois law grants permission to individuals to do as they please, limited only by these requirements. The distinctive form of freedom it generates is self-will. This is not freedom as the relentless pursuit of self-interest; rather, it is the freedom to exercise one's will without constraint, whether in the interests of self or the interests of others. Freedom as self-will has two aspects: a negatively construed freedom of choice and a positively construed freedom to realize these choices within the prescribed limits. The dual aspect of property rights reflects these two sides of bourgeois freedom. Bourgeois property is both a space of freedom, a domain for the exercise of self-will unimpeded by social control and, as private wealth [*Vermögen*], an instrument of freedom – a means for realizing individual choices. The institution of property rights serves to justify rights of political participation, since the right to dispose over property, which entails the right to realize one's choices, also entails the right to participate in collective decisions over the distribution of social means. This view of law is common to both liberal versions of democracy, which prioritize freedom of choice over the freedom to realize choices, and socialist versions, where the emphasis is on ensuring ability to realize choices through welfare provisions and the regulation of commerce. Although neither side recognizes their commonality, they share a view of law as a mechanism for protecting and enabling the self-will of individual subjects, irrespective of the content of their willing (Menke 2020, 214–16).

Menke's account of the bourgeois idea of freedom as self-will not only complements Taylor's narrative of the process of secularization in Western modernity; it shows, in addition, how a view of human agents as self-sufficient authorities in matters of ethical value is not just predominant in Western modern moral and political theory, but also underpins and structures Western modern institutions of law and politics.

In my opening remarks to this chapter I identified two features of the exclusive humanist perspective on human freedom that I consider especially troubling. One was its instrumentalist approach to what I call entangled human agency. The other was its idea of autonomy as an intramundane mode of self-authorship. By this I mean an understanding of autonomy in which humans, individually or collectively, are the self-sufficient authors of the moral norms and principles that bind them. I now clarify my objections to these two features.

Intramundane transcendence

I begin by explaining the limitations of intramundane conceptions of transcendence and their troubling consequence for the modern ideal of moral and political self-authorship.

In contemporary critical theory in the Frankfurt School tradition, Habermas is the champion of intramundane or 'this-worldly' transcendence. As discussed briefly in Chapter 2, he construes the transcendent power of human reason in a postmetaphysical sense that involves no appeal to any reality or authority that is not humanly generated. He argues that, in European modernity, in the course of secularization processes accompanied by the 'linguistification' of the lifeworld, the context-transcending moment of human reason is de-transcendentalized, in the sense of made part of the human world (Habermas 1987; 2017; Cooke 2019b). Habermas describes his postmetaphysical understanding of the 'Wholly Other' as 'deflationary' and as 'this-worldly' ['*diesseitig*'] or 'intramundane' ['*innerweltlich*'] (1991a [Mendieta 2002]; 1996; 2003b). It is noteworthy that its context-transcending normativity is generated from within the resources of European modernity. As Habermas sometimes puts it, European modernity takes on the task of generating its own normativity, by which he means its own standards for rational critique (1990, 7).

According to his postmetaphysical account of human reason, as discussed earlier, only claims to truth and moral rightness are potentially universally valid and, in consequence, have an unconditionally binding force. This is because only these claims can be validated by human reasoning in 'this-worldly' terms, which is to say, without appealing to an idea of normativity whose origins are not within the human world. In the case of claims to moral rightness, which is most relevant for present purposes, argumentatively achieved universal agreement *defines* their validity. Habermas writes: '[Idealized] warranted assertibility is what we *mean* by moral rightness . . . it exhausts the meaning of moral rightness itself' (2003a, 258; emphasis in original).

In Chapter 2, I drew attention to one unwelcome implication of Habermas' intramundane interpretation of context-transcending validity. For Habermas, ethical claims – claims about the good life for humans – are not universal validity claims; they are irreducibly local, bound to the evaluative horizon of particular communities and groups. This means that no argumentatively reached agreement among all humans as to their validity could ever be reached, even under idealized circumstances. It also implies that the inhabitants of modernity have no way of rationally assessing the claims to validity raised (implicitly or explicitly) for ethical arguments and, by extension, for the ethical-existential-political claims made by critical theory for its emancipatory projections. This is one reason why a decentring, expansive, exploratory mode of critical theorizing requires an expanded version of Habermas' model of intersubjective argumentation.

A further unwelcome consequence of Habermas' account of 'this-worldly' transcendence is a closure of the horizons of modernity against claims to ethical-existential-political validity that are universal in scope but do not conform to his particular postmetaphysical understanding of such validity (Cooke 2019a, 78–9).[10] When applied to the emancipatory claims of critical theories, this evidently privileges theories whose philosophical legacy is European modernity.

There is yet another reason why Habermas' 'this-worldly' view of context-transcending validity is inadequate for the decentring, expansive, exploratory mode of critical theorizing that I advocate. His position is not just Eurocentric; it is also perniciously anthropocentric. It conceives of context-transcending validity entirely in human terms, as a purely human construction, thereby blocking educative, self-transformative learning by humans through engagement with the normativity of other-than-human agencies. This pernicious anthropocentrism results from his epistemic-constructivist account of morality, according to which moral validity is generated through the exchange of arguments under ideal communicative conditions aimed at determining the universalizability of the interests of the participants. It is important to notice that it is not a consequence of his *argumentative* approach to context-transcending validity (which I endorse for reasons explained in Chapter 2); rather, it is due to his view of context-transcendent normativity as *humanly* generated. I discern this troubling feature also in the *non-argumentative*, 'materialist' view of context-transcending normativity, which Peter Gordon (2023) finds in Adorno's writings.

Like many in the Frankfurt School tradition, Gordon emphasizes the importance of the immanent moment of critical social theorizing. He holds – correctly, in my view – that social critique and social change must proceed by drawing on the normativity available to us in the society we inhabit. He offers a reading of Adorno's philosophy along these lines. Distancing himself from those who maintain that Adorno cannot locate any reliable sources of normativity within the existing world, such as Habermas (1984) and Fabian Freyenhagen (2013),[11] Gordon argues that Adorno's writings are animated by a normative commitment to happiness (in the capacious sense). Moreover, on his reading Adorno seeks to disclose within existing social reality glimpses of a better world – 'fragments of normativity that point beyond the landscape of our current suffering' (Gordon 2023, 3). I am in broad agreement with Gordon's reading of Adorno up to this point.

On occasion, however, Gordon asserts a stronger version of the thesis of immanent transcendence. This is evident, for example, when he endorses the intramundane – 'this-worldly' – conception of critique that Habermas derives from the idea of self-authorization, citing Habermas' view of modernity approvingly: '[Philosophy] must discover within our experience itself the normative resources it needs to gain leverage against it' (Gordon 2023, xvii). By 'self-authorization', Gordon means justification on the basis of self-imposed principles and norms; evidently, it is closely connected with the Kantian idea of autonomy as self-authorship, which, as I noted in Chapter 1, is at the heart of Habermas' writings on law and politics. Self-authorization is also the core of Habermas' discourse ethics, and forms the basis of his account of context-transcending moral validity (Cooke 2020b). In a review essay on German idealism, Gordon references Habermas, writing that modernity 'carries its warrant in its own pockets' (2005, 121). In the same essay, he explicitly welcomes the 'modernist breakthrough from a "metaphysical" conception of self-creation to a "normative" conception of self-authorization' (ibid., 137), and applauds modernity's 'poignantly twofold message that everything should stand before the tribunal of reason, but the tribunal of reason answers only to itself' (ibid., 122). In short, there can be little doubt that Gordon embraces a view of self-authorization in which the transcending moment is 'this-worldly'. It is not surprising, therefore, that, on another occasion, he takes Habermas to task for undermining the self-authorization thesis by acknowledging the possibility of an *extra*mundane source of authoritative value (2016, 471–3).

Here, Gordon astutely notes a shift in Habermas' postmetaphysical thinking. As discussed, Habermas had previously insisted that the transcendent power of communicative rationality is 'this-worldly' – intramundane – as opposed to 'otherworldly' – extramundane. He had consistently emphasized that critical theory rejects metaphysical transcendence, embracing instead what he also refers to as 'transcendence from within' (Mendieta 2002). However, in his writings on religion since around 2010, Habermas seems to pull back from his emphatic affirmation of 'this-worldly', postmetaphysical transcendence (2017; 2019). Gordon observes, in my view correctly, that Habermas 'appears to surrender the pragmatic and forever unfinished ideal of Enlightenment self-authorization' that had inspired his own and other secularizing philosophies within European modernity (2016, 472; cf. Cooke 2019b; 2023c). Gordon's interpretation of Adorno may be read as a 'this-worldly' reading of context-transcending normativity that tacitly rebukes Habermas for reneging on the promise of self-authorization issued by (European) modernity.

Whether dialogical or 'materialist', 'this-worldly' approaches to context-transcending validity are at odds with the decentring, expansive and exploratory mode of critical theorizing that I propose.[12] 'This-worldly' approaches inhibit educative, self-transformative learning by critical theories (and human agents) from human experiences of the normativity of other-than-human agencies. They are also hostile to learning by humans from their experiences of human-transcending powers that are neither created by nor belong to any particular agency, human or other-than-human. In short, 'this-worldly' accounts of transcendence may be described as ideologically closed.

Gordon is certainly alert to the risk of closure. He underscores Adorno's view that all theory is open and must remain as open as experience itself (2023, 117; citing Adorno 2017b, 98). He also emphasizes the distance between Adorno's negative dialectics, which refuses to unify human experience by assigning to it a single meaning, and Hegel's dialectics, which follows a logic of reconciliation that culminates in the elimination of non-identity and becomes 'a nightmare of thoroughgoing closure' (ibid., 46–57; here p. 47). Furthermore, Gordon offers a careful and nuanced analysis of the similarities and differences between Kant's 'thing-in-itself' and Adorno's 'non-identical', understood as that which lies beyond the intelligible and hence escapes the net of conceptuality (ibid., 113–18). He also reminds us of Adorno's concern to develop a new style of philosophy that 'will fasten our attention on those places where "irreducible reality breaks in upon it [human reason]"' (ibid., 48; citing Adorno 2000b, 38). In the same vein (as noted in Chapter 2), Gordon offers an illuminating account of Adorno's idea of normatively rich or 'emphatic' experiences, in which humans are afforded a glimpse of the non-identical (ibid., 116). He draws attention to Adorno's insistence on the need for humans to open themselves in genuine vulnerability to the non-identity of the object and offers an insightful interpretation of his idea of mimesis along these lines. He writes that Adorno assigns enormous philosophical importance to the enduring bond between humans and nature, a responsiveness that cannot be construed in purely instrumental terms. Instead, it is 'a deep or even "archaic" feature of human experience that is anterior to all considerations of utility' (ibid., 130–2; here p. 130).

However, Gordon's welcome emphasis on the openness of Adorno's philosophy to experiences of the non-identical is in tension with the view of immanent normativity he imputes to him. Gordon takes 'the absolute' to mean 'the unrealized future' (2023, 46). Given his appreciation of the openness of Adorno's philosophy we may assume that he understands this as an unrealized future that is indeterminate. However, although indeterminate in content, for Gordon it is a future whose determination relies entirely on human thought and action. He understands Adorno's materialism 'in a broad and non-doctrinal sense' as the thesis that 'this-worldly and sensuous being [is] the locus of all human fulfilment' (ibid., 105). His reading of 'the absolute' in Adorno as 'the unrealized future' projects a future that is materialist in this sense: a condition of human fulfilment that is complete in itself, entirely self-sufficient, with no need of anything beyond the human world. In other words, it is perfection in 'this-worldly' terms. However, his interpretation of what Adorno means by 'the absolute' does not fit well with his account of emphatic experiences in Adorno's writings, in which 'irreducible reality breaks in upon' supposedly self-sufficient human reason.[13] On a more plausible interpretation of 'the absolute' in these writings, emphatic experiences afford glimpses of an *irreducible* reality – a reality that may not be reduced to human fulfilment within the human world. In other words, they are experiences of extramundane transcendence. Importantly, as I observed in Chapter 3, due to the dual perspective on normativity that I adopt, the transcending moment I build into ethical agency is readily compatible with self-determining agency. Thus, it does not undermine the intramundane, 'this-worldly', emancipatory aims of critical theories. Such extramundane experiences may nourish human endeavours to change existing social reality in ways that will enable human happiness and freedom within 'this world'; at the same time, they remind us that human fulfilment is never *completely* humanly generated, but is dependent on human relationships with other-than-human beings and experiences of other-than-human powers, and that humans can learn in an ethical-existential-political sense from these relationships and experiences. Exclusive humanism is closed to this possibility. This is what makes it perniciously anthropocentric.

Subtractive freedom

I turn now to the second, connected, feature of the exclusive humanist perspective that I find troubling: its denial of, or disregard for, the ethical dimension of what I have called the constitutive materiality of humans – the ethical significance of the entanglements between human agency and other-than-human agencies.

The exclusive humanist perspective on freedom is 'subtractive'. Taylor uses the term to describe self-dissociation by humans from what they have come to perceive of as constraints. Subtraction stories explain modernity in general, and modern secularity, in particular, in terms of 'humans having lost or sloughed off, or liberated themselves from certain earlier, confining horizons, or illusions, or limitations of knowledge' (2007, 22). In the context of anthropogenic ecological depredation, the subtractive perspective is worrying because it uncouples human freedom from 'nature', disregarding the multiple, complex entanglements between ethical agency and other-than-human agencies. Earlier, I suggested that Adorno's view of human 'naturalness' is a helpful reminder of the constitutive materiality of human agency and, hence, of these entanglements. However, their significance may be understood in two quite different ways. The significance of the entanglements between human and other-than-human agencies may be understood either in a way that reinforces the exclusive humanist perspective, or in a way that breaks with this perspective. To explain what I mean and why this matters, I discuss the reconfigured account of autonomy I find in the writings of the political theorist, Pierre Charbonnier.

In his book *Affluence and Freedom: An Environmental History of Political Ideas*, Charbonnier critically discusses the liberal conception of freedom, which he characterizes as 'extraction autonomy' (2021, 89–92). Extraction autonomy depends on a mode of relating to the world that is similar to the relation characteristic of the sovereign human subject in Horkheimer and Adorno's *Dialectic of Enlightenment*. In both cases, 'nature' is treated as an inexhaustible resource, in Charbonnier's discussion it is a resource for the realization of the (Western) modern value of freedom. In his account, the modern project of liberty founders on its 'inability to give political meaning to the interdependencies between modern society and its world, its resources, its environments, and its spaces, which has left the field open to ecological predation' (ibid., 93). Extraction autonomy is inattentive to, and indeed obscures, the ecological dynamics that allows human societies to reproduce themselves socially, culturally and economically (ibid., 238). Put differently, human freedom, when construed as extraction autonomy, conceals the *material* dimension of the Western project of emancipation.

Taylor's term 'subtractive' adds an inflection that is missing in Charbonnier's account. Unlike 'extraction', it has a connotation of possible loss or impoverishment. Understood in this way, subtractive freedom is not just an error; it also diminishes possibilities for the free development of human agency. By contrast, in Charbonnier's political history, extraction autonomy refers in the first instance to a functionally problematic mistake or illusion. He criticizes liberal freedom for impairing the proper functioning of the social system of industrialized capitalism, for which the value of individual freedom is an integral part. In other words, for Charbonnier, liberal versions of the modern project of autonomy make the mistake of thinking that freedom involves the removal of all material constraints on society: they extract 'nature' from 'society', in the sense that they uncouple the two domains, conceiving of each as essentially separate. However, such liberal interpretations of the modern emancipatory project are based on an empirical error: they uncouple 'society' and 'nature', failing to realize that they cannot be uncoupled without undermining the functioning of the social system on which the emancipatory project depends. This dooms them to failure from the outset. So long as they continue to uncouple the two realms, modern societies will at some point prove unable to reproduce themselves socially, culturally and economically – they will become unsustainable, ceasing to function as they should.

The alternative proposed by Charbonnier is an 'integrated' view of autonomy. He claims that the early socialists construed human freedom in this way. For them, the modern ideal of freedom as self-authorship involves the integration of effective relationships with the world:

> The energy of fire, machinery, the division of labour, the exploita-tion of the land and labour in any shape or form comprise the frame of reference necessary for the ideas of equality and liberty. In other words, and contrary to what happens in the liberal tradi-tion, collective relationships with the world take on a political significance. (2021, 116)

Charbonnier points out, however, that socialist conceptions of autonomy as originally construed, although they do not uncouple 'nature' and 'society', for the most part remain bound to a paradigm, in which growth of the economy through the exploitation of natural resources, albeit for the benefit of all humans, is the main criterion of a well-functioning social system. He argues that humans today need a reconfigured version of socialism detached from this 'productivist' framework. He takes the view that the reality test imposed on us by the new climate regime means that we need to rethink the idea of self-preservation as one that extends to the entire planet and is not exclusively human-centred. For the same reason, socialism must adopt a new perspective on freedom that no longer insists on endless production and growth as the salient criteria for successful social reproduction.

Accordingly, Charbonnier calls for a reconfigured version of socialism in which the reproduction of human society is viewed as a matter of collective control by humans over their future, which requires the integration of a certain number of ecological norms and thresholds. In short, he envisages a new perspective on human freedom, which is based on a reversal of a functionally problematic uncoupling of 'nature' and 'society' and is, moreover, detached from the productivist paradigm of endless economic growth.

However, in at least one respect Charbonnier's reconfigured version of integration autonomy seems strangely similar to the extraction autonomy he rejects. It appears to share with liberal versions of freedom the exclusive humanist perspective that facilitates a purely instrumentalizing perspective on 'nature', reducing other-than-human agencies to lifeless objects to be used by human agents as they will and lending itself in turn to capitalist exploitation and extractivism. Certainly, integration autonomy, as rearticulated by Charbonnier, is significantly different from extraction autonomy in assigning humans the role of stewards of nature. For Charbonnier, stewards are necessary to ensure provision of the material goods humans require if they are genuinely to realize the emancipatory promise of European modernity and actualize individual human freedom in existing social reality. Otherwise, the social systems they inhabit will cease to function properly. Capitalism, due to its inherent drive towards maximizing profit, has proved to be incapable of achieving this goal. Charbonnier is confident, however, that a properly functioning socialist system would be able to do so. This is why I read his functionalist argument for integration autonomy as a reconfigured socialist version of the liberal conception that retains its instrumentalist perspective: he exposes the dysfunctionality of the liberal conception, not its ethical deficiencies.

Our contemporary situation of anthropogenic planetary destruction calls for more than a critique of dysfunctionality. It also calls for more than environmental stewardship based on a clear perception of the realities of our disastrous environmental situation. It is not enough to recognize the material dependency of humans on their nonhuman environments. What is required, in addition, is a decisive break with the hubristic belief in the self-sufficiency of the human ethical will characteristic of exclusive humanism and the instrumentalizing stance towards 'nature' that it fosters. Alongside this there is a need for further exploration of the entangled relationality of human and other-than-human agencies and the normative implications of this relationality.

In sum: I contend that acknowledging the entangled interdependencies between human and other-than-human agencies is important in the first instance neither instrumentally, as a necessary precondition for the realization of freedom, nor functionally, because the successful reproduction of human societies depends on the material goods provided for humans by their nonhuman environments. Rather, attentiveness to these entangled interdependencies is important primarily because human freedom itself, as I reimagine and rearticulate it, depends on engagement with other-than-human (as well as human) agencies that have their own normativity. In the next chapter, I elaborate on my proposed reimagining and rearticulation of freedom.

Neither functionalist nor instrumentalist reasoning should be dismissed out of hand. Each may contribute indirectly to bringing about relations between human agents and other-than-human agencies that are *not* perniciously anthropocentric. For this reason, environmental policies implemented for functionalist or instrumentalist reasons may be welcomed cautiously. For example, policies aimed at replacing fossil fuels with the 'green' energy of solar power and wind and wave power, or policies to increase biodiversity. Such measures, even when in the service of human interests in their own survival on the planet or, indeed, even for the purposes of the continued functioning of industrialized capitalism, may nonetheless result in fundamental shifts in ethical perceptions that help to dismantle exclusive humanism and other pernicious kinds of anthropocentricism. In general, however, societies in which the dominant logics and vocabularies are instrumentalist and/ or functionalist will be hostile to the decentring, expansive, exploratory mode of critical theorizing that I propose and incompatible with the kind of self-determining, self-transforming, ecologically entangled ethical agency that I envisage.

The constitutive materiality of ethical agency

Despite his neglect of the ethical-existential-political dimension of the multiple, complex entanglements between human agency and other-than-human agencies, Charbonnier's critique of extraction autonomy is welcome for highlighting the constitutive materiality of human agency, inviting further consideration of this dimension.

In the Frankfurt School tradition, there are various senses in which critical theories characterize themselves as materialist, several of which have been mentioned in the preceding chapters. To begin with, there is materialism in the Marxist sense that reality is historically produced through human action in the world. As discussed in Chapter 1, Marx criticizes Feuerbach's materialism for failing to recognize this.

Horkheimer makes historical materialism a cornerstone of critical theory when he writes that it takes as its object humans as producers of their own way of life in its totality.[14] Frankfurt School critical theories often understand themselves as materialist in the further sense that they give voice to human experiences of unfreedom and injustice within existing social realities. As I pointed out in Chapter 1, Hegelian idealism could also be said to be materialist in this sense. Unlike Hegel's idealist approach to history, however, Frankfurt School critical theories are materialist in a third, distinctively Marxist, sense: they attribute to theory the power to change empirical reality. This too was discussed in Chapter 1.

In tune with the materialist method, which they take over from Marx and adapt in various ways, Frankfurt School critical theories also understand ethical agency in materialist terms. Most fundamentally in the sense that human agency is constituted in historical processes of social, cultural and economic reproduction.[15] For Horkheimer, the relationship is co-constitutive: human agents are constituted in continuous dialectical interaction with 'the material and spiritual culture of humanity as such' and, in turn, react back on it (2018, 113). Given the Marxist explanatory framework of Horkheimer's research programme, it seems safe to assume that 'material' here means the 'forces of economic production'.

Horkheimer's emphasis on the *dialectical*, co-constitutive movement involved in the production of human agency is important for the 'transformation' component of the conceptualization of freedom that I develop in the following chapters. This is because it establishes a dynamic relationship between transformation of 'selves' through the impact of the specific 'material and spiritual culture' they inhabit and the power of 'selves' to transform the lives of other agents, human and other-than-human, as well as their material and spiritual environments. It provides the basis for a dimension of my discussion of individual freedom that so far has not come into view: the ethically significant, co-constitutive relationship between social institutions and ethical agency. I come back to this in Chapter 7.[16]

Put differently, Horkheimer's dynamic, dialectically materialist perspective on the constitution of human agency attributes to it a material dimension that has some independence of human history and the social processes that constitute it. As discussed in Chapter 1, for Horkheimer, as for Marx, human nature is not *entirely* socially produced; rather, it is socially produced within the limits of certain natural facts about humans as a species. In this sense, his account can be said to take human naturalness [*Naturwüchsigkeit*] into consideration.

This relevant independence is also present in Adorno's and Menke's respective accounts of the constitution of subjectivity, in their case explained by a pre-social drive. For all three theorists, human agency is constituted in significant measure by material forces that have some independence of human history and activity.

However, what is missing in Horkheimer's dialectical materialist account of the constitution of human agency is a human-transcending *ethical* dimension. There is a similar omission in Adorno's and Menke's respective conceptions of human naturalness in terms of a pre-social 'drive'. In all three accounts, for different reasons, the constitutive materiality of human agency does not contribute *constitutively* to its free development as an ethical agent: it is not constitutive of *ethical* agency. By contrast, in *Dialectic of Enlightenment*, Horkheimer and Adorno hint at the ethical significance of the constitutive materiality of human agency when they call for recollection of 'nature within' by self-reflective human subjects (2002, 32), inviting consideration of the possibility that such recollection will contribute constitutively to the free development of ethical agency. This suggestive remark fits well with my perspective on ecologically entangled human agency.

In the next chapter, I fill in the picture of ethical agency I have sketched so far, explaining why an argumentative, dialogical approach to self-determination is important, why self-transformation has to be thought together with self-determination and how self-determining self-transformation can result from epistemically and ethically significant encounters with other-than-human agencies.

5

Freedom as Ethical Agency: Explorations

Individual human freedom, as I picture it, is self-determining, self-transforming ethical agency that is entangled in multiple complex ways with other-than-human agencies. Crucially, there is an ethical dimension to these entanglements: humans can learn in an educative, self-transforming, ethical-existential-political sense from their communicative engagements with other-than-humans. By this, I mean that communication with other-than-human agencies contributes substantively to the free development of humans as *ethical* agents. One important presupposition here is that other-than-human agencies, too, have their own normativity. *There is normativity on both the human and other-than-human sides.*

In this chapter, I fill in the picture of freedom as ethical agency that I have sketched so far. Highlighting its key features, I explain the sense in which self-determination is relational, why it is dialogical and why self-determination and self-transformation are inseparable moments of ethical agency. I then address the question of how human agents can be transformed in an ethically significant and epistemically relevant sense through communicative engagements with other-than-human agencies.

Reconfiguring relational freedom

My proposed perspective on freedom as ethical agency is relational. Moreover, it belongs to the family of 'positive' conceptions of freedom (loosely interpreted).[1] Here I recall Isaiah Berlin's distinction between negative and positive liberty (1969). In the terms made famous by Berlin, the 'positive' conception of liberty 'derives from the wish on the part of the individual to be his own master. I wish my life and decisions to depend on myself, not on external forces of whatever kind. I wish to be the instrument of my own, not of other men's, acts of will' (1969, 8). This is autonomy as self-authorship, self-legislation or self-determination, as articulated by Kant. Berlin is wary of positive liberty, maintaining that it leads easily to self-abnegation, on the one hand, and self-surrender to authoritarian leaders or political institutions on the other (ibid., 10). He juxtaposes it with negative liberty, which he clearly favours. Negative liberty is the area within which a human agent can act unobstructed by others: 'If I am prevented by others from doing what I could otherwise do, I am to that degree unfree' (ibid., 3). For Frankfurt School theorists, by contrast, the positive conception of liberty as individual and collective self-authorship is the most fitting expression of the ideal of freedom. As observed in Chapter 1, Habermas describes collective self-authorship as the dogmatic core of his normative theory of law and democracy; in the same vein, Adorno holds that 'the power of . . . self-determination' is the 'single genuine power standing against the principle of Auschwitz' (2005, 195).[2]

Both relational and 'positive' conceptions of freedom are vulnerable to the objections I raised against exclusive humanism in Chapter 4. Accordingly, although I construe individual human freedom as relational and as self-determination, I take two decisive steps beyond contemporary theories that advance a similar view. By contrast with other relational, 'positive' approaches, I understand relationality to include relations between human agents and other-than-human agencies, and hold that its ecological entanglements are ethically significant for self-determining agency.

My relational account of freedom as self-determination builds on some fruitful reconceptualizations of freedom as autonomy in the Frankfurt School tradition from Habermas onwards. With his 'communicative turn', Habermas offers a social-relational account of self-determination that dialogically recasts the Kantian conception of moral autonomy. For Habermas, as for Kant, humans are the authors of the moral law to which they are subject; however, for Habermas, self-authorship takes place in intersubjective processes of argumentation. This enables him to avoid some serious objections that have been directed against Kantian versions of moral autonomy. For the most part, these objections, which were picked up and developed by communitarian, feminist and poststructuralist critics in the 1980s and 1990s, have to do with connotations of self-ownership and self-mastery that the concept of autonomy acquired in the course of capitalist modernity. Thanks to his relational approach, Habermas' conception of moral autonomy is able to avoid these unwelcome connotations, while nonetheless accommodating the self-determining component of the ideal (Cooke 1992; 1999a; 1999b).

Following Habermas, there have been a number of fruitful attempts within critical theory to rethink the idea of individual freedom in social-relational terms (e.g. Young 1990; Benhabib 1992). More recently, Axel Honneth (2014) has offered a Hegelian social-relational account and Rainer Forst (2012) a Kantian one. In my own writings over the past decades, I too have adopted a social-relational approach to autonomy (e.g. Cooke 1992; 1997; 1999a; 1999b; 1999c; 2006a).

For some time, the distinctive feature of my relational approach to autonomy was the ethical-existential component that I build into self-determination. I then became aware that my relational approach, which focused exclusively on relations between humans, was open to objections of anthropocentricism and, by extension, Eurocentrism. In my more recent work, accordingly, I have sought to expand my relational approach in ways that acknowledge the importance of human relations to other-than-human entities (Cooke 2020a; 2023a; 2023b). This book may be read as an effort to explore further this line of thought and its implications for critical theorizing.

Self-evaluating agency

In my efforts to reimagine and rearticulate the idea of self-determination in a more encompassing relational sense, I begin with Marx's writings on alienated (estranged) labour in his 1844 *Economic and Philosophic Manuscripts* (2000c). One of the forms of alienation Marx describes in these early writings is alienation of humans from their 'species-being', by which he means alienation of humans from their capacity for freely purposive, creative, self-reflective activity. As I observed in Chapter 1, the early Marx understands freedom not only as the capacity of humans to set goals and pursue them without being bound by biological necessity; he also understands it as the capacity of humans to make their life-activity into the object of their will and consciousness. In other words, to assert themselves as human subjects and to direct their life-activity intentionally and reflectively. Marx does not satisfactorily develop this thought in his early manuscripts. Charles Taylor's view of the modern self as a strong evaluator helps to explicate it (1989).

Taylor holds that humans are self-interpreting creatures. By this, he means that human relationships to the world are never simply given, but are constantly articulated, reconstituted, negotiated and transformed through individual and cultural processes of interpretation. Furthermore, human interpretations of the world are always also interpretations of the self (and vice versa). The process of self-interpretation is driven by what Taylor calls 'strong evaluations'. At any given time, these strong evaluations constitute evaluative roadmaps for human individuals. Stable identities and intentional human action are inconceivable without such roadmaps, which depict substantial ethical conceptions that embody ideas of the good: ideas about what is important, what really matters (1989, 63). In other words, the good is that which is picked out as incomparably higher in a qualitative distinction and in this sense is a 'higher good' (ibid., 62–3). Higher goods depend in turn on constitutive goods. Examples of constitutive goods include God, history, reason, art and nature. They command moral allegiance and as such are 'moral sources' (ibid., 91–107). Accordingly, strong evaluation has an integral receptive element, calling for openness to experiences in which the power of moral sources makes itself *present* to human subjects, requiring in turn flexibility, open-mindedness, sensitivity to others and imaginativeness. Nonetheless, strong evaluation is also a mode of self-determination. This is because it requires human agents to ascertain for themselves what kind of person they would like to be and what paths they should pursue if they are to become that kind of person; furthermore, it requires them to take responsibility for their evaluative judgements. In addition, critical reflection is an integral part of strong evaluation; self-determination calls for evaluative discrimination by human agents among the aims in life they consider worth pursuing. In short, strong evaluation is an ethical-existential process guided by a critically reflective concern for a good life.

However, to all appearances Taylor's account of strong evaluation has a serious lacuna: it seems not to *require* communicative engagement with other human agents in argumentation. If this is so, ultimate authority for the validity of evaluative judgements is handed over in principle to the individual agents who make them, rendering the practice of strong evaluation open to the objections of subjectivism and solipsism that I raised against Karl Jaspers in Chapter 3. However, in this respect Taylor's account manifests a certain ambivalence (Cooke 2021a). On the one hand, he describes strong evaluations as tracking some mind-independent reality and resting on the conviction that 'there is supposed to be a truth of the matter;' it 'lies in their nature as strong evaluations to claim truth, reality, or subjective rightness' (2011, 297–8). But, like Habermas in his writings about ethical-existential-political validity, as discussed in Chapter 2, Taylor appears to rule out any prospect of critical assessment of such claims that is not simply particularistic, determined by subjective experiences interpreted against the background of the norms and values prevailing in a historically specific sociocultural context. In other words, he seems to conceive of strong evaluations as ethical-existential claims that are determined subjectively and contextually. Accordingly, the self-reflexivity he builds into strong evaluation may be described as monological rather than dialogical.

The non-dialogical perspective he appears to hold may be due in part to his philosophical method. Taylor's method is distinctive, an 'interwoven type of argument' interlacing historical, ontological, phenomenological, hermeneutical, theistic and ethical strands (Meijer 2017, 372; quoting a verbal remark by Taylor characterizing his arguments about strong evaluation). However, the phenomenological strand often takes precedence. This results in an overreliance on a phenomenology of self-interpretations, which makes the ethical commitments and convictions held by actual people in the historical context in question the basis for sociocultural and philosophical critique.[3]

Whatever the reason, if Taylor's account of strong evaluation is monological, as it seems to be, it is troubling from the point of view of the self-transforming aspect of self-determination as I envisage it, for it fosters ideological closures. Moreover, it tacitly supports the exclusive humanist picture of normatively self-sufficient human agency that I target in these chapters with the help of his writings. In short, it threatens to close the transcendent window that both he and I seek to keep open.

Resonant human agency

Hartmut Rosa's writings on resonant relationality are open to a similar objection (Cooke 2025b). This is surprising, since he proposes an understanding of individual human freedom as resonant self-efficacious [*selbstwirksam*] subjectivity that in many respects is close to the self-transforming ethical agency I depict. On the face of it, Rosa's conception of resonant agency is diametrically opposed to the modern Western ideal of the autarkic human subject, who decides and chooses just as it pleases, subject only to general legal and moral constraints. Instead of self-will [*Eigenwille*][4] and self-sufficiency, Rosa emphasizes openness, receptivity and willingness to be changed through encounters with others, human and other-than-human. He emphasizes, moreover, the importance for human agency of recognizing the other's fundamental inaccessibility [*Unverfügbarkeit*, also translatable as 'unavailability' or 'uncontrollability'],[5] as opposed to seeking to control and dominate the other. Furthermore, as I explain below, his normative theory of resonant human agency, especially his concepts of adaptive transformation [*Anverwandlung*] and partial uncontrollability [*Halbverfügbarkeit*], contributes helpfully to explicating an idea of self-determining human agency that involves self-transformation through experiences of a human-transcending power and encounters with other agencies, human and other-than human.

Resonance is the key category in Rosa's critical social theory (2019a). He uses this acoustic phenomenon to formulate a social-scientific tool of analysis that is at once descriptive and normative (ibid., 220). On a purely descriptive level, he seeks to show that resonance is a necessary condition both for identity and sociality. His normative claim is that humans are existentially shaped by their longing for resonant relationships. Here, he employs the concept of resonance as a 'metacriterion': as the measure of a good life, in the ethical sense of a well-lived one [*ein gelingendes Leben*], within a corresponding good society, again in an ethical sense (ibid., 577).

On occasion, Rosa makes clear that he views resonance as the promise of the modern idea of freedom. Characterizing the project of Western modernity as a dialectical movement between desire for mastery of the world and desire for resonance through adaptive transformation of the world, he writes:

> The project of modernity is defined by the strategy of increasing humanity's share of the world, but it is motivated by the hope of adaptively transforming [the] world. *That we can go out into the world to find the place that 'speaks to us' or 'appeals to us', where we can feel at home, that we can make our own* – this is the promise of the modern idea of freedom. 'Finding our place' here means establishing vital relationships in all dimensions. (2019a, 461; emphasis in the original)

Rosa's critical sociological diagnosis is that Western capitalist modernity is currently in a situation that may be described as a resonance catastrophe (ibid., 397–460). Following Max Weber, he maintains that modernity 'seeks to make the world predictable, controllable, comprehensible, calculable, and thus *accessible* [*verfügbar*]' (ibid., 418). An accessible world is supposed to enable resonant world relations. However, its promise of accessibility (in the sense of *complete* availability or controllability)[6] turns into the opposite: the world becomes ever more *un*controllable, producing angry citizens, who feel threatened by the world (2019b, 46, 10). From a sociological perspective, it produces a widespread state of alienation. Rosa here adopts Rahel Jaeggi's definition of alienation as a 'relation of relationlessness' (Rosa 2019a, 228; Jaeggi 2014). In Rosa's account, alienated subjects encounter a mute world, a world that does not sing back to them, a world bereft of qualities. In their state of alienation, the only kinds of relationships to the world available to them are either withdrawal from, or instrumentalizing control over, the segment of the world in question.

It is important to recognize that Rosa attributes this widespread state of alienation to capitalist modernity's promise of *complete* controllability rather than controllability *simpliciter*. Its error is a failure to acknowledge the moment of constitutive unavailability *in the things themselves* (2019b, 52). Human agents have resonant relationships with counterparts or events that have something like their own will or character and, accordingly, speak with their own voice. Resonant subjectivities intervene in the world with a willingness to put themselves at risk through the resulting contact and to change themselves. This is the moment of adaptive transformation, mentioned above, which is an integral part of resonance (Rosa 2019a, 53, 236). This is why resonant relationships cannot be brought about purely intentionally, in a planned manner. However, it would be wrong to think that resonance is something that is completely *un*controllable (Rosa 2019b, 48). Following the publication of *Resonance*, Rosa proposes a qualified notion of (un-)controllability [*Un-Verfügbarkeit*], which he calls 'semi-controllability' [*Halbverfügbarkeit*] (ibid., 56). He argues that humans can enter into resonant relationships with others, human and other-than-human, and with events, if they move between complete controllability and total unavailability (ibid., 48; cf. p. 120). He explains what he means by introducing a new distinction between availability and accessibility [*Erreichbarkeit*]. While availability expresses a desire to acquire, enforce and control, accessibility in the sense of *Erreichbarkeit* is a responsive, open-ended process.

The term 'semi-availability', also translatable as 'partial controllability', not only expresses the difference between availability and accessibility as *Erreichbarkeit*; it also conveys the moment of *self-efficacy* contained within the concept of resonance. For Rosa, in contrast to the modern ideal of the autonomous subject (as he understands it), the resonant self-efficacious subject is characterized not by its ability to control the course and outcome of its activity, but by its ability to *respond to the call of the other entity or event* (2019b, 50). This ability in turn presupposes the ability to be reached by something or someone in a responsive and open-ended manner (ibid., 61).

Overall, Rosa's multidimensional and rich account of resonant subjectivity is a fruitful resource for conceptualizing ethical agency in ways that break with the exclusive humanist idea of normative self-sufficiency. However, it too suffers from a serious weakness. Like Taylor's apparently monological understanding of strong evaluation, its interpretation of 'the promise of the modern idea of freedom' as resonant self-efficacy lacks the argumentative critical reflexivity required for ethical-existential-political self-transformation oriented by a human-transcending idea of 'the good'. In contrast to Taylor, Rosa makes this quite clear. Indeed, in certain places he seems to be hostile to any kind of critical reflexivity. As a result, like Taylor (to all appearances), he ends up affirming the exclusive humanist picture of human agency that is the opposite of the picture of resonant agency he envisages.

This is a consequence of Rosa's emphatic rejection of any attempt to conceptualize freedom as self-determination – as autonomy in a Kantian sense (2019a, 233–4). He argues that the nonrelational character of the concept of autonomy, which he insists is part of its very concept, makes it unsuitable for defining resonant subjectivity (ibid., 249–50n90). This is why he replaces autonomous agency with resonant self-efficacy.

In elaborating his alternative idea of individual freedom, Rosa draws explicitly on Taylor's concept of strong evaluation. However, at times at least, his interpretation of it is strangely nonrelational, even static (Cooke 2020c, 375). In Rosa's account, strong evaluations gain their meaning from a moral source, which is an 'independent source of value that confronts [human subjects] as valuable and important *as such* and concerns them in some way' (2019a, 170). He writes that strong evaluations involve 'discriminations of right or wrong, better or worse, higher or lower, which are not rendered valid by our own desires, inclinations, or choices, but rather stand *independent* of these and offer standards by which they can be judged' (ibid., 134). With this account, Rosa seems to rule out critical interrogation by individual human subjects of the validity of moral sources, irrespective of whether such interrogation is monological (as it appears to be in Taylor's account of strong evaluation) or dialogical, by way of the exchange of reasons in argument (broadly understood). Worryingly, he suggests at times that critical reflexivity is not necessary for resonant self-efficacious agency, and is even bad for it. Resonant self-efficacious agency, Rosa declares, is not about critical self-interrogation but rather about establishing vital relationships in all dimensions that enable human subjects 'to feel at home in the world'. Critical reflection by human subjects on their deeper purposes with a view to embracing them as their own is not a necessary condition for being-at-home in the world in this way; on occasion he even suggests that it is undesirable, since it involves self-control. He views this as tendentially a form of alienation from oneself, observing that 'people frequently feel the least alienated . . . precisely when they *lose* control over themselves, their lives, or their circumstances' (ibid., 226; see Cooke 2020c, 375).[7]

Rosa is not entirely consistent in his rejection of the need for critical reflexivity. On occasion, he suggests that self-efficacious subjects are not indifferent to the epistemic quality of their ethical decisions, judgements, actions and practices and, due to their fundamental engagement with the world, feel compelled to judge them as good or bad on the basis of critical self-reflection in which affective and rational motivations and reasons are interwoven (e.g. 2019a, 239–40). Crucially for present purposes, however, such critical reflexivity is not argumentative; it does not involve the intersubjective exchange of reasons oriented by a concern for 'the good'. The unwelcome – and quite likely unintended – consequence of his position is that individual human subjects (or particular communities of human subjects) are granted sovereign control over the validity of their ethical-existential-political judgements, decisions, actions and behaviour (Cooke 2025b). So long as they do not violate the prevailing laws and generally accepted ethical norms, they are entitled to judge, decide and act as they please in ethical matters, without challenge or protest from others. In other words, Rosa's resonant subjectivities are normatively self-sufficient. Accordingly, his hostility towards conceptions of freedom in terms of critical reflexivity has an unhappy result. It leads him to propose an alternative conception of individual freedom as resonant self-efficacious subjectivity that inadvertently reproduces the figure of normatively self-sufficient human agency, which disposes as it pleases over its ethical-existential-political judgements, decisions and actions, subject only to general moral and legal constraints. Thus, Rosa's account of resonant subjectivity, like (to all appearances) Taylor's account of strong evaluation, stands accused of exclusive humanism and its closure of 'the transcendent window' that he too undoubtedly seeks to keep open.

If modified to allow for self-determination and self-transformation in argumentative engagement with other humans, Rosa's conception of resonant agency would be a congenial partner for my account of self-determining, self-transforming ethical agency. Indeed it would enhance it. Among other things, his concept of adaptive transformation describes a kind of attentive and responsive attitude that elucidates the relationality of ethical agency in a way that is significantly different to Heideggerian conceptions of attunement.

Relationality and attunement

The relationality of self-determining, self-transforming ethical agency is complex. Rosa's theory of resonance elaborates many facets of it, complementing and supplementing my account. Up to now, I have used words and phrases such as 'attentiveness' and 'responsiveness' to convey the attitudes towards others, human and other-than-human, appropriate for self-determining, self-transforming ethical agents as I envisage them. In previous writings, I have also used the word 'attunement', a term that chimes with Rosa's concept of 'resonance' (Cooke 2020a; 2023a; 2023b). However, through its employment by Martin Heidegger (1962), and in the reception of his work, the term 'attunement' has acquired certain socially conservative undertones, raising doubts about its suitability. One cause for concern is its connotation of 'letting be'. As I explain below, when understood in this way, attunement encourages unquestioning acceptance of the way things are, fostering an uncritical attitude towards prevailing social systems, structures, institutions and sociocultural practices, in turn facilitating perpetual reproduction of everything that is wrong with them from an ethical-political and ethical-existential point of view. It is also hostile to the argumentative evaluation of ethical-existential-political claims to validity, and the possibilities for educative, self-transformative learning opened by such evaluation, which is centrally important in the conception of ethical agency I propose. In sum, attunement as 'letting be' in a Heideggerian sense is hostile to the transformative aspect of self-determining agency as I depict it.

The unwelcome conservative tendencies contained within the concept of attunement, when understood along Heideggerian lines, are visible in Jarret Zigon's relational ethics, as developed in his book *How Is It Between Us?* (2024). Such tendencies are at odds with the socially progressive, transformative impulse clearly motivating the ethics he develops. His provocative proposal for an ethics of ecstatic relationality challenges prevailing ethical-political norms and conventions and, overall, like Rosa's proposal, is a congenial partner for my efforts to develop a decentring, expansive, exploratory mode of critical theorizing. However, it falls prey to a danger that I seek to avoid.

Zigon argues that the ethics the world demands today is one that responds in an attuned manner. He calls it an ethics of the 'between', which enacts attunement and openness by linking together anthropology and phenomenological hermeneutics. His main concern is social transformation: he seeks to show the import of an ethics of the 'between' for responding to contemporary ethical-political challenges relating to truth and justice, ranging from drug and alcohol abuse, through algorithms and big data, to climate change. To this end, he develops his account using ethnographic vignettes, intended to illustrate how his ethics of the 'between', and the attunement it demands, can be used in actual social practices in concrete cases, for instance, as a contribution towards harm reduction in the case of substance abusers.

In his relational ethics, living a good life in an ethical-existential-political sense is an open process with no *telos* or predetermined ethical principles or values. Rather, it is a matter of inhabiting the ephemeral space of the 'between'. Zigon underscores the radicality of the question that is the title of his book: how is it between us? He contrasts it with the questions: 'What is the good?' or 'Did she act rightly?', claiming that such questions assume that there is something called 'the good', the 'whatness' of which we can use as the measure for answering the questions definitively (2024, 12). He views 'the good', instead, as a matter of interpretation that calls for ongoing, attuned responses to particular situations and to the unknowability of the others to whom one is exposed.

In this ethics, beings, including human beings, do not exist as singular existents prior to their intertwining and they conduct their lives in existential processes in which they are ecstatically intertwined. I understand this to mean that beings – existents – are entangled with each other in successive situations in which each is ecstatic. I take 'ecstatic' to mean a movement outwards and beyond, in this case outwards from and beyond where they were prior to a given situation; the movement is towards others in the situation and towards the situation itself. Accordingly, Zigon describes such an ethics as a movement towards an 'otherwise' that calls for ongoing, never-ending attunement to '*the between of the situation*' (2024, 16–17, 13; emphasis in original).[8]

At first glance, Zigon's relational ethics seems to fit very well with my account of ethical agency, especially with its 'ecological entanglements' and, more generally, with its antipathy to exclusive humanism. His ecstatic ethics calls on human agents to acknowledge their constitutive dependency on others, human and other-than-human and, with this, their lack of self-sufficiency. Furthermore, it fosters openness and receptivity, requiring human agents to engage consciously and intentionally in continual processes of mutual encounter, in which they are receptive, attentive and responsive to others and the situations of reciprocal relationality in which they find themselves. Such an ethics is diametrically opposed to the idea of the sovereign human subject and an ethics of self-ownership, and is characterized instead by mutual care and concern. It is 'an ethics that lets-be and attunes rather than projects and controls' (2024, 95). Yet another congenial feature of Zigon's ethics is that it encompasses human as well as other-than-human entities. He describes it as an ethics of open hospitality that welcomes all exist- ents into human worlds *without* reducing them to a human conception (ibid.).

However, Zigon's Heideggerian interpretation of attunement limits the critical force of his ethics. This is evident in a vignette he offers. He describes how Downtown Eastside Vancouver (DTES), a district of Vancouver on the west coast of Canada, has been redesigned as a 'world of nonjudgment, where drug users are let be to dwell' (2024, 22). He depicts this space of attunement as a 'nonjudgmental site of potentiality' that allows those who find themselves there to become relationally ethical (ibid., 23): 'To practice harm reduction is to let-users-be, attune, and to build worlds that are open to this letting-be' (ibid., 20). He explicitly acknowledges his intellectual debt to Heidegger, explaining that his interpretation of attuned relationality as mutual 'letting be' is connected with a Heideggerian view of truth as 'unconcealment' [*alētheia*].[9] Zigon elucidates this relational attunement as letting 'beings be the beings they are' (ibid., 35). Furthermore, he appears to endorse Heidegger's view that the essence of truth reveals itself as freedom and writes that 'freedom "lets beings be the beings they are" to disclose themselves as such' (ibid.).

Certainly, letting 'beings be the beings they are' may be an important first stage in harm-reduction practices. In a similar vein, I have argued in earlier writings that 'spaces of one's own' are a necessary condition for self-determination, by which I mean spaces that facilitate the unfolding and development of creative, receptive, contemplative and critically reflective capacities (Cooke 1999c). In these writings, I emphasize the importance for self-determining agency of 'spaces of one's own', but I also caution against retreat into a sealed-off space of self-referential self-authorship. The example I give is Helmut, a central character in Martin Walser's novella *A Runaway Horse* (Walser 1987; Cooke 1999c, 31–2). However, although I criticize Helmut's retreat in Walser's story, I make the point, in the spirit of Herbert Marcuse, that his withdrawal into a self-enclosed space can be interpreted as a desperate attempt 'to maintain a private sphere of personal authenticity in the face of the commodification of every aspect of personal identity and experience that has become a feature of life in advanced industrialized societies in the late 20th century' (Cooke 1999c, 38; cf. Marcuse 1991). Thus, my objection is not to 'letting beings be' per se, but to the Heideggerian view that such letting be, understood as letting 'unconcealment unfold' (Zigon 2024, 35), constitutes human freedom. What is missing from this conception of freedom, or more generally ethical agency, is critical reflexivity and the concern to learn from others that, in my conception, motivates ethical-existential-political self- and social transformation. I maintain that a potential for such transformation is inherent in encounters between (human) beings that are receptive, attentive and responsive to one another. In this respect Rosa's concept of adaptive transformation, combined with his concept of partial uncontrollability, could help to avoid the socially conservative tendencies of the Heideggerian conception of attunement that Zigon favours, although it is in evident tension with his own socially and politically engaged stance.

As discussed above, the resonant self-efficacious human subjects envisaged by Rosa form attentive, receptive and responsive relationships with counterparts or events that are partially uncontrollable. As he puts it, these counterparts or events have something like their own will or character and, accordingly, speak with their own voice. Resonant self-efficacious subjects are always willing to allow themselves to be changed through the contacts they establish with others or their immersive experiences of events. Change can occur in both directions. Not only may human agents change themselves in response to their experiences of a partially uncontrollable world; the world itself – being partially controllable – may also change in response to human agency. Rosa's suggestive tuning-fork metaphor, which he uses to explicate the phenomenon of resonance, illustrates the reciprocal movement of adaptive transformation. When placed in close proximity, the vibration of one tuning fork prompts the other to vibrate at its own frequency; each then speaks with its own voice. Moreover, the vibrations of the two forks can mutually reinforce each other, their amplitudes growing ever larger (Rosa 2019a, 213–14). This is attunement in a mobile (and literal) sense that conveys the energetic reciprocity of the relationship between the agents involved. Its energy and mobility suggest generativity – the emergence of something new as a result of the encounter. The generativity of the relationship is part of the self-transforming aspect of self-determination, mirroring the (re-)generative power of social criticism to which I drew attention in Chapter 2, and is an integral feature of the decentring, expansive and exploratory mode of critical theorizing developed in this book. It is the dimension missing in Zigon's account.

Rosa's idea of partial uncontrollability also helps to clarify the dynamic, ethically charged relationship between human agency and other-than-human agencies that I envisage. As discussed in the previous chapter, I interpret this in terms of an idea of naturalness [*Naturwüchsigkeit*] that has a double aspect. On the one side, it refers to a dynamically co-constitutive relationship between human and other-than-human agencies. So far I have used the term ecological entanglement to describe this aspect of the relationship (later I extend the idea of entanglement to include social institutions). On the other side, it refers to an unsettling drive, force or energy within human will-formation that propels humans to transgress existing normative orders and boundaries (as explained, I diverge from Adorno and Menke by characterizing this transgressive energy as an ethical impulse). Rosa's concept of partial uncontrollability fits well with the first aspect in particular. If understood as designating a movement between intentional creative action on 'nature' by humans, on the one side, and flexible responsive reaction to 'nature' by humans, on the other side, it testifies to the reciprocally constitutive, normatively entangled relationality between human and other-than-human agencies. This aspect, too, is missing, from Zigon's account of relational attunement.

However, as observed, Rosa's account of the mutual constitution of agencies, human and other-than-human, lacks the ethical-existential-political dimension of educative learning from others, human and other-than-human, that is a central component of my account of freedom as self-determination. On the other hand, making sense of learning of this kind is challenging. In previous chapters, I acknowledged the problem of mutual intelligibility that arises for my argumentative approach to ethical learning, and made some suggestions for how to address it. In the remaining pages of this chapter I consider a related, but somewhat different, set of questions: What does it mean to say that humans learn ethically from their encounters with, and experiences of, other-than-human agencies? Furthermore, how can they make sense of such encounters and experiences to themselves and to others, for otherwise they will not be able to evaluate them argumentatively? In addressing these questions, I begin with an ethnographic vignette.[10]

Self-transforming ecologically entangled agency

The vignette tells the story of an encounter between the French anthropologist Nastassja Martin and a brown bear, which took place when Martin was conducting an ethnographic study with the Even, an indigenous people in North-East Siberia. In her autobiographical book *In the Eye of the Wild* (2021), she relates how the encounter left her almost dead, with her face as well as other body parts severely mutilated. The book begins at the moment when she is airlifted from the scene by a Russian army helicopter. She undergoes operations, first in Russia and later in Paris, in which the surgeons patch her up more or less effectively. As she describes her transformation, she is changed into a Cyborg, a being that is supplemented technologically, giving her a new, hybrid identity as part human, part machine. However, her new hybridity has a further component, which is foregrounded in her narrative: she has become a being that is not just part-human and part-machine, but also part-*bear*. She struggles to learn what it means to inhabit her new complex hybridity, which she comes to understand as a matter of learning how to answer the ethical-existential questions posed to her by the bear.

Martin's psychiatric advisers and therapists in Paris suggest to her various interpretations of the encounter – for example, that the bear is a symbol of power and sexual desire. None of the interpretations helps her, and she continues to be troubled by disturbing dreams.[11] Against the advice of her advisers and friends, and to the distress of her mother, she decides to return to the Even. Following her encounter with the bear, the Even have given Martin a new name, *Medka*, which means half-human, half-bear.[12] Realizing that the bear's questions to her will be mediated through the interpretations of them by the Even, Martin attempts to learn from *them* what her new name means and how to live her life as this new hybrid being.[13] She learns among other things that inhabiting her new identity does not mean the death of her human self but, rather, a process of co-constitution between her human-machine-self and her bear-self. The cosmology of the Even, in particular their circular understanding of reality, helps her to envision an other-than-human intentionality that impacts on her human one.[14] It is noteworthy that Martin's learning process also involves changes in her relationship to her body. She gradually realizes that the pain her body expresses connects her closely to the world, giving her a new feeling of responsibility for her body. In the terminology I have been using, this could be described as a new awareness that she is not a 'self-sufficient normative authority' concerning the needs of her body. She comes to realize, instead, the need to be *responsive to* her body, to attend to how it communicates with her and what it has to say. She develops an understanding that her body is not something that she owns or has the right to control, but something that has its own agency and from which she can learn if she is attuned to it and cares for it attentively. However, her body is not just communicating with her about its own agency; it is also a site for *inter-agential* communication. She perceives her body as 'a territory where Western surgeons parley with Siberian bears. Or rather, where they try to establish communication' (2021, 44).

What could it mean to 'establish communication' between Western surgeons and Siberian bears or, more specifically, between

Nastassja Martin's machine-human-self and bear-self? Evidently, making sense of this is crucial not just for Martin's future work as an anthropologist, but also for her attempt to live her new hybrid identity. In addition, it is important for understanding the self-transformative component of self-determining ethical agency and for making sense of what it means for critical theories to learn in an educative, ethical-existential-political sense through communicative engagements with the inhabitants of radically different worldviews and cosmologies. This is because it raises questions about intelligibility similar to ones I discussed in previous chapters. I acknowledged that, at any given time, in any given place, the vocabularies human agents have at their disposal may prove inadequate for articulating their experiences in ways that are linguistically intelligible to other humans, or indeed to themselves, which is a precondition for the argumentative evaluation of these experiences. Argumentative evaluation is, in turn, a precondition for educative self-transformative learning.

In response to this difficulty, I suggested in Chapter 3 that Karl Jaspers' concept of 'cipher' and my own concept of fictions in critical theorizing could provide some help. In Chapter 2, I referred to exploring possibilities for ontological openings that could enable playful 'world-travelling', as described by María Lugones (1987). By this, Lugones means a form of non-arrogant (she calls it 'loving') perception involving epistemic movements between different 'worlds', recommending it as a 'skilful, creative, rich, enriching and, given certain circumstances, a loving way of being and living' (ibid., 3). As Kristie Dotson explains, such fluency is developed through the wilful exercise of a flexibility in moving between constructions of life in which one feels (more or less) at home and those in which one feels an outsider (2012, 34).

In addition, I recommended a view of argumentation as a process of making partial epistemic connections between apparently incompatible worldviews, as opposed to a procedure that demands full intelligibility or complete understanding. This recommendation is especially relevant to the question of learning from encounters with other-than-human agencies, as in Nastassja Martin's case. The anthropologist Marisol de la Cadena expands on it fruitfully.

As part of her ethnographic fieldwork in the Andes, de la Cadena for several years conducted research in Peru in a small village, Pacchanta, about fifty kilometres from Cuzco. During this time, she established a close friendship and working relationship with two members of the indigenous community, Mariano Turpo and his son Nazario Turpo. She refers to their working relationship as 'co-labouring'. This is de la Cadena's name for the 'practices among us (conversations, sensations, feelings, observations, intuitions) that composed a complex togetherness: a contact zone . . . in which we *understood each other and did not understand each other* (2021, 247; my emphasis). She characterizes them as practices of 'not knowing: in the presence of . . .' (ibid.). Presence is the relation within which 'not knowing' happens, and in her specific case it includes Mariano and Nazario. Presence involves a certain mode of relationality. As de la Cadena puts it, 'them' also includes her. When she is 'co-labouring' with Mariano and Nazario, she is them and they are her: no separable 'other' exists in this 'presence' (ibid., 246). 'Not knowing: in the presence of . . .' calls for a readiness to live 'in equivocation', to understand, while not understanding. Over the years, her conversations with Mariano and Nazario became the *shared* site where their worlds diverged as they emerged in and with their constitutive differences (2017, 5). She describes it as a site for 'ontological openings' (ibid., 2).

Co-labouring, accordingly, is an ethnographic mode that 'required a different *we*: not me with ethnographers, but me and the Turpos. Co-laboring required my categories and Mariano's stories even if they clashed – or as I learned, better if they clashed – for this would not stop the conversation. It would continue and yield unexpected possibilities and the unexpected as possibility' (de la Cadena 2021, 248). De la Cadena refers to her ethnographic method as an analytics of 'partial connections' (2017, 4–5). Such an analytics involves learning how to share a condition where equivocations and their control (when possible) are enacted. It involves controlling, without negating (she calls it 'cancelling') the use of categories or concepts or practice of analytics that may overpower or even kidnap the situation that is up for description. The result is a better description that indicates the limits of the 'controlled' categories, concepts or analytics.[15] These limits are also an 'excess' that, while present yet controlled, does not explain away the situation in question. This excess resists closure, remaining open for a subsequent better description (2021, 249).[16]

De la Cadena became aware of the importance of this method of ethnographic practice in her efforts to understand the radically different relationality that constituted the worldviews inhabited by her, on the one side, and the cosmology inhabited by Mariano and Nazario, on the other (de la Cadena 2015). In Mariano and Nazario's cosmology, *tirakuna* (a Quechua word[17]) are earth-beings (or mountains‡). *Runakuna* are humans (or humans‡), who, emerging together with *tirakuna*, form *ayllu* (clan‡).[18] The relationality referenced by the Quechua words differs radically from relationality in de la Cadena's own worldview. She describes it as a kind of emergence in which detachment from an origin is impossible.[19] Translating *tirakuna*, *runakuna* and *allyu* as mountains, humans and clan is not wrong according to de la Cadena; nonetheless, the translations presuppose dualities and other separations that inhibit the ethnographic practice of co-labouring (2021, 247).

De la Cadena's method of ethnographic practice helps to cast light on what it means for human agents to be transformed in an ethical-existential-political sense – to learn something about the conduct of a good human life and the kind of society conducive to it – through encounters with agencies that are other-than-human. She invites us to think of educative, self-transformative, ethical learning as, on occasion, a matter of *understanding,, while not understanding*, and as requiring a willingness to live in a state of equivocation. Learning of this kind is *Bildung*, in the broadly Hegelian sense in which I have been using it. It belongs to a process of the free development of ethical agency which, in this specific case, involves engagement by de la Cadena with an ontology 'in which there is no clear separation between subject and object, receiver and sender, but in which being takes place in togetherness and learning is a matter of understanding, while not understanding – of "not knowing: in the presence of . . .'''. Ethical-existential-political learning in this mode takes place through practices such as co-labouring in the case of de la Cadena as ethnographer; but also through existentially challenging encounters with bears, facilitated by the interpretations of the Even, in the case of Nastassja Martin.[20] It presupposes an understanding of human agency in which humans determine their ethical-existential-political life-trajectories in communicative engagement with other-than-human agencies. By contrast, in a worldview in which human agents are normatively self-sufficient, learning about the meaning of the good life and good society through encounters with other-than-human agencies is not just unnecessary, it is fantastical.

Nonetheless, it is important to notice that Martin's and de la Cadena's learning processes are, in each case, mediated by indigenous ontologies and epistemologies, in which the relationality between human and other-than-human agencies is understood in ways very different from the 'exclusive humanist' worldview. Contemporary Frankfurt School theories for the most part share such a worldview. Due to this sociocultural heritage, even the decentring, expansive, exploratory critical theories that I envisage will require the interpretative help of the inhabitants of cosmologies alien to them in their efforts to learn from the normativity of other-than-human agencies. The same holds for self-transforming, self-determining ethical agents. In both cases, for now at least, *Bildung* will depend on the mediating powers of human agents whose ontologies and epistemologies are widely divergent from the exclusive humanist worldview predominant in Western moral and political theories in general, and also shared by many inhabitants of capitalist modernity.

In the remaining three chapters my focus shifts to the question of fundamental social transformation. As before, I consider the question from the point of view of self-transformative, ethical learning by critical theories from their interlocutors and by human agents from other agents, human and other-than-human. In Chapter 6, I consider contemporary Frankfurt School critiques of capitalism from this viewpoint, in the context of ongoing anthropogenic planetary devastation.

6

Critiques of Capitalism: Decentrings, Openings, Explorations

In the opening paragraph of *The Communist Manifesto*, Marx and Engels present their readers with a stark alternative. Throughout history, they write, oppressor and oppressed 'stood in constant opposition to one another, carried on an uninterrupted, now hidden, now open fight, a fight that each time ended, either in a revolutionary reconstitution of society at large, or in the common ruin of the contending classes' (1967, 79). The manifesto makes clear that communism demands the revolutionary reconstitution of society at large.[1] Their call invites consideration of what is politically at stake. For Marx and Engels, the fundamental political problem was the impossibility of actualizing their vision of individual and communal free development within bourgeois capitalism, in which the only form of freedom available was *bourgeois* freedom. This is the freedom of capital: 'free trade, free selling and buying'. Capital is free – it is independent and has individuality – but 'the living person is dependent and has no individuality' (ibid., 98).[2] Not only does capitalism rob humans of their freedom through relations of dependency that inhibit their free development as creative individuals; it prevents them establishing relations with other humans that would foster this individuality.[3] Furthermore, it substitutes a perverted, debased form of freedom in place of the free development of creative individuality in relationships with other humans.

This perverted form of freedom is what Christoph Menke describes as self-will [*Eigenwille*]: it grants permission to individuals to do as they please, limited only by requirements of security and stability.[4] Rejecting this as a travesty of genuine freedom, Marx and Engels call instead for an association that would ensure the free development of each individual as the condition for the free development of all.[5] However, the authors hold that modernity's emancipatory promise will never be realized without a break with the capitalist mode of economic production

and its reduction of the free development of human agency to bourgeois freedom. This is because the logic of capitalism is totalizing in the
sense of all-encompassing and all-consuming. It is omnivorous, indis-
criminately extracting and exploiting whatever is available for its own
purposes.[6] Marx and Engels write: 'The need of a constantly expanding
market for its products chases the bourgeoisie over the entire surface
of the globe. It must nestle everywhere, settle everywhere, establish
connections everywhere' (1967, 63).[7] Accordingly, capitalism can never
be contained. Instead it must be dismantled or overcome, leading to the
fundamental reconstitution of society as a whole.

The rapid advancement and expansion of capitalism to all parts of the
planet since the 1840s lends credence to Marx and Engels' view. Indeed,
in the meantime the reasons to radically reconstitute capitalist society
have become even more numerous and even more pressing. Above all,
the apparent inseparability of capitalism from anthropogenic ecological depredation means that not just the possibility of human freedom
and happiness is at stake, but the survival of any human societies. The
question, therefore, is not *whether* to reconstitute capitalist society. The
question is what reconstituting it *means*. In the next chapter, I develop
the conceptual framework for a model of fundamental institutional
transformation as 'revolutionary reconstitution from within'. In the
final chapter, I explore some implications of the model I propose. In
the present chapter, I address Marx and Engels' call for 'revolutionary
reconstitution' as a 'message in a bottle' for future critical theorizing
about capitalism.[8] In the contemporary context of anthropogenic planetary depredation, I read it as a message enjoining critical theories to
decentre and open their critical perspectives in ways that take account
of the multiple complex entanglements between human and other-
than-human agencies and open critical theories to learning in an ethical
sense from protests against capitalism based on ontologies and epistemologies alien to the inhabitants of secularized Western modernity.

Read in this way Marx and Engels' message to future critical theories
requires a fundamental reconfiguration of the exclusive humanist and
productivist version of socialism they developed.[9] These troubling
elements are readily visible in Marx's early writings. His critique of
religion leaves no doubt as to his exclusive humanist perspective and to
his tacit affirmation of the picture of normatively self-sufficient agency
fostered by it. He begins his 'Towards a Critique of Hegel's *Philosophy
of Right*: Introduction' with the words: 'The criticism of religion is the
presupposition of all criticism' (2000d, 71). Elaborating, Marx claims
that humans, when they discard religion, regain their senses; they begin to
think, act and fashion their reality so that they revolve around themselves

as their 'real sun' (ibid., 72). In the same vein, he writes that the 'criticism of religion ends with the doctrine that *man is the highest being for man*' (ibid., 77). In other words, he holds that humans create their own values; what humans find ethically important is made by humans for humans.

Productivism is a further troubling feature of Marx's emancipatory vision.[10] From a productivist perspective, growth of the economy through the exploitation of natural resources is the main criterion of a well-functioning social system that serves the interests of all its members equally. Marx's productivist view is evident in his characterization of the 'species being' of humans. The early Marx distinguishes humans from other animals due to their interest in production independently of physical need; this explains his view of freedom as free creative activity. It is unsurprising, therefore, that Marx and Engels applaud the unleashing of human productive powers by capitalism, depicting them as potentially emancipatory (1967, 80–94). Nor is it surprising that Marx in his later writings, most notably his 1875 'Critique of the Gotha Program', envisions a communist future in which labour will become 'life's prime want'.[11]

This has consequences for emancipatory reconfigurations of socialism envisaged in contemporary Frankfurt School theorizing. Decentring, expansive, exploratory critiques of capitalism of the kind I advocate, which are guided by an idea of self-transforming, self-determining ethical agency that is attentive to the ethical significance of its multiple complex entanglements with other-than-human agencies, must be alert to possible ideological closures arising from allegiance to Marxist versions of socialism. Moreover, they must recognize that exclusive humanism and productivism, although related conceptually and often combined in Marxist versions of socialism, are separate phenomena and need to be addressed separately. This is why, as I pointed out in Chapter 4, rejecting the productivist paradigm does not necessarily entail rejecting an exclusive humanist perspective.[12]

The target of Marx and Engels' critique is bourgeois market capitalism. Since the 1840s, capitalism has undergone many permutations. One transformation took place in Europe in the period after World War Two. This was the incorporation within a capitalist socioeconomic order of 'the Welfare State', following on from the 'New Deal' enacted under President Franklin D. Roosevelt in the USA in the 1930s after the 'Great Depression', and building on systems of social insurance established to a greater or lesser degree in various European countries from the nineteenth century onwards. Another, more recent, permutation is due to the 'digital revolution', which over the past decades has led to the decentring of manufacturing in the Global North, the rise of the knowledge economy together with the centrality of finance, information technology and, most recently, Large Language Models (LLMs) and Artificial Intelligence (AI). However, these major historical shifts in how capitalism operates seem to have strengthened it, not weakened it. Indeed, as Albena Azmanova observes, capitalism as an engine of prosperity is doing well (2020, 2). According to her critical analysis, even the Great Recession of the early twenty-first century brought about not a crisis *of* capitalism, but a crisis *for* capitalism – it merely set roadblocks on the path of the competitive production of profit that capitalism is already finding ways to overcome (ibid, 190).

Although, initially, capitalism was the central focus of critique in Frankfurt School critical theory, from the mid- to late 1980s onwards it appeared to fade into the background. In their conversation about capitalism, Rahel Jaeggi and Nancy Fraser attribute this to the impact of Habermas' *Theory of Communicative Action* (Fraser and Jaeggi 2018, 4–5; Habermas 1984/1987). They agree that Habermas' book was the last great systematic attempt to ground normative critical theory in a large-scale social theory. But they also agree that it was a turning point in critical theory, since its thesis of the 'colonization of the lifeworld' by the administrative and economic 'subsystems' effectively removed the economy from the realm of normative criticism. As a result, rather than generating successor works of comparable ambition and breadth, its legacy proved to be a major increase in disciplinary specialization among Habermas' followers. The negative effect, according to Jaeggi and Fraser, was abandonment of Horkheimer's original research programme, in which critical theory was an interdisciplinary project aimed at grasping society as a totality.[13]

Within the Frankfurt School tradition, Fraser is one of the few contemporary theorists who has demonstrably been concerned for decades to renew a critique of capitalism and reposition it at the centre of critical social theorizing. One of her earliest published essays (1985) took Habermas to task for de-politicizing critical theory through his colonization thesis, an unwelcome consequence of which was to sideline the question of gender domination. Over many years, she has sought to disclose the multiple complex links between the capitalist economy and its invisible 'others', which give rise to a host of interlocking injustices and irrationalities (1990). Her book *Cannibal Capitalism* (2022) astutely analyses and elegantly exposes the moral, political and functional failings of capitalism, arguing eloquently for a new eco-socialism for the twenty-first century.

Although certainly one of the most powerful contemporary contributions to criticisms of capitalism, Fraser's critique falls short from the point of view of the decentring, expansive and exploratory critical theorizing that I propose. Its shortcoming is a methodological closure to protests against capitalism that cannot be articulated in the normative-functional analytics she employs. I show that Fraser's critique shares this limitation with Charbonnier's critique of capitalism, as discussed in Chapter 4. I then argue that a similar objection can be raised against Jaeggi due to the ethical-functionalist approach that she adopts. Despite significant differences between the two approaches, in each case a functionalist argument limits the scope of their critical perspectives, for it restricts criticism to problems with capitalism that can be articulated within the worldview of Western modernity. I then consider Azmanova's nonfunctionalist critique of capitalism, which makes it more open in principle to decentrings and expansions, but requires further development in this respect.

Functionalist critiques of society find the normative criteria for a properly functioning social system within the society they criticize. In this sense, they are versions of an immanent mode of social critique. Not all functionalist critiques combine their immanent critiques with a context-transcending perspective. However, in the Frankfurt School tradition, as I emphasized in Chapter 3, critical theories have always been concerned to sustain a dialectics between immanence and transcendence. I observed, however, that they have not found it easy to navigate the tensions between the two moments, often weakening one at the expense of the other. In the case of Fraser's and Jaeggi's respective approaches, the context-transcending moment of critique is weakened at the expense of the immanent one. Fraser's critique appeals to the normative promise of Western modernity – universal freedom, equality and solidarity – arguing that capitalist societies, due to their structural and systemic features, make it impossible to realize these values. The context-transcending moment resides in the gap between this promise, as Fraser interprets it, and the possibilities for freedom, equality and solidarity actually available within advanced capitalist societies. The context-transcending moment of Jaeggi's critique resides in the discrepancy between deep potentials for resolving the problems confronting a given form of life that have evolved within the history of that form of life, on the one side, and, on the other, awareness by the inhabitants of the given form of life that they already possess the resources for correctly grasping and responding to the problems in question.[14] Since capitalism blocks this awareness, immanent critique for Jaeggi has an ethically disclosing, educative, self-transformative function. However, in both cases, the context-transcending moments in their respective critiques of capitalism appeal to normative potentials made available historically through the development of Western modernity. In other words, their context-transcending critical perspectives remain immanent to the normative frame of the kind of society they criticize. This makes them vulnerable to accusations of Eurocentrism and anthropocentricism and closes them to possibilities for self-transformative ethical learning through communicative engagements with protests against capitalism that are based on worldviews and cosmologies with quite different ontologies and epistemologies.

Azmanova's critique of capitalism is normative-empirical as opposed to normative-functionalist. As a result, her critical approach is better able to avoid these objections of Eurocentrism and anthropocentricism and more open to self-transformative ethical learning. Nonetheless, in its present version it too falls short from the point of view of the mode of critical theorizing I propose. The court of appeal for the validity of her critical diagnoses, and the normative basis for her recommendations concerning social transformation, is the lived experience of human agents within the advanced capitalist societies of Western modernity. Due to her explicit adoption of a purely immanent approach, however, her critique as it stands fails to acknowledge that a critical perspective on the iniquities of capitalism can and must learn through communicative engagements with the inhabitants of worldviews and cosmologies who understand human relationality very differently from the inhabitants of the capitalist society whom Azmanova describes and, in consequence, conduct their lives as ecologically entangled agents in quite different ways.

My discussion focuses on Fraser's critique of capitalism, offering briefer comments on comparable shortcomings I discern in the critiques of Jaeggi and Azmanova. To illustrate my reasons for rejecting all three approaches, I start once more with an ethnographic vignette, this time depicting a protest against capitalist extractivism by indigenous people in Peru.

Anti-extractivist protests in a cosmological perspective

As noted in Chapter 4, I distinguish 'worldviews' from 'cosmologies', using the latter term to designate perspectives in which there is no sharp divide between human and other-than-human agencies and in which human existence is open, porous and vulnerable to a world of spirits and powers. Following Linda Martín Alcoff, I use the term 'extractivism' in a general way to mean legally sanctioned practices of extracting value from the formerly colonized areas of the planet. These include mineral and plant resources as well as timber, fossil fuels and animal products that are then monetized and exchanged. Both land and peoples are treated primarily as resources. This typically happens in countries with rich mineral deposits, fossil fuels or plant resources such as Bolivia, Columbia, Ecuador and Peru (but there are many examples of such practices elsewhere). Martín Alcoff emphasizes that transnational corporations enrich not only foreign nationals, but also domestic elites. To complicate matters further, extractivist projects may bring significant employment to locals in the region as well as large payments which may be used by progressive governments for public goods (2022, 3–4).

However, as I now explain, this is not the only problem. Indigenous protests against capitalist extractivism do not only run up against the complication that domestic elites have a stake in the game, claiming that the projects in question increase public goods and are therefore in everyone's best interests (claims that may carry conviction to some of those they address). They also run up against the problem that their protests are likely to be misconstrued, recast in a normative vocabulary that completely misses the substance of their objections. In Chapter 2, I called this 'epistemic imperialism' (in contemporary social epistemology it is sometimes referred to as 'epistemism'). These terms designate onto-epistemic denials and exclusions that happen when individuals and groups make knowledge-related assertions that deny or make invisible modes of knowing, and, by extension, modes of being, that do not fit with their underlying worldview. It thus establishes, maintains and reinforces epistemic hierarchies.[15]

There is a wealth of contemporary ethnography, elucidated by politically engaged anthropologists such as Marisol de la Cadena, Marilyn Strathern, Mario Blaser and Helen Verran, which draws attention to this problem. For the sake of simplicity, I take my example from one of de la Cadena's ethnographic studies, which I discussed in a different context in the previous chapter. There, I sought assistance from her method of 'not knowing: in the presence of . . .' in order to make sense of learning in a self-transformative, ethical-existential-political sense through encounters with other-than-human agencies. (I emphasized, however, that, for inhabitants of 'the immanent frame' of Western modernity, such learning will normally be *mediated* through interpretations by the inhabitants of cosmologies who understand human agency and relationality in ways that make no clear distinction between human and other-than-human agencies.) In this chapter, I show the relevance of de la Cadena's work for the critique of capitalism, using an example she provides of anti-extractivist protests by indigenous people in the small village of Pacchanta near Cuzco in Peru, the site of some of her ethnographic fieldwork.

De la Cadena relates an episode in struggles over many years to prevent international corporations, supported by the local government, from extracting minerals in the area. The episode she discusses happened in Cuzco in 2006. It took the form of a demonstration in the main square, which followed a petition to the president of the region by representatives of a local coalition against the proposed mining operations. Nazario, an indigenous member of the Pacchanta village community and her 'co-labourer' in her ethnographic work (as explained in the previous chapter), was part of both the delegation and the demonstration. The proposed mines were to be opened at Ausangate and Sinakara. For some members of the delegation, including Nazario, Ausangate and Sinakara were at once mountains and *tirakuna* (earth-beings).[16] For the others, both in the meeting with the president and at the demonstration, they were simply mountains. As I sought to convey in the last chapter, understanding the meaning of *tirakuna* involves inhabiting a radically different cosmology, with a radically different understanding of relationality, in which detachment from origin is impossible and in which some mountains may be earth-beings and some humans may be *runakuna* (humans‡) who, emerging together with *tirakuna*, form *ayllu* (clan‡). For Nazario, and some other *runakuna* demonstrators and members of the delegation, protests on behalf of earth-beings were not equivalent to protests on behalf of particular mountains and particular humans or even on behalf of a particular indigenous community. This was because Nazario and some other *runakuna* inhabited a cosmology in which earth-beings resist the very distinction between human agents and other-than-humans agencies. In consequence, Ausangate and Sinakara, as earth-beings, were more than particular mountains and their power was diminished when reduced to that ontological category. However, it was not just the representatives of the international corporation, the president of the region and the local government officials who were unable to acknowledge this; others in the political struggle against the proposed mining operation were likewise incapable of doing so, including other anti-extractivism activists on the Left (with whom de la Cadena herself would have identified prior to her fieldwork in Pacchanta). De la Cadena's awareness of the chasm separating Nazario and some other *runakuna* from their co-protestors was awakened only when she happened to meet Nazario at the 2006 demonstration. During the weeks that followed, she learned that, for Nazario and other *runakuna* (humans‡), what to her was a mountain was, in addition, an earth-being (*tirakuna*). De la Cadena also learned that this was not a matter of disagreement about different perspectives on the same thing. It was an onto-epistemic gulf. For one side, Ausangate was *only* a mountain; for the other side, Ausangate was an earth-being *and* a mountain. In addition, one side denied the very existence of earth-beings. This side – comprising not just state officials but also some of the anti-extractivism protestors – could 'respect Ausangate as a cultural belief but could not accept its reality' (de la Cadena 2017, 7). De la Cadena continues: 'I was privy to a politics of *what* could be, where *who decided what was* could not be in question: an ontological politics at the limits of state recognition' (ibid.). Heated debates had already taken place about how best to phrase the protestors' demands. At the insistence of a local NGO, the decision was made to phrase it as an environmental concern, a cause the state could recognize and perhaps even accept as righteous (ibid., 3–4). The villagers achieved one of their aims; no mine was opened in Ausangate.[17] However, de la Cadena points out that, while the mining corporation lost and the mountain won, Ausangate the earth-being was rendered invisible. Its *political* presence was withdrawn by the protesters who were defending it. Victory for the mountain was bought at the expense of earth-beings (*tirakuna*), for the mountain's win diminished their power. De la Cadena concludes: 'To save the mountain from being swallowed up by the mining corporation, activists themselves – runakuna included – withdrew tirakuna from the negotiation. Their radical difference exceeded modern politics, which could not tolerate their being anything other than a cultural belief' (2015, 4). Furthermore, since *tirakuna* (earth-beings) form *ayllu* (clan‡) with *runakuna* (humans‡), the wellbeing of *tirakuna* impacts on the totality of *ayllu*, which includes *runakuna*.[18]

Fraser's critique of cannibal capitalism

With this example in mind, I return now to Fraser's critique of capitalism. Her main thesis, developed most comprehensively in *Cannibal Capitalism*, is that capitalism is not an economy, but a type of *society* – one in which an arena of economized activities and relations is marked out and set apart from other, non-economized zones. The economized zones depend on the non-economized ones, but they disavow their dependency (2022, 96). Proposing an enlarged view of capitalism, Fraser shows how the capitalist economy depends structurally on its 'others', specifically the unwaged activities of social reproduction that form and sustain those who perform wage labour; the legal orders, repressive forces and public goods that underpin private property and contractual exchange; and the natural processes that assure availability of vital inputs, including raw materials and sources of energy. She argues that these 'non-economic' factors are not external but integral to capitalism; they constitute its essential conditions (ibid., 61). This is what Fraser calls 'division', the first of several 'D's' that constitute the internal contradictions of capitalism. By *division*, she means capitalism's institutional separations of production from reproduction, economy from polity, and human society from nonhuman nature; these divisions did not exist in previous social formations. Far from being historical universals, they are artefacts of capitalism. However, capitalism *disavows* its *dependency* on these 'others'. Its dependency and disavowal are two other D's that distinguish capitalism as a social formation (Fraser and Jaeggi 2018, 153–4). From this, Fraser draws the consequence that a 'socialism for our times' must overcome not only capitalism's exploitation of wage labour, but also its unacknowledged free-riding on unwaged care work, public powers and wealth expropriated from racialized subjects and non-human nature (2022, 94). For Fraser, capitalism is not just omnivorous, as depicted by Marx and Engels; in addition it systematically destroys the conditions that enable its voracious appetite – it is primed to devour its own substance. It is at once a cannibal and an ouroboros that eats its own tail (ibid., 12).[19]

Furthermore, Fraser views capitalism as a profoundly crisis-ridden regime (2022, 11–13). She holds that the deepening turbulence of our times should be read as a crisis of the form of capitalist society we inhabit today. Her distinctive contribution to contemporary critiques of capitalism is to stress the multidimensionality of the present crisis. Departing from Marx and Engels, and, indeed, the first generation of Frankfurt School theorists, she argues that the internal contradictions of capitalism, at least in the present day, are not only economic and financial, but also ecological, political and social. Accordingly, its crisis tendencies consist in the complex interrelationship of multiple iniquities such as care deficits, climate change and de-democratization (ibid., 2).[20]

One of the strengths of Fraser's critique of 'cannibal capitalism' is her concern for its destruction of the natural environment. She draws attention to capitalism's inherent tendency to ecological crisis (2022, 60), which is compounded by the interrelationship between this domain and the other non-economic domains on which it depends yet disavows. Capital avoids paying anything close to the true replacement costs of the inputs it takes from nonhuman nature; instead, it depletes the soil, befouls the seas, floods carbon sinks and overwhelms the carbon-carrying capacity of the planet. Helping itself to natural wealth while denying the latter's repair and replacement costs, it periodically destabilizes the metabolic interaction between the human and nonhuman components of nature (ibid., 58).

Developing this point in the context of the present general crisis, Fraser explicitly calls for a (new) eco-politics. She points out that present-day eco-politics hides a 'roiling dissensus beneath a superficial consensus' (2022, 60). While many people are concerned by global warming, and other threats to life as we know it on the planet, they do not share a common view of the socioeconomic forces that drive environmental degradation, and of the changes required to stop it. For the most part, moreover, they do not connect their ecological diagnoses to other vital concerns (ibid., 58–9).[21] Consequently, in present-day eco-politics, many people fail to grasp the importance of a political movement that is both 'anti-capitalist and trans-environmental' (ibid., 59). What is needed, in Fraser's view, is a new, counterhegemonic common sense, with anti-capitalism as its central organizing motif (ibid., 58–9). This new common sense would see through capitalism's divisions and disavowals, recognizing the links between multiple strands of injustice and irrationality, environmental and non-environmental.

For Fraser, the problem with capitalism is not just that it is inherently dysfunctional and crisis-prone. In her diagnosis, a functionalist line of criticism is linked to a normative line of criticism, leading her to theorize the effects of its dysfunctionality in the 'interpreted and norm-laden social worlds in which capitalism's subjects actually live' (Fraser and Jaeggi 2018, 119). She describes this normative line of criticism as both moral and political. The moral argument highlights capitalism's exploitative and extractivist character: the private appropriation of society's surplus in capitalist societies entrenches deep-seated relations of domination along lines of class, gender, race and empire, while also allowing a small group of private individuals and firms to usurp what is actually the collective wealth (ibid., 130). The political argument criticizes capitalism's structural tendency towards de-democratization: it undermines the political infrastructure and institutions it needs for its operations, compromising political autonomy in the sense of collective self-authorship, thereby denying the capacity of humans to participate in fundamental decisions about who they are or want to be, and about what their form of life is and should be (ibid., 131). As observed at the start of this chapter, the context-transcending moment in Fraser's critique resides in its exposure of the discrepancy between the modern 'enlightenment' ideals of freedom, equality and solidarity and the moral and political defects of advanced capitalist societies. She holds that the moral and political lines of critique must be used together with the functionalist one as a toolkit (ibid., 178).

However, it is important to notice that Fraser's critique is, in the first instance, functionalist rather than normative. The normative line of her critique is directed at capitalism's failure to fulfil modernity's promise of a kind of society in which freedom, equality and solidarity would be realized. But, similar to Charbonnier in his critique of 'extraction autonomy',[22] Fraser attributes this normative failure to the dysfunctionality of capitalism as a type of society. In other words, the normative deficiencies of capitalist societies follow as an inevitable effect of capitalism's internal contradictions. Moreover, like Charbonnier, Fraser uncovers a fundamental illusion that renders capitalism dysfunctional. In Charbonnier's case, the illusion is to think that realizing human freedom involves extracting 'society' from 'nature', in the sense of removing all material constraints on autonomy. In Fraser's case, the illusion is to deny the dependency of social reproduction upon multiple non-economic spheres. In both cases, the resulting dysfunctionality of capitalism means that it is incapable of realizing modernity's promise of freedom, equality and solidarity. For both theorists, realization of this promise would mean rectifying the dysfunctionality of the system by replacing it with a properly functioning socialist alternative. However, neither interrogates the values promised by Western modernity from the point of view of what I call ecologically entangled ethical agency, resulting in a disregard for the ethical significance of the multiple complex entanglements between human and other-than-human agencies. In consequence, Fraser's functionalist approach leaves no room for protests against capitalist exploitation and extractivism that cannot be articulated within the Western modern secularized worldview (this also holds for Charbonnier's). This not only opens her critique to accusations of Eurocentrism and anthropocentrism; it also results in ideological closures that block self-transformative ethical learning by human agents through communicative engagements with the inhabitants of cosmologies with radically different ontologies and epistemologies, such as Nazario and other *runakuna* in the vignette I offered earlier.

Fraser does not champion what I have referred to in the previous chapters as an exclusive humanist worldview. Indeed, at one point in her conversation with Jaeggi, she rejects conceptions of human agency that celebrate human sovereignty and self-sufficiency. She distances herself from such 'Promethean' perspectives that assume the possibility and desirability of human mastery of contingency, contrasting them unfavourably with strands of ecological thought in which humans are not separated from nature, but remain part of it to the very end (Fraser and Jaeggi 2018, 135). In the same vein, she thinks that there may be 'something worth salvaging' from Horkheimer and Adorno's critical account in *Dialectic of Enlightenment* of the process 'by which we split ourselves into two: on the one hand, a master and subject, apart from nature; on the other hand, nature as the object which we seek to master and which we rush to leave behind, but which then "bites back"' (ibid.). While Fraser doubts that human and nonhuman nature can ever harmonize perfectly and queries the suitability of reconciliation or harmony as a frame for human aspirations, she holds that capitalism pits human and nonhuman nature against one another in an unnecessarily sharp and dangerous way. She concludes that the tensions in the relation between society and nature could and should be lived in a less antagonistic manner (ibid.).

However, it becomes clear in *Cannibal Capitalism* that, for Fraser, a less antagonistic way of living this relation does not fundamentally change the prevailing Western secularized understanding of the relationality between human agents and other-than-human agencies. The main problem with capitalist extractivism in her view is that it treats nature as an *inexhaustible* treasure trove from which it can *endlessly* extract monetized value (2022, 96). As I read Fraser, living the relation between human society and nature less antagonistically means acknowledging nature as a treasure trove – a stock or store of valuable things – that is *exhaustible*. The fundamental change she envisages is a new awareness that human societies need to *re*stock and *re*store the trove of treasure that nature affords them. However, this kind of less antagonistic relation between society and nature, based on awareness of the need for society to replenish and repair nature, articulated in terms of sustainability, does not question the prevailing assumption that nature is essentially a resource *for* humans to use judiciously. (I raised a similar objection to Charbonnier's call for environmental stewardship in Chapter 4.)

Indeed, despite the distance she takes from 'Promethean' perspectives on human agency, Fraser seems at home in the exclusive humanist worldview characteristic of capitalist societies. A core thesis in her critique of capitalism is that socialism 'encapsulates real, historically emergent possibilities: potentials for human freedom, wellbeing, and happiness that *capitalism has brought within reach but cannot actualize* (2022, 95; my emphasis).

Fraser evidently takes the view that the eco-socialism she espouses has the potential not only to restore the emancipatory meaning that the normative goals of 'liberty, equality and fraternity' had for revolutionaries in the eighteenth century; she attributes to it the potential to address the iniquities of capitalism, overcome its internal contradictions and allow for the realization of these normative values in the lives of all humans on the planet. While she acknowledges that ecological depredation is not unique to capitalism, she claims that only capitalism drives ecological destruction non-accidently, by virtue of its very structure. She claims that nothing in the inherent dynamics of either pre-capitalist or self-proclaimed post-capitalist societies spawned the ecological damages they effected.[23] She suggests that the *right kind of post*-capitalist socialist societies would develop sustainable patterns of interaction with nonhuman nature, while the same cannot be said for capitalist societies (2022, 59–60).

I agree with Fraser that future, reconfigured socialist societies are conceivable, desirable and perhaps even possible, in which ecological degradation is not a structuring principle, whereas it is virtually impossible to imagine future capitalist societies of this kind. I take the view, however, that, for eco-socialism to be desirable, it would have to fulfil a condition towards which Fraser's approach as it stands is inhospitable. The condition is that the envisaged socialist societies would not be post-capitalist, at least not in the sense of *following on* from capitalism; they would be '*de*-capitalist'. I mean by this a radically reconstituted society that does not simply *make good* the promises of the old capitalist one, thus uncritically reproducing its exclusive humanist worldview. However, to all appearances this is what Fraser seeks when she calls for 'deep structural transformation'. The counterhegemonic project of eco-political social transformation that she envisages aims at *actualizing* the potentials for human freedom and happiness that capitalism has 'brought within reach'. This requires 'reinventing the institutional divisions that constitute capitalist society' (Fraser and Jaeggi 2018, 223). However, to all appearances it does not require 'reinventing' the exclusive humanist worldview that spawned both capitalism and socialism in the same secularized bed within European modernity.

By contrast, the *de*-capitalist society that I envisage would involve a 'revolutionary reconstitution' of the promises of capitalism and, as part of this, 'reinvention' of the dominant exclusive humanist pictures of human agency. The exclusive humanist perspective facilitates an instrumentalizing stance towards other-than-human agencies and, as the evaluative horizon implicitly framing Fraser's critique of capitalism, limits her critique to humans who share this perspective. In consequence, it is vulnerable to accusations of Eurocentrism and anthropocentrism and also, tendentially, epistemically imperialist.

Fraser is likely to resist accusations of Eurocentrism, anthropocentrism and imperialism (Fraser and Jaeggi 2018, 187–8). She can certainly defend herself up to a point. She explicitly criticizes 'the NGO-ization of politics', drawing on support from a study by Sonia Álverez, which casts doubt on the contribution of NGOs in promoting a feminist politics and bringing about social change (ibid., 182; Álverez 1999). (Recall the comparable accusation that de la Cadena raises against the NGO members of the protest coalition in the vignette I presented earlier in this chapter.) Fraser bolsters her defence against such accusations by referring to fruitful alliances between Western traditions of capitalism critique and the protests currently voiced and practised among multiple indigenous peoples. Rejecting the supposition that the Marxist framework is inherently Eurocentric, she claims that, in the Andean countries, the Quechua catchphrase *sumak kawsay* (usually translated as '*buen vivir*' in Spanish) is 'used in an interesting way: not to demand preservation of traditional life forms, but rather to transform present-day capitalist society for everyone's benefit'. The phrase is used, she continues, 'to promote a form of life that is "modern" in the sense of being gender-egalitarian and democratic, but also ecologically sustainable' (Fraser and Jaeggi 2018, 188).

Fraser is right to highlight the dynamism and openness of learning by indigenous peoples through engagements with Western modernity. In many cases, this has resulted in fruitful incorporations within their respective cosmologies of Western modern developments such as gender and political egalitarianism; such learning processes are still in train. Nonetheless, the cited passage demonstrates that Fraser does not share my view that ecological sustainability – like environmental stewardship – is a questionable goal for a newly reconfigured socialist society, at least when construed in functionalist terms that do not challenge the exclusive humanist perspective. Furthermore, she disregards the difference between a society based on ecological sustainability and a society that seeks to learn ethically-existentially-politically *from* indigenous peoples, who are more attuned, responsive and attentive than the inhabitants of Western modernity to the ethical significance of the multiple complex entanglements between human and other-than-human agencies. In this respect, Fraser's critique, like Charbonnier's, is vulnerable to the accusation of epistemic imperialism: the imposition of a particular epistemic-ethical vocabulary of environmental stewardship and sustainability on peoples whose understanding of ecologically entangled agency renders this interpretation normatively troubling.

Not surprisingly, given her interpretation of *buen vivir*, Fraser is hostile to contemporary movements that call for *de*-colonization as opposed to *post*-colonization. She criticizes some strands within these movements for seeming to imagine that it is possible (and desirable) to 'purify' indigenous culture, to purge the Western influences that have 'contaminated' it, and thereby to return to something pristine (Fraser and Jaeggi 2018, 189). For similar reasons she is hostile to *de*-growth as opposed to *post*-growth movements (ibid., 184).[24] She is likely to be equally suspicious of my advocacy of *de*-capitalization. However, Fraser's critical remarks on de-growth and de-coloniality may miss something important. Rather than simply romanticizing indigenous cultures, these movements are motivated, at least on occasion and at least in part, by a concern to learn from the radically different ontologies and epistemologies of indigenous peoples; importantly, this is not learning in an extractivist mode, which appropriates discrete elements of indigenous cosmology for use for one's own purposes within one's own worldview; rather, it is educative, self-transformative, ethical learning in the sense in which I have used it throughout this book. In cases such as these, it seeks to establish mutual points of connection between diverging worldviews and cosmologies, while also acknowledging the points of disconnection – a process of 'understanding, while not understanding', as de la Cadena puts it. De la Cadena ends her ethnographic study on a note that strikes this tune. Following a brief discussion of *buen vivir* as a 'project for a Good Life that is an alternative to both capitalism or socialism', she favours an interpretation of it as *cosmovivir*. Understood in this way, it is a proposal for 'a partially connected commons achieved without canceling out the uncommonalities among worlds . . . a commons across worlds whose interest in common is uncommon to each other' (2015, 13–14).

In sum, it is easy to imagine a *post*-capitalist socialist society along the lines envisaged by Fraser that would *not* adequately have confronted its capitalist history of colonialism, racism and ecological depredation and would therefore remain open to accusations that it is perniciously Eurocentric and anthropocentric, and perhaps also epistemically imperialist. By contrast, if my argument in this book holds, there is a reasonable expectation that a *de*-capitalized socialist society would address these troubling aspects of its capitalist past through acknowledging the need for ethical learning in communication with the inhabitants of radically different worldviews and cosmologies. This opens possibilities for fundamental ethical self-transformations and for the kind of revolutionary reconstitution of capitalist society 'from within' that I advocate in the next two chapters.

Critique of capitalism as a form of life

At first glance, Jaeggi's *ethical* critique of capitalism, as it emerges from her conversation with Fraser, seems more promising than Fraser's normative-functionalist one. It seems to allow for a critical stance towards capitalism that adopts a decentring, expansive perspective on what constitutes a good life for humans, without presupposing the validity of the Western modern worldview. In contrast to Fraser, Jaeggi emphasizes that the normative component of her approach to a critique of capitalist society is ethical rather than moral or political.[25] According to her definition, ethical critique reveals capitalism to be a bad form of life, destroying essential components of the good life. Ethical critiques target the way capitalism changes our everyday lives and the value things have for us, along with the ways we relate to them, to the world and even to ourselves (Fraser and Jaeggi 2018, 116, 127). Accordingly, Jaeggi's ethical approach addresses the negative impact of capitalism not just on the fabric of everyday life, but also on human self-understandings and perceptions of relations with others, human and other-than-human (at least potentially). It is noteworthy, in addition, that Jaeggi is not apparently wedded to the worldview of secularized European modernity, hinting on occasion that critical theory may need to revisit the conception of modernity that has shaped its critical diagnosis of capitalism and projections of a better alternative. She acknowledges that critical theory's conception of modernity may be sectarian, biased against legitimate and desirable views of a good life (ibid., 185–90). Indeed, she raises the possibility that this is the case not just for the 'enlightenment' versions of critical theory that have followed in the wake of Habermas' *Theory of Communicative Action*, but for *socialist* versions as well (ibid., 186). Not surprisingly, therefore Jaeggi is less hostile than Fraser to de-colonial and de-growth movements and seems more receptive to possibilities for social learning through engagement with such movements as well as from indigenous ones (ibid., 185–90).

Jaeggi adopts a 'form of life' approach to social critique (2018). To understand capitalism as a form of life is to treat it as an ensemble of social practices and institutions that links together social, economic and cultural dimensions. This ensemble is constituted by normative criteria of appropriateness. To criticize the capitalist form of life involves examining it with regard to its ability to solve normatively predefined problems, and to enable appropriate processes of learning and experience. Examination of this kind discloses the capacities or incapacities of a given form of life to make sense of the contradictions posed by its own social practices and to transform itself accordingly (ibid., 159). In other words, it not only permits functional and normative defects in the shape and content of economic practices and institutions to come into view (Fraser and Jaeggi 2018, 137); it shows that the form of life in question has the resources to address the identified defects.

In her conversation with Fraser, Jaeggi describes her critical approach as an 'immanent crisis critique' or 'crisis-oriented version of immanent critique' (Fraser and Jaeggi 2018, 138). In her view, part of the task of critical theory is to expose the functional disturbances – 'contradictions' – and, hence, the irrationality, of a given form of life (ibid., 137). Thus, its task comprises two tightly woven strands. One strand is an ethical, disclosing critique in which the critical theorist enables the inhabitants of capitalist societies to recognize how capitalism blocks their awareness of the resources they would need in order fully to grasp the problems they are confronting, in turn hindering their ability to come up with adequate solutions to certain kinds of crises (ibid., 58). Alongside this, it is a functionalist critique of the irrationality of the capitalist form of life, its incapacity as a system to solve normatively predefined problems, and to enable appropriate processes of learning and experience (ibid.). The ethical, disclosive strand of critique uncovers deep potentials that have evolved historically in the given context. Jaeggi writes: 'The contradiction between forces of production and relations of production is not in the end a story about false promises; it is about there being actual capacities and possibilities for us to do something and live up to something, which we are not fulfilling' (ibid., 139). Accordingly, the disclosive strand of her ethical-functionalist critique of capitalism has an educative, self- and socially transformative, function.

This also explains why critique of this kind does not rely on the givenness of social struggles and conflicts that are already in the open. Instead, it allows for latent crises or crisis tendencies. As Jaeggi puts it, it is a way of theorizing about deep conflicts and deep crises that allows the critical theorist to make judgements about the social order that are not superficially reliant on a social movement showing up at a certain point or moment (Fraser and Jaeggi 2018, 160). As mentioned earlier, this is the context-transcending moment in her immanent critique. She acknowledges that ethical critiques are often conservative, nostalgic or even reactionary. Nonetheless, she insists on the importance of this kind of ethical critique of capitalism – but only when its ethical strand is coupled with a functionalist one, demonstrating the ways in which capitalism is intrinsically dysfunctional and crisis-prone.

This is precisely the problem. Jaeggi's critique of capitalism is not an ethical critique *simpliciter*. It is an *ethical-functionalist* one. Qua functionalist critique, it repeats the problem I identified in Fraser's approach: its context-transcending critical perspective remains immanent to the normative frame of the kind of society it criticizes. In other words, it finds the normative criteria for a properly functioning social system *within* the society whose deficits it diagnoses – in Jaeggi's case, these are deep potentials buried within the history of Western modernity. Qua functionalist critique, it leaves no room for fundamental critical interrogation of these normative criteria. This closes her critique of capitalism, like Fraser's, to educative, ethical learning through communicative engagement with the inhabitants of worldviews and cosmologies that understand human agency and relationality in radically different ways to the Western modern one. It renders it impervious to critical impulses that are not and have never been part of social practices within Western modernity, for example, forms of life in which *tirakuna* (earth-beings) emerge together with *runakuna* (humans‡) to form *ayllu* (clan‡). It also makes her critique, like Fraser's, vulnerable to accusations of Eurocentrism and anthropocentricism.

Thus, despite the merits of Jaeggi's approach, in particular, its attentiveness to history and the latent contradictions within it, its concern with social learning and its explicit ethical-existential-political orientation, its functionalist framing limits its critical perspective with the result that it falls short of the kind of critical theorizing that I advocate.

Critique of capitalism as subversion from within

Not all immanent critiques of capitalism are functionalist. Azmanova emphatically rejects what she considers a crisis-fixation in contemporary critiques of capitalism. She proposes instead a focus on the singularity of the present times in order to discern tendencies within capitalism based on actual lived experiences of what is wrong with it that contain opportunities for overcoming it, as opposed to stabilizing or overthrowing it (Azmanova 2020).[26] By 'overcoming' capitalism, she means subverting it from within through radical practices, based on real experiences, that strike at the very constitutive dynamics of capitalism, which is the competitive production of profit (ibid., 190).

Azmanova's book, *Capitalism on Edge* (2020), analyses the transformation of democratic capitalism in the early twenty-first century, telling a story about how neoliberal capitalism mutated in this century into the new, more malignant form of capitalist society we inhabit today. Her name for this more malignant variant is 'precarity capitalism'; one of its distinctive features – and for her the salient one – is the universalization of insecurity, which has come to afflict the majority of the inhabitants of capitalist societies, including those in more prestigious types of employment and with higher income levels. In consequence, the winners as well as the losers are now suffering. The result is a new multifaceted general discontent and feelings of aggrievement about the impact that the competitive production of profit is having on human lives as well as on their social and natural environments. In Azmanova's view, this multifaceted discontent is shaping a powerful political force, which can be mobilized for social change, indeed even for fundamental social transformation that would result in overcoming capitalism. She concludes: 'Mobilized in a mundane and inglorious anticapitalist revolution, these forces can perform a social change yet more radical than any proletarian class struggle could ever achieve' (ibid., 196).

Azmanova describes her critical approach as 'an internal (immanent) critique of lived experiences of injustice originating from the key contradictions of contemporary capitalism', (2020, 191). She makes it no secret that her critical perspective is purely immanent, dispensing with the context-transcending moment I identified in Fraser's and Jaeggi's critiques. Accordingly, the court of appeal for the validity of her critical diagnoses, and the normative basis for her recommendations for socially transformative mobilizations, is the lived experience of human agents within the advanced capitalist societies of Western modernity.

Azmanova's experience-based critique of capitalism connects with the early Marx's 'bottom-up' understanding of critical philosophy,[27] moving it in the direction advocated by Lois McNay.[28] As discussed, McNay accuses contemporary Frankfurt School critical theories of weakening the immanent moment of social critique and abandoning critical theory's original emphasis on the connection between social criticism and subjective human experiences in favour of a paradigm-led mode of critical social theorizing. Azmanova's approach is not open to this objection. Furthermore, her interpretation of 'overcoming' capitalism in terms of subverting it from within fits well with the model of institutional reconstitution 'from within' that I develop in the next chapter. In addition, unlike Fraser's and Jaeggi's approaches, Azmanova's critical model is normative-empirical as opposed to normative-functionalist, rendering it expandable in principle to include *all* subjective experiences, even those based on ontologies and epistemologies that are radically alien to human agents within the normative frame of secularized Western modernity. This makes her critique less vulnerable to accusations of Eurocentrism and anthropocentricism. Nonetheless, in the end her critical approach, too, falls short of the kind of critical theorizing about capitalism that I envisage. If not in principle, *as a matter of fact* Azmanova's critique makes no attempt to explore the normative significance for 'subverting' capitalism of the multiple complex entanglements between human and other-than-human agencies. Indeed, it shows no awareness of the relevance for this kind of revolutionary endeavour of ecologically entangled agency. Therefore, despite the important difference between her normative-immanent approach and Fraser's and Jaeggi's normative-functionalist ones, her critique of capitalism is similarly limited in scope and, to all appearances, unconcerned with learning in an ethical sense from the inhabitants of different worldviews and cosmologies who may wish to subvert capitalism for quite different reasons. By contrast, I envisage a critique of capitalism that is attentive to lived experiences in all their planetary multiplicity and richness. Due to its human-transcending idea of 'the good', it is open to learning, in a self- and socially transformative ethical sense, from protests against capitalism by human agents (such as *runakuna*) who live their lives more attuned to their ecologically entangled agency than the inhabitants of Western modernity.

In the next chapter I turn to critiques of politics. I explore two concerns for critical theories of politics that adopt the perspective on individual human freedom that I propose. One is the question of political freedom as an ethical-political mode of self-transforming, self-determining, ecologically entangled agency. The other is the question of institutional transformation. Here, I take initial steps towards developing a conceptual framework for the 'revolutionary reconstitution of society at large' that construes it as a process of transformation *from within*.

7

Critiques of Politics: Decentrings, Openings, Explorations

The Communist Manifesto summons critical theories to heed its call for 'a revolutionary reconstitution of society at large' and invites them to consider what this means. In broad terms, I hear the call as a demand for fundamental social transformation on a planetary scale – a demand with profound consequences for the self-understanding, conceptual framework and methodology of critical social theorizing.

In the first five chapters of this book, I presented key elements of a decentring, expansive and exploratory mode of critical theorizing appropriate for fundamental social transformation in the context of anthropogenic planetary devastation. I underscored the ethical-existential-political dimension of the emancipatory impulse driving critical theorizing, exploring what this means for theories of the kind that I advocate. I proposed an understanding of freedom as self-determining, self-transforming ethical agency that is ecologically entangled, entwined in multiple, complex, ethically significant ways with other-than-human agencies. I argued that only a human-transcending conception of 'the good' permits educative, self-transformative, ethical learning by ecologically entangled human agents in their communicative engagements with others, human and other-than-human.[1] I emphasized, however, that the human-transcending moment of ethical normativity goes hand in hand with a view of ethical normativity as humanly constructed in social practices in existing social realities. In Chapter 3, in loose analogy with Marx's dual perspective on the human 'essence' in his sixth thesis on Feuerbach, discussed in Chapter 1, I described this as a dual perspective on ethical normativity. As I observed in the Introduction, 'dual' is understood not statically but dialectically, as a continuous movement between two separate yet interconnected moments. In this perspective, as in Marx's perspective on the human 'essence', ethical normativity is socially constructed *in its reality*. In other words, its actual meaning and content is a human product. This is the context-immanent moment of my dual perspective, which I also referred to as intramundane or 'this-worldly'. However, ethical normativity is not entirely determined by actual, substantive human interpretations of it at any given time. As elucidated in Chapter 3, it is animated by human experiences of an ethically unsettling human-transcending (and other-than-human-transcending) power, and kept alive by reflective recollection of these experiences. This is the context-transcending moment of my dual perspective, which I also referred to as extramundane or 'other-worldly'. Understood in this way, ethical normativity does not originate in human agency (or in any other specific agency), but its meaning and substance are the result of human agency.

My dual perspective on ethical normativity is antithetical to what I have called the 'exclusive humanist' perspective (building on Charles Taylor's account of Western modern secularization processes). The exclusive humanist worldview rejoices in the self-sufficient power of human reason, understanding the moral order as a self-sufficient framework within which to find the standards of social, moral and political life. Accordingly, in the exclusive humanist perspective, humans are normatively self-sufficient in an ethical-existential-political sense: they are the creators of 'the right', 'the just' and 'the good'.

In the previous chapter, I considered the limitations of contemporary critiques of capitalism. My focus there was their inability or unwillingness to engage with, or learn, from protests against capitalism based on ontologies and epistemologies radically different from the exclusive humanist worldview. I contended that this ideological closure restricts the scope of their socially transformative imaginations and limits their critical, emancipatory power.

In this chapter, I extend my account of ethical-existential agency to agency in the political realm. Accordingly, I construe political freedom as ethical-existential-political agency that is entangled in multiple complex ways with other-than-human agencies with their own distinctive normativity. I draw out the implications of this for some key questions for critical theories of politics. Once again, the motif of human-transcendence, with its interlocking components of ecologically entangled human agency and a human-transcending conception of 'the good' ('the just' or 'the true'), is to the fore.[2] Here, too, the question of fundamental social transformation frames my reflections. In the second part of the chapter, I consider the mutually constitutive relationship between political agency and political institutions (in the broad sense) that provides the conceptual framework for an account of the 'revolutionary reconstitution of society at large' *from within*, some implications of which I explore in the final chapter.

Democracy

I focus my reflections on democratic politics. For decentring, expansive, exploratory critical theories, the question of the kind of political order most conducive to their emancipatory intentions is an open one. For Frankfurt School critical theories, there is a strong prima facie argument in favour of some kind of democratic politics. The ethical-political values that inspired the revolutions of the seventeenth, eighteenth and nineteenth centuries in Europe and America, laying the bedrock for modern democracy, are freedom, equality and solidarity; these are precisely the values embedded in Marx and Engel's 1848 revolutionary vision. Accordingly, 'Liberté, Égalité, Fraternité', the slogan of the 1789 French Revolution, could serve as the emancipatory motto for *The Communist Manifesto* as well.[3] This is not coincidental. The political thinking of the early Marx was profoundly influenced by the revolutionary movements that ended centuries of divinely authorized, oppressive political regimes in Europe, replacing the subjugating divine right of the monarch with emancipatory rule by the people. Indeed, in his posthumously published 'Critique of Hegel's Philosophy of Right' (2000b), Marx famously declared that democracy is the 'truth of monarchy', not only abolishing the subjection of the people to the laws of the constitution imposed through the might of the monarch, but making the constitution a process of self-constitution by the demos of the demos. He writes: 'in democracy the constitution appears . . . as the self-determination of the people. In monarchy we have the people of the constitution, in democracy the constitution of the people. Democracy is the resolved mystery of all constitutions' (ibid.). He then explains why democracy resolves the 'mystery of all constitutions'. It is because it returns the constitution to 'its real ground, actual man, the actual people' and reveals it to be the continuous self-constitution of the people and, hence, to be the people's own work (ibid.).[4]

Critical theories in the Frankfurt School tradition overwhelmingly endorse Marx and Engel's vision of an association of free and equal individuals, who are conscious that their freedom as individuals is the condition for the freedom of everyone (and vice versa). This helps to explain the fundamental commitment by Frankfurt School theories to a form of democratic politics in which the value of freedom has a central place, together with equality and solidarity as its necessary presuppositions. However, as discussed, theories in this tradition have always also engaged in robust critical interrogation of the prevailing interpretations of freedom (as I do in this book by way of a critique of the exclusive humanist perspective).

It may be helpful to distinguish between democracy as a normative idea and democracy as the constitution of political authority, although the two are closely interrelated. In the contemporary context of anthropogenic planetary depredation, both aspects demand critical interrogation, together with imaginative exploration of how they could be reconfigured and renewed. The discussions in the preceding chapters take some steps that help to reconfigure and renew democracy as a normative idea. When human agency, as I propose, is understood as ecologically entangled agency, and these entanglements are held to be ethically significant for the free development of such agency, the idea of democracy as the self-constitution by the people of the people gains a dimension that is lacking in Marx's 1843 characterization of it. The interdependence of human and other-than-human agencies means that 'the people', too, is ecologically entangled. In the perspective on critical theorizing that I advocate, this opening of the exclusive humanist worldview towards the normativity of other-than-human agencies is accompanied by an opening towards unfamiliar, uncongenial, even partly unintelligible ontologies and epistemologies. Such openings in the modern democratic imagination push democratic theories towards openness in their definitions of citizenship, altering the question of who is to be included in the demos. In the contemporary geopolitical context of mass migrations (likely to increase as the effects of planetary environmental depredation intensify), this is a central concern for contemporary democratic theory and politics (Benhabib 2004; Celikates 2019; Landemore 2020). Decentred, expansive and exploratory theories of the kind I envisage are likely to view the question of inclusion not as one of principle but, rather, as a pragmatic, contextual one. When inclusion in the demos is viewed as a principled matter, *certain categories* of persons are included or excluded (for example, migrants or refugees or convicted criminals, or, in some constitutions, mountains or lakes[5]). When it is viewed as a pragmatic, contextual question, by contrast, everyone is included in principle, but for practical, contextual reasons, due to contingent exigencies of the given political situation such as availability of material resources, not everyone can in fact by included; however, the exclusion of some can be justified only on grounds of contextually specific practical constraints and is always merely provisional.

At the same time, in my account, the inclusion in principle of everyone in political law-making, decision-making and policy-making processes extends only to human agents. It does not include mountains, lakes or any other other-than-human agencies either directly or as represented by human agents. This is because only self-transforming, self-determining human agents are *ethically* engaged, reflectively and discursively concerned with questions of what it means to live a good life in association with others. Accordingly, only human agents can perform the ethical-political activity of self-constitution – the activity of constituting the people. However, since ethical-political agency as I construe it is also ecologically entangled in an ethically significant sense and, moreover, depends for its development on communicative engagement with other-than-human agencies, this does not imply a view of political agency as a superior form of agency or establish a hierarchy in which human agency is elevated above other-than-human agencies. Thus, although my view of democratic agency is unambiguously human-centred, I maintain that it is not perniciously anthropocentric – unlike the exclusive humanist view.[6]

Reimagining the idea of democratic agency as ecologically entangled ethical-political agency has consequences for the question of the constitution of democratic authority. Over the course of recent centuries, democratic authority has come to be closely associated with government through citizen representation by elected members of parliament. Representative democracy can take more or less open forms, concerning both who is eligible to be selected as a representative of the people and the openness of deliberations among the selected representatives to the input of every citizen. At least since Habermas' major work on democratic politics (1996), Frankfurt School critical theories have argued forcefully for maximizing openness in both respects. Thus, Cristina Lafont (2019) calls for a form of participatory democracy that engages public opinion as the voice that needs to be heard, contested and suitably transformed in order to achieve politically successful and normatively better laws and policies. While her envisaged model of citizen participation does not abolish political representation, it views every citizen equally as an active contributor in the political process.[7] Lafont highlights the institution of judicial review as a site for the self-constituting power of the citizenry, writing that citizens must feel empowered to 'put on their robes' in order to show how the policies they favour are compatible with the equal protection of the fundamental rights of all citizens, to which they are all committed as democratic citizens (2017; 2019, 219–42). In her model, political representatives, too, should be viewed simply as citizens with no elevated status, who assume the responsibility of channelling the opinions of other citizens into formalized political processes, then passing laws, making decisions and formulating policies on the basis of these opinions.[8]

For reasons discussed in previous chapters, a decentred, expanded understanding of ethical-political agency as ecologically entangled agency complicates participatory deliberative democracy, increasing the likelihood that the contributions of some citizens will not be readily intelligible to others. However, the decentring and expansive mode of argumentation I propose in these chapters also helps to address such difficulties. Moreover, as I have argued, these difficulties are a sign of the vitality of the deliberative process and not obstacles to its proper functioning.

Decentring, expansive and exploratory theories of politics must be open towards new imaginings of representative government, and indeed new nonrepresentative modes, guided by the normative aim of the free development of each ethical agent through participation in political life. As things stand, maximally open, participatory, deliberative forms of democratic government seem best suited for this purpose, whereby a decentred, expansive, exploratory model of participatory deliberative democracy is required. Theories that approach democracy as the exercise of constituent power are a good starting point for further explorations of the constitution of democratic authority, since they share the dynamic and radically transformative, self-determining impulse of the mode of theorizing that I propose.

Constituent power

Theories of constituent power distinguish between 'constituted power', which refers to the authority of established institutions,[9] and 'constituent power', which refers to collective political agency as the normative basis for this constituted authority. In other words, the concept of 'constituent power' expresses the democratic idea that a constitutional order – a legitimate political association – is one that rests upon the activity of the people. Earlier, I quoted Marx's 1843 view of democracy as 'the truth of monarchy' and attributed to him exactly this thought: democracy is an activity of self-constitution by the people of the people.

The idea of constituent power gained currency through the writings of Emmanuel ('Abbé') Sieyès, a theorist of the French Revolution, who argued for the centrality of the people in the creation of a constitutional system (2003). Peter Niesen elucidates Sieyès' idea as follows:

Modern constitutionalism is based on the notion of constituent power. Constituent power signals that constitutional orders are made, not found, and that their authorship of last resort lies with the people. The notion connects the idea that all government needs to be subjected to formal legal rules with a commitment to popular sovereignty, such that without eventual recourse to an authorizing people, or against its authoritative expression, claims to constitutional validity will be fraudulent or void. (2017, 222)

On this view, constituent power is the source of constitutional authority. However, constitutional authority is not established once and for all in a single historical moment but relies on the continued engagement of the people with those who are constitutionally entrusted with governing as well as with the structure of the system (Lang 2017, 20). Accordingly, it has a dynamically self-constituting, self-transforming moment.

Niesen acknowledges Ingeborg Maus as one of the staunchest defenders among contemporary democratic theorists of the constituent power of the people (Niesen 2019, 32). For Maus, constituent power expresses the idea of popular sovereignty. It is a version of the horizontal social contract proposed by Rousseau (Maus 2011, 79). As such, it is an extra-legal category that designates a constitution-making subject as pre-existing the legal order and continuing to exist beside it. The people can activate constituent power at all times, and not just when there is reason to suspect that government is abusing its power. Maus underscores the importance of Sieyès' view that the people themselves can never be peremptorily bound by their constitution, whereas, by contrast, no constituted authority may change the terms of the constitutional order without authorization by the people.

Niesen highlights the advantages of the language of constituent and constituted power for explaining the normative basis of constitutional orders and for criticizing 'fraudulent or void' claims to constitutional validity. For present purposes, one of its additional strengths is to configure 'the people' as an active, not reactive, force, without which the entire legal and constitutional order would have no validity; this is why, as Maus emphasizes, constituted power is valid only so long as the people have not yet changed it. Connected with this is a further advantage: it establishes a dialectical relationship between political agency and institutional agency congruent with the co-constitutive perspective on the development of ethical agency that I propose. I come back to this point later in the chapter.

Constituent power has what Niesen calls a creative side that can never fully be institutionalized (2017, 231; citing Maus 2011, 91). It not only locates political authority in the collective will of the people, and thus horizontally through their interconnections as opposed to a vertical relationship from the top to the bottom; it also designates a space within a constitutional order in which the people realize their power collectively to change that constitutional order (Lang 2017, 28). To this I add that its self-constituting dynamics prevents it from *ever* fully being institutionalized. As a never-ending process of ethical-political self-constitution, constituent power is a generative, transgressive force that pushes beyond all established institutional frameworks, conceptual frameworks and habitualized patterns of thinking and action. Although it is not a component of most (or perhaps any) contemporary theories of constituent power, the dual perspective on normativity that I propose, which incorporates a human (and other-than-human) transcending moment, helps to explain this generative, transgressive force.

Despite the potential fruitfulness of their approach for critiques of politics as I envisage them, theories of constituent power have not always been sufficiently attentive to the normative ambivalence of the generative, transformative power of 'the people'. Political developments within contemporary democratic societies remind us that the demos does not automatically act in the service of the good. It is readily apparent, as it was in the 1930s when Horkheimer was developing his research programme for a critical theory of society, that the power of the people can effect fundamental changes to the political order that are for the worse rather than for the better.[10] These troubling developments have revitalized theories of democratic defence (Nitzschner 2024). Such theories were initially formulated under the heading 'militant democracy' in response to the dismantling of democracy by (formally) democratic means in the Weimar Republic, ending in Adolf Hitler's election to power in 1933 (Loewenstein 1937). Militant democracy persists as an influential strand within contemporary theories of democratic defence. These theories continue to grapple with the apparent 'paradox of democracy' (Schupmann 2024; Nitzschner 2025). The paradox is that citizens may legally pursue antidemocratic aims by using democratic means; formal democratic institutions permit their own abolition if the means of abolishing them do not contravene legally established democratic criteria such as inclusion, equality and nonviolence. While this is legally permissible, it is generally held to be normatively undesirable. For this reason, the militant democratic strand of theories of democratic defence argues in favour of democratic regimes that are willing to adopt pre-emptive, prima facie illiberal measures to prevent those aiming at subverting democracy with democratic means from destroying democracy – for example, party bans and other repressive measures. This adds a new dimension to the relationship between constituent power and constituted power. By pointing out that the transformative power of the demos can be destructive of democracy, militant democratic theorists raise the possibility that the repressive force of governmental institutions could be normatively justified in certain cases. This would hold even if, contrary to the views of Maus and Sieyès, the constituted authority changed the terms of the constitutional order without authorization by the people. This is not a thought congenial to the theoretical approach I advocate. It runs counter to my ethically self-transformative approach to political agency and, in particular, for reasons I presently explain, to my call for political institutions that contribute to the development of such agency. Accordingly, I take the view that a critical theory of politics framed in terms of constituent power must explore alternative ways of responding to the militant democratic challenge. My discussion of institutional transformation in the final part of this chapter takes some steps in this direction.[11] I draw attention to how political institutions, which I characterize as other-than-human yet humanly constructed agencies, contribute to the constitution of human freedom, understood as the development of self-transforming, self-determining, ecologically entangled ethical agency. However, I also point out that they are endemically prone to impeding the development of such agency. This calls for models of politics in which perpetual public contestation of institutional agency is a core component. Crucially, since institutional agency has an ethical component, which contributes to the free development of human agency, contestation is aimed not at *controlling* institutional power, but at *transforming it for the better from within*.

From the theoretical perspective that I propose, approaches to democracy in terms of constituent power require development in yet another respect. As things stand, they tend to appeal unreflectively to self-authorship and popular sovereignty as the emancipatory ideas at work in normative accounts of democracy. Thus, Maus holds that constituent power expresses the democratic ideal of popular sovereignty; likewise, Niesen refers to 'popular authorship', 'constituent authorship' and 'popular sovereignty as though their normative value were self-evident (2017, 222). Seeing no need to interrogate critically collective self-authorship and popular sovereignty as democratic ideals, they run the risk of uncritically reproducing the exclusive humanist versions of freedom predominant in contemporary mainstream political theory. As I explained in previous chapters, the exclusive humanist perspective on human agency construes it as normatively self-sufficient, denying or disregarding the ethical significance for humans of their ecologically entangled agency. As a result, it facilitates a purely instrumentalizing stance by human agents towards other-than-human agencies, as well as to the biospheres that sustain all agencies, even in cases where careful maintenance of them is advocated. This is what makes it perniciously anthropocentric. Frequently used catchwords are 'environmental stewardship' and 'sustainability'. As I point out, stewardship is deemed important only because it protects and secures the material infrastructure necessary for the exercise of human self-authorship (this is how I read Charbonnier's position in Chapter 4); other-than-human environments remain a resource to be used (sustainably) by humans for their own purposes, which may of course be moral-political (this is how I read Fraser's position in Chapter 5). However, as far as I can judge, neither Maus, Niesen nor theorists of constituent power in general are wedded to this particular understanding of self-authorship; it seems to me a contingent feature that could be eradicated at no cost to their theories. Over the course of the preceding chapters, I have argued for a reimagined and rearticulated conception of self-authorship (self-determination), highlighting its radically self-transformative dimension. The dual perspective on normativity I adopt enables me to construe self-authorship in a way that breaks with the exclusive humanist trope of normative self-sufficiency, allowing me to envisage human freedom as self-transforming, self-determining, self-authoring, ecologically entangled ethical agency that develops in communicative engagement with other agencies, human and other-than-human. I see no reason why theories of constituent power could not embrace this dual perspective, together with the view of human freedom as self-transforming, ecologically entangled, ethical-political self-authorship it enables. Indeed, this conception of ethical-political agency fits well with their view of the demos as always in process of self-constitution.

Embracing my dual perspective would encourage theories of constituent power to expand their conceptions of ethical-political agency to include in principle all humans on the planet. As observed previously, awareness of the interdependence of human and other-than-human agencies potentially expands the category of 'the people', opening the democratic imagination and pushing it towards a maximally inclusive conception of the demos. However, I cautioned against taking the ecological entanglements of human agencies as a reason to include other-than-human agencies directly in political processes of legislation, decision-making and policy formulation (or as represented by human agencies). I observed that only human agents are ethically engaged, reflectively (and, in my account, also dialogically) concerned with questions of what it means to live a good life in association with others, human and other than human. Accordingly, only human agents can perform the ethical-political activity of self-constitution by the people of the people. At the same time, I have emphasized throughout that the constitutive relationship between human freedom, as a mode of ethical agency, and the normativity of other-than-human agencies is centrally important from an ethical-existential-political point of view. As a result, the ecologically entangled dimension of human agency is highly relevant in political legislation, decision-making and policy formulation processes – even if, as I contend, this does not mean including other-than-human agencies in such political processes. Instead, it calls on the human agents involved to bring with them to democratic processes of legislation, decision-making and policy formulation their experiences of, and insights into, the ecological entanglements of their agency. This itself decisively changes the conduct and content of political deliberation.

Thus, my ecological perspective on self-authorship does not unreservedly support theories of constituent power that extend it directly to other-than-human agencies, or to their human representatives. For the same reason, it does not unreservedly support political theories that call for recognition of the 'rights of nature'. In contemporary legal and political theory, there are new, in several respects commendable, efforts to develop legal frameworks that inscribe rivers, mountains, lakes and similar other-than-human entities as nonhuman persons (Wesche 2023). Indeed, as mentioned earlier in this chapter, such legal inscription of other-than-human agencies is in some places already a legal fact. Alongside my argument that ethical agency is distinctively human (which I claim is anthropocentric in a relatively benign sense), an additional reason not to support such initiatives unreservedly is the danger that the rights they grant remain trapped in the view of agency underlying the (Western) modern conception of subjective rights. The modern system of subjective rights, as discussed previously,[12] permits the rights-holders to choose and act as they please, subject only to certain, very general, moral and legal constraints. Understood in this way, rights are essentially noncommunicative and nongenerative; they safeguard a space in which agents have no obligation to explain or account for their actions to others and are free to act as they please. Freedom in this sense is what Christoph Menke calls 'self-will' [*Eigenwille*] and a variant of the exclusive humanist view of the normatively self-sufficient will that I emphatically reject.[13] When detached from an exclusive humanist worldview, theories of constituent power are likely to welcome epistemic and ethical inputs of all kinds into the process of political self-constitution. However, for the reason given previously, I argue against welcoming all kinds of agencies.

Nonetheless, in Chapter 4 I cautiously welcomed environmental policies introduced for instrumentalist or functionalist reasons, such as replacing fossil fuels with the 'green' energy of solar power and wind or wave power, as well as policies to increase biodiversity. While rejecting the instrumentalist or functionalist reasoning often driving such policies, I acknowledged that they may *indirectly* contribute to fundamental shifts in thinking and behaviour that help to dismantle exclusive humanism and instil awareness of the ethical significance of the ecological entanglements of human agency. On the same grounds I accept the possibly educative, ethically transformative effects of the new legal frameworks that have already emerged, and others that may soon do so, and recognize that they may contribute indirectly to the required fundamental transformation of society on a planetary scale. Emille Boulot and Joshua Sterlin strike a similar note when they write that rights of nature inclusions permit 'the leaking of Indigenous legal and ontological orders into the legislation of the nation-state' (2022, 16). While pointing out that 'this dynamic is not without a multiplicity of issues', they take the view that, by renegotiating colonial relations, some state legal systems have initiated a process potentially more profound than has been acknowledged so far in the current theoretical literature. Thus, in their opinion, the inscription of 'nonhuman natural subjects' into the legal orders of some modern states has been a far more radical inclusion than has previously been recognized, for the realities and beings that are described by these cases exceed the theoretical discourse that has sought to describe and extend them (ibid., 22–3).

Beyond sovereignty

The normatively self-sufficient human agent of exclusive humanism has a close cousin: the sovereign human subject.[14] In this section, I show that even political theorists who reject the ideal of sovereignty may nonetheless unquestioningly reproduce the exclusive humanist worldview.[15] My examples are Hannah Arendt's and Sofia Näsström's rejection of the idea of sovereignty as a democratic ideal. Their critiques are instructive, demonstrating that dismantling the exclusive humanist worldview involves more than repudiation of the idea of the sovereign human subject: it also involves acknowledging the ethical significance of the multiple, complex entanglements between human and other-than-human agencies, which requires, in turn, a human-transcending perspective on ethical normativity.

In contemporary political theory, the sovereign people is usually regarded as the normative benchmark of democracy. The discussion in the previous section showed that theories of constituent power, too, make use of this vocabulary. This also holds for theories of politics in the Frankfurt School tradition. Habermas asserts, for example, that when read in discourse-theoretical terms, 'the principle of popular sovereignty states that all political power derives from the communicative power of citizens' (1996, 170). According to this view, democracy's liberatory promise resides in its replacement of a divinely appointed sovereign by the people, who declare *themselves* sovereign and assert their right to be their own source of authority in political affairs. Accordingly, sovereignty is understood as collective self-authorship (or self-legislation or self-determination) and equated with political freedom.

In her writings on freedom and revolution, Hannah Arendt takes issue with the concept of sovereignty (2006a; 2006c). Defining sovereignty as 'the ideal of a free will, independent of others and eventually prevailing against them', she declares that the 'identification of freedom with sovereignty is perhaps the most pernicious and dangerous consequence of the philosophical equation of freedom and free will' (2006c, 163, 164). For Arendt, freedom is neither a property of the human will nor the exercise of it. Instead, it is a form of natality (1998). Just as each birth represents a new beginning and the introduction of novelty in the world, freedom is an action that performs something unexpected, thereby starting something new. Freedom calls into existence something 'which did not exist before, which was not given, not even as an object of cognition and imagination, and which therefore, strictly speaking, could not be known' (2006c, 151). In other words, freedom for Arendt is generative as well as generated. It is also performative in the sense that it exists only when enacted. She writes: 'Men *are* free . . . as long as they act, neither before nor after; for to *be* free and to act are the same' (ibid., 153; emphasis in original). Moreover, freedom is inherently relational, existing only when humans *act together*. In addition, freedom requires plurality. It exists only when performed among a plurality of humans, who, from their different perspectives, can judge the quality of what is enacted. Finally, it must be performed in *public* spaces. The raison d'être of the political is to 'establish and keep in existence a space where freedom as virtuosity can appear' (ibid., 154). In sum, freedom for Arendt is generated horizontally through communicative relationships between a plurality of humans, who act in concert in the public realm and thereby bring something new into the world.

Näsström shares Arendt's antipathy to sovereignty as a political ideal. Rejecting the widespread preoccupation with popular sovereignty in contemporary democratic theory, she seeks to recover the radical spirit that animates modern democracy, as expressed in the revolutions of the eighteenth century, and explore how it could be reinvigorated under contemporary conditions. In *The Spirit of Democracy* she argues that recovering the spirit of democracy requires a new vocabulary (2021, 2). Drawing on the political writings of Baron de Montesquieu, she aims to revitalize its revolutionary, emancipatory animus by replacing normative accounts of democracy in terms of popular sovereignty with a spirit-oriented one. Drawing together Montesquieu and Arendt, she contends that understanding democracy in terms of the prerogative of sovereign peoples to control and decide their own affairs undermines the commitment needed to uphold what Montesquieu describes as a democratic political *lifeform*. In his 1748 treatise *The Spirit of Law* (1989) Montesquieu writes that all political forms – be they monarchies, republics or despotic regimes – are guided by a dominant principle of action and judgement that gives them their distinctive spirit and shapes them in their entirety. Näsström contends that the spirit of modern democracy is the spirit of emancipation. Emancipation in the modern democratic sense means exit from a condition in which the basic purpose and direction of society is decided for subjects by their rulers. Furthermore, its emancipatory spirit is revolutionary, again in the modern sense. Following thinkers such as Arendt (2006a) and Reinhardt Kosellek (2004), who observe that prior to the revolutions in the late eighteenth century, the term 'revolution' signified a process of circulation, or a return to the same, Näsström highlights the experience of novelty and radical political change with which it is associated today (2021, 73). Accordingly, she connects emancipation with a new perception of the radical openness of the course of human history, citing Arendt's characterization of revolution as the sense that 'an entirely new story, a story never known or told before, is about to unfold' (Arendt 2006a; quoted in Näsström 2021, 73).

In these ways, Näsström joins Arendt in rejecting sovereignty as a democratic ideal and as the basis for political freedom. With Arendt, she understands freedom instead as a form of natality, as the capacity to start anew, as generated through human action, as relational, as requiring plurality and as something that manifests when humans act together in public spaces to determine the shape and structure of their collective lives. In Arendtian mode, she writes that freedom 'exists in the space that opens up between people, and as such it depends on us caring for the world, and not merely for our own private happiness or material interests' (2021, 90).

Näsström perceives a downside to the exhilarating new awareness of human freedom that comes with the political revolutions of European and American modernity.[16] Its negative side is a fundamental existential uncertainty about the purpose and direction of social life (2021, 73). Drawing on Claude Lefort (1988), Näsström argues that, when the divinely appointed monarch is toppled through the revolutionary act, it gives rise to feelings of profound uncertainty on the part of the newly liberated human subjects. This is a burden that the democratic lifeform must deal with. Every political lifeform can be understood as a way of coping with existential uncertainty, but the post-revolutionary evacuation of the place of power occupied by the divinely sanctioned monarch opens a veritable abyss of freedom and responsibility. Näsström claims, however, that the post-revolutionaries have an important resource on which they can draw to mitigate this heavy burden. This resource is equality. Rule by divine right is toppled but it is toppled through appeal to the Judaeo-Christian message that 'all human beings are considered equal under God' (2021, 80). She takes this to mean that all human beings are equally finite and fallible and hence equally situated in relation to the abyss of freedom and responsibility that is opened up by the revolutionary act. By sharing and dividing the burdens of this existential uncertainty equally, humans are able to embrace their newly achieved freedom rather than being overwhelmed by the manifold responsibilities that come with it. But to do so, they need laws, institutions and policies that ease their burdens of responsibility.

Coping with uncertainty is one reason that Näsström gives for establishing freedom-enabling laws, institutions and public policies. Another connected but separate reason is that, in democracies, institutions and public policies 'give everyone equal time and space to explore the diversity of experiences and expectations that make up their common world, in the political as well as in the social realm' (2021, 122). When laws, social institutions and public policies fail to do this, democracy becomes corrupted and threatens to disintegrate. In Näsström's view, this is happening at the moment. The contemporary world is characterized by a present-centredness that manifests politically as the 'tyranny of novelty', the reduction of democracy to what is immediately present (ibid., 145; cf. Hartog 2015). It stems from a failure of people to grant each other equal time and space for judging and deciding the purpose and direction of society.[17] The contemporary privatization of responsibility is, in her view, a further manifestation of democratic corruption.[18] Using freedom in the sense of individual choice as a ploy, democratic governments make citizens solely responsible for their life situations, their life prospects and their wellbeing.

At first glance Arendt's and Näsström's critiques of sovereignty complement and enhance my critique of the exclusive humanist perspective on freedom. Certainly, all three of our critiques share a decentring impulse. In my case, it is a matter of decentring the exclusive humanist view of political freedom by making human self-authorship dependent on reflective communicative engagement with the ethical significance of the multiple complex entanglements between human and other-than-human agencies; in Arendt's case, displacing the sovereign human will as the locus of human freedom, indeed dispelling the belief that freedom has a locus by arguing that it exists only in the generative interrelationality of a plurality of humans acting in concert in the public realm; in Näsström's case, in a similar vein, relocating power from the place evacuated by the divinely appointed monarch to a plurality of citizens acting together reflectively and creatively in public spaces.

However, closer consideration reveals that Näsström and Arendt, despite their vehement rejection of conceptions of freedom in terms of the sovereignty of the human will, have not severed links with the exclusive humanist worldview – evidently in the case of Arendt and apparently in the case of Näsström. The core problem in Arendt's case is the anthropocentrism of her political theory, which, as she makes quite clear, is based upon the anthropological category of human action. Arendt, as is well known, distinguishes 'action' from the categories of 'labour' and 'work', singling out 'action' as the activity that distinguishes humans from other animals and from the gods (1998). There can be no doubt, therefore, that her account of freedom is anthropocentric. This is not necessarily a serious objection. Earlier in this chapter, I acknowledged the anthropocentrism of my view of ethical-political agency, but, for reasons discussed in Chapter 4, I described it as relatively benign. In itself, Arendt's anthropocentric view of 'action' is likewise relatively benign: as I pointed out in my earlier discussion, claims to human distinctiveness are not necessarily claims to human superiority. (I cautioned, however, that they lend themselves easily to supremacist thinking and open the door for the kind of pernicious anthropocentrism I discuss under the heading 'exclusive humanism'.[19]) The problem, accordingly, is not Arendt's explicitly anthropocentric view of 'action' per se. Her anthropocentrism is pernicious only when 'action' becomes the basis for her characterization of freedom. Her emphasis on the openness of history and on the generative power of humans acting together threatens to obscure the fact that freedom as natality is understood as *entirely* the product of human activity. In Arendt's perspective, humans develop their ethical agency through communicative interactions only with other *human* agents. The implicit assumption is either that other-than-human agencies lack normativity that is ethically significant for human agents, or that human normativity is inherently superior to the normativity of such agencies. This makes Arendt's account of freedom perniciously anthropocentric in my terms. It closes off possibilities for ethical learning in reflective communicative engagement with the ethical significance of the ecological entanglements of human agency. It is unclear whether Näsström is committed to this feature of Arendt's account. Certainly, she does not share her anthropocentric view of human *action*.[20] At the same time, she expresses no reservations about the anthropocentrism of the concept of natality. It seems to me that nothing in her approach weds her to the Arendtian version of natality and that she could avoid its pernicious anthropocentrism by adopting the dual perspective on normativity that I propose. Doing so would enable her to acknowledge the ethical significance for humans of the normativity of other-than-human agencies, but would also require her to embrace a conception of normativity with an integral transcending moment that radically decentres it, pushing it beyond the normativity of all specific agencies, human or other-than-human.

There is an evident analogy between a conception of freedom as natality, which is generated entirely through human interrelationality by way of intersubjective performances in public spaces, and Habermas' view of freedom, which is generated entirely though human interrelationality by way of the intersubjective exchange of reasons in moral and political discourses in public spaces. In my discussions in the previous chapters I objected to Habermas' intramundane, 'this-worldly' perspective on moral normativity, which I characterize as exclusively humanist, for blocking possibilities for self-transformative ethical learning by human agents from other-than-human agencies and increasing the risk of ideological closures in critical theorizing. Even though, unlike Habermas, Arendt rejects the idea of sovereignty, I raise the same objections against her conception of freedom – and Näsström's insofar as she endorses it. My objection, to be clear, is not to Habermas', Arendt's or Näsström's emphasis on the *generativity* of human action. To the contrary, I consider this a strength of their respective approaches. My objection, rather, is to the position that the meaning of 'the good' ('the just' or 'the true') is *completely* determined by the generative activity of humans. My position, to repeat, is that such normative determinations, which are generated through human action, point beyond themselves to a human-transcending 'moral source', in the phrase used by Charles Taylor.[21] I have argued that the ethically unsettling power of moral sources, when experienced by humans, impacts on them affectively and intellectually; moreover, that recollection of experiences of this power can be retrieved reflectively by human agents, informing the ethical conduct of their lives (Chapter 3).

Alongside the objections to the exclusive humanist idea of freedom I articulated in previous chapters, I now add a further unwelcome effect: it limits the democratic imagination concerning possibilities for fundamental social transformation and to possibilities for such transformation that are immanent within the existing social structures and institutions.

I have stressed the importance, in the contemporary historical situation of anthropogenic ecological depredation, of transformations in self-understandings, normative vocabularies and ontologies and epistemologies as a precondition for the fundamental transformation of society that our disastrous situation demands. *Pace* Arendt (and perhaps Näsström), such transformations call for a conception of human freedom in which humans develop their ethical agency not just in communicative interactions with other *human* agents, but also through communicative engagement with other-than-human agencies (although, as I pointed out, for many inhabitants of the Western modern worldview, engagement with other-than-human agencies will require the mediating powers of human agents whose ontologies and epistemologies are widely divergent from their exclusive humanist perspective). As I articulate it, freedom is the free development of ecologically entangled human agents who are concerned to live good lives in association with all others, human and other-than-human. I have underscored, furthermore, that this implies the ethical significance of other-than-human agencies and, in turn, a conception of ethical normativity with a human-transcending moment. Expanding the concept of human freedom in this way calls for political institutions (and social institutions in general) that are attuned to the multiple, complex ways in which the good for human agents is entangled with the good for other-than-human agencies, open to educative learning about what this means and to transforming themselves accordingly when pressured to do so. Thus, I combine this with a perspective on social institutions in which they too are self-transforming agencies and have an ethical dimension. The proposed view of social institutions goes further than Näsström's, who, as mentioned, attributes to them the role of *enabling* human freedom. Instead, the perspective I propose calls for a view of institutions as contributing to the very constitution of freedom. Moreover, it emphasizes the reciprocally constitutive relationship between human agency and institutional agency and attributes to both a transformative ethical power. It attributes to institutional agency the power of authority, which fosters the free development of ethical agency and changes it for the better; it attributes to human agents the power to change social institutions for the better through contestation, contributing to their more or less fundamental reconstitution from within. In the remainder of this chapter I explain what I mean.

Institutions as humanly constituted other-than-human agencies

My first step is to clarify the ontological status of social institutions as I construe them.[22] Up to now, when referring to other-than-human agencies, I meant other-than-human entities that are *not* humanly fabricated. In mainstream Western moral and political philosophy, these entities, together with the biospheres that sustain them, are usually called 'nature' (theorists inspired by Marx's dialectical materialism often refer to 'material environments'). However, in my discussions so far I have left aside the question of the ethical-existential-political significance of the multiple interactions between human agents and *fabricated* entities: the 'things', humanly produced and maintained, on which humans depend in their everyday lives. For Arendt, as Bonnie Honig observes, the world consists of 'things' produced by human activity (Arendt's examples include shoes, tables, craftwork, sculpture and art). Honig, drawing on Arendt and Donald W. Winnicott, sketches a thought-provoking picture of the 'thing dependency' of human existence, arguing that without public things, possibilities for acting together politically in public spaces are undermined and the signs and symbols of democratic life are devitalized (2017, 39; referencing Arendt 1998). This invites consideration of the ways in which material 'things' in general, humanly fabricated or not, can contribute to the development of ethical agency (and also threaten it or impair it). In Chapter 4, I quoted Honig's observation that 'things' in the 'natural world' – her example was the corn plant – can give us instruction, which she (correctly in my view) took to mean that such 'things' have agency. I understand 'agency' to imply normativity – in this case, the distinctive normativity of the corn plant.[23] In the following, I extend this point to some *humanly fabricated* 'things'. I claim that at least some such 'things' have agency and can instruct us – educate us and change us for the better. As I now explain, social institutions are 'things' that belong to this category, with important implications for critical theories of politics.

Institutional self-transformation

Classical sociological accounts of institutions define them as socially constructed, supra-individual entities (Berger and Luckmann 1967). I conceive of social institutions as humanly constituted other-than-human agencies that interact with human agents in processes of reciprocal self-formation. Moreover, I attribute to institutions a distinctive ethical normativity, which has some independence of the ethical normativity of the human agents that co-constitute then. The co-constitutive relationship is dynamically dialectical: the two sides have relative independence of one another, but they are permanently reciprocally engaged. I attribute this relative independence to the human-transcending (and other-than-human transcending) moment in ethical normativity as I conceive of it. In the account I offer, to recall, ethical normativity is not entirely socially constituted. Its constitution in social processes, which makes it *in its reality* an 'ensemble of the [prevailing] social relations' (Marx 2000e, 172), is animated by reflective recollection by human agents of experiences of a human-transcending power. This is why ethical agency in general, be it the agency of institutions or of individual and collective human agents, is not *generated* through the co-constitutive processes that I describe, although it becomes a social reality only through such processes. The implication I draw is that self-determining agency is not *enabled* by institutions, it is *formed and shaped* by institutions in ethically significant ways; conversely, self-determining agents form and shape institutional agency in ethically significant ways. In other words, both sides of the relationship have an ethically relevant mutually transformative power.

I use the term 'institution' in a broad sense to encompass both formal political institutions and the multiple other kinds that make up what Hegel calls '*Sittlichkeit*' (Neuhouser 2003). As mentioned, Näsström, following Montesquieu, calls this institutional complex a 'lifeform'. Examples of institutions are families, schools, sports clubs, parliaments and churches.

I follow Luc Boltanski in the view that institutions primarily serve the function of shaping and stabilizing social meanings. As he puts it: 'To institutions falls the task of saying and confirming what matters' (2011, 75). He points out, furthermore, that they give an enduring semantic shape to reality, 'they seem removed from the corruption of time' (ibid.).

Boltanski's account of social institutions is helpful for its emphasis on the role social institutions play in shaping and stabilizing social meanings as well as on their relative inertia − their persistence over time. However, it pays no attention to the *ethical* dimension of the meanings they shape and stabilize. By contrast, I emphasize the role of institutions, individually and in configuration, in constituting webs of ethical meanings (Cooke 2020d).[24] In my account, social institutions are incorporations of often diverse and sometimes conflicting ethical meanings, which form a multilayered and multidimensional sedimentation. This sedimentation is the complex historical product of human ethical agency in interactions with institutions; it is the humus that nourishes institutional agency. Moreover, it gives them an ethical dimension, enabling them to provide ethical guidance and orientation. They may do so tacitly, by inculcating certain modes of thought and behaviour, or expressly, by way of laws, ordinances, policies, prescriptions, mission statements, recommendations and other directives. Political institutions in the narrow sense of governmental agencies do not only provide ethical orientation and guidance; they have other tasks such as policing and administration, each of which exercises a different kind of power. My concern here is solely with the ethical power of institutions, which I refer to as authority.

Authority is a distinctive form of power, differing, for example, from domination. In contrast to power as domination, authority depends on the acknowledgement of an obligation to obey on the part of those over whom it is exercised. Furthermore, it is an obligation that is in some sense self-imposed. This means that it has an integral moment of freedom. Arendt draws attention to this, observing that it 'implies an obedience in which men retain their freedom' (2006b, 106). Here, she makes explicit a connection between authority and freedom that others, too, have noted. Herbert Marcuse, for example, observes that the concept of authority has a moment of freedom built into it that is lacking in domination: at a minimum, authority involves freedom in the sense of voluntary recognition and affirmation of the bearer of authority (2008).

However, neither Arendt nor Marcuse attends to the ways in which institutionalized authority is potentially freedom-constituting, in my sense of contributing to the development of self-transforming, self-determining, ecologically entangled, ethical agency. In Marcuse's case, this is a consequence of his failure to differentiate between non-authoritarian ('authoritative') and authoritarian authority. But Arendt, too, neglects the ethical-existential aspect of authority. She cites the definition of authority given by Theodor Mommsen, the nineteenth-century German historian, apparently approvingly. Mommsen writes that authority is 'more than advice and less than a command, an advice which one may not safely ignore' (1888, 1034; cited in Arendt 2006b,

123).[25] But she passes over the ethical-existential component in his definition. As I read Mommsen, he suggests that authoritative advice is rationally and affectively compelling – the message conveyed to the agents addressed makes sense to them, connecting with intuitions or ideas that they already have, though they may not be aware of them. Even if they do not want to hear the advice or follow it, they *know* that they cannot 'safely ignore' it. The phrase 'safely ignore' [*füglich entziehen*] is ambiguous – it has both an ethical-existential and a prudential meaning. In the case of authority, I understand Mommsen to mean that it has both: ignoring authoritative directives is unwise because it is detrimental to the good conduct of life by the human agents concerned and also because they would be judged negatively by other human agents for not following it.

This picture of institutional agency assumes that humans in their capacities as ethical agents construct an agency with an ethical power ('authority') that is qualitatively different from their own ethical agency. How is this possible? Émile Durkheim's writings on the generative power of collective moral activity help to make sense of it. In his account of such activity, be it religious or secular (for him this is unimportant), human agents generate a transcendent being, moral in character, that is qualitatively different from each of them as individuals as well as from the aggregate of their individual beings (1965, 51). For Durkheim, this transcendent moral entity has the characteristics of a sacred object, inspiring feelings of fear or respect, but also arousing feelings of love and awakening desires and aspirations; it both keeps the human agents concerned at a distance and draws them towards itself (ibid., 48). The collectively acting agents perceive its power as superior to their own, attributing to it a moral authority.[26] It may be helpful to think of social institutions along these lines. Although not all social institutions inspire awe and arouse affection to the same degree, at least on occasion their power may be experienced as a moral presence. For present purposes, the important point Durkheim makes is that collective human activity, when ethically motivated, can generate a transcendent ethical entity that is qualitatively different from the individual ethical agents involved in the collective activity and also different from the aggregate of these agents. What remains unexplained is the ethical quality of the power of the transcendent being that is produced. A conception of 'the good' such as I propose, which transcends the generative activity of all particular human (and other-than-human) agencies, helps to answer this question.

Institutional authority slides easily into authoritarianism. This is due in part to the role social institutions play in stabilizing social meanings and to the inertia arising from their persistence over time. As a result, the social side of the constitution of institutional agency – its human fabrication – is easily obscured, or at least often not readily visible, impeding protest against and resistance to institutional authoritarianism and its detrimental effects. If institutions are to exercise power that is authoritative, yet nonauthoritarian, they must be opened to change in response to objections to, and protests against, their ethical agency, objections that may target their mode of operation, their organization, the ethical meanings sedimented in their institutional identities and/ or the specific ethical contents of their directives. In other words, authoritative yet nonauthoritarian institutions must perceive themselves, and be perceived by those affected by them, as in a permanent process of self-transformation through ethically motivated contestation. In contemporary democracies, in which there are multiple diverging and often conflicting ethical-existential-political perspectives, the process of institutional self-transformation is likely to be antagonistic rather than harmonious. Nonetheless, the co-constituting agencies involved in the process – the institutional agencies on the one side and the human agents affected by them on the other – are part of a common project of mutual constitution that is always potentially transformative of both agencies.

I describe this reciprocal process of transformation as 'self-transformation' in the sense of internal transformation or 'from within'. By this, I mean that even the most fundamental and far-reaching changes are not imposed externally by either side of the co-constitutive relationship; instead, they are made by the agencies themselves, typically as a result of an ethical learning process. On the one side, institutional authority provides orientation and guidance to human agents that, in the words of Mommsen, is 'more than advice and less than a command'; it is experienced by them as a directive that they cannot 'safely ignore', calling upon them to act in accordance with it and, if necessary, to develop new ways of thinking and behaving. On the other side, institutional agency is contested and protested by human agents when it becomes oppressive or repressive; however, since the contesting agents acknowledge its potential contribution to the constitution of their own ethical agency, they do so with a view not to dismantling or abolishing the institution in question, but in order to change it for the better. Importantly, contestation of this kind presupposes a sense of inclusion within the institution. For this reason, its precondition is often a political struggle for inclusion, in which excluded agents insist that they too belong to the institution. But even here, the aim is not to dismantle or abolish the institution but to be included within a newly configured, better version of it, to be achieved in part through the protests and challenges of those previously excluded from it.

In *The Souls of Black Folk* (2007), W. E. B. Du Bois attributes to the 'American Negro' a striving for inclusion in the US society of his time that illustrates what I mean. He describes a desire for inclusion that seeks fundamentally to change the existing institutions in ways that would merge the American Negro's unhappy 'double selves' – the only selves available to them under the prevailing social conditions – into 'a better and truer self', in which 'neither of the older selves' would be lost. Institutional transformation, which would be radical, would neither 'Africanize America, for America has too much to teach the world and Africa', nor would it 'bleach' [the American Negro] soul in a flood of white Americanism, for he [the American Negro] knows that Negro blood has a message for the world' (ibid., 2–3).

My proposed account of institutional self-transformation does not hold for all social institutions under all conditions, but only for institutions that serve the purpose of fostering human freedom (and equality and solidarity as its preconditions). This is why the institution of slavery in the United States could only be abolished, not reconstituted through transformation from within.

Furthermore, on occasion, even institutions whose identity is built on the normative aim of fostering human freedom may become so degenerate and corrupt that they must be 'de-instituted' before they can be 're-instituted', in the words used by Sarah Garton Stanley and Owais Lightwala in *Manifesto for Now* (2023). However, as Garton Stanley and Lightwala also observe, institutions are 'our memories'. I take this to mean depositories of the ethical hopes and aspirations of the past that have made us who we now are. Thus, re-institution following de-institution is likewise a process from within. In such cases, institutional self-transformation involves efforts to retrieve buried ethical hopes and aspirations from the institutional ruins. I return to this in the next, final, chapter.

My picture of ethically self-transforming institutional agency is utopian, but not *abstractly* so. It has a basis in existing social practices, recalling historical initiatives and social movements that, following social struggles often demanding inclusion, strove to reconfigure the existing institutions from within. Examples include the English, American and French revolutions between the seventeenth and nineteenth centuries, which sought successfully to reconstitute institutions such as government and the law from the point of view of freedom, equality and solidarity. Feminist movements from the late nineteenth century onwards provide a further example, in this case the institutions of bourgeois marriage and the nuclear family. Figures such as Johann Pestalozzi in the late eighteenth century and Wilhelm von Humboldt in the early nineteenth century strove to transform the institutions of early childhood education and the university in ways that would foster the free development of ethical agency. This is also true for religious movements such as Lutheranism, Calvinism, Pietism and Liberation Theology, which reconstituted institutionalized Christianity from the sixteenth century onwards.

In the perspective I have offered, institutions are agencies, with their own specific ethical normativity, who contribute to the ethical constitution of human agents, who in turn contribute to the ethical constitution of institutional agency. My co-constitutive model builds a self-transformative ethical dimension into institutional and political agency that diverges from most accounts in contemporary political theory, even from those such as Näsström's, which, like my own, stress the positive role of social institutions and view freedom dynamically and relationally. My account is distinctive in two main respects. First, in its call for reconstituting institutional agency *from within*; second, in its emphasis on the *ethical* dimension of such reconstitution. Brief consideration of freedom-enabling approaches to political institutions, which at first glance appear to fit well with the perspective I propose, helps to illustrate these distinctive features.

In Philip Pettit's neo-republican theory of freedom and government (1999), political institutions are freedom-enabling, but only when they are *externally* checked and controlled. For Pettit, as for Näsström, it is the task of the state to provide the protection and empowerment necessary for political freedom through its institutional framework and government policies (2019, 15). Accordingly, he calls for a mixed constitution, which implements a system of checks and balances on state power by way of a number of mutually constraining, multiple representative centres of power. Furthermore, the state enables political freedom when it checks and controls the citizenry and the citizenry checks and controls governmental institutions. Control is necessary on both sides. The state controls its citizens by tracking their 'common avowable interests'. Common avowable interests are interests that individual citizens have good reasons to embrace as collective ones. On the one side, the state employs mechanisms of checking and control to guard against the disjunction between their common avowable interests, as determined through the appropriate procedures, and their self-serving interests (Pettit 2012, 132–3). On the other side, citizens, by way of a mixed constitution and through exercising permanent vigilance and contestation, control the state by forcing it to track their common avowable interests in ways that avoid domination.

In Sharon Krause's critical theory of eco-emancipatory politics (2023), political freedom is likewise enabled by political institutions in ways that involve checking or controlling institutional power from the outside. In her account of environmental domination, Krause demonstrates the diverse ways in which dominating power structures human relationships with other-than-human entities, generating environmental problems and undercutting the abilities of humans to deal with them effectively. She calls instead for a politics of eco-emancipation that would involve practices of care for the planetary ecosystem along with institutions that protect it from exploitative human power. Accordingly, she identifies institutional mechanisms in politics that could formally check and control the exploitative power that people have over nature and incorporate other-than-human entities, along with all human agents, as valued members of political communities (2020, 461).

However, such freedom-enabling models of political freedom based on checking and control are conceptually closed towards possibilities for educative learning and self-transformation that arise when the co-constitutive relationship between human and institutional agency is recognized. Theorists such as Pettit and Krause are correct to insist that the freedom-enabling functions of political institutions go hand-in-hand with the exercise of dominating power. But when they respond by calling merely for control of such power, they throw out the baby with the bathwater. In my terms, they throw out authoritative authority together with its authoritarian perversions. As I observed earlier, authoritarianism is endemic to institutional authority. This is due to the tendential inertia of institutions, coupled with their functions of policing and administration, which makes them susceptible to entrenched power hierarchies whose authority appears to be unshakeable. Although, following Mommsen, we may criticize authoritarian authority as a perversion, this does not alter the fact that institutions are, at best, sites for continual battles between authoritarianism, on the one side, and, on the other, ethical-political self-transformation, with the outcomes weighted to the former side. Nonetheless, in the model I propose, the co-constitutive relationship between ethical-political and institutional agency attributes a politically transformative power to institutions that is missing in freedom-enabling accounts. Such accounts are alert to the ways in which institutional power is prone to authoritarianism. However, they seek to constrain it purely externally, through checks and controls.[27] The problem, to repeat, is that external control not only curtails the institution's oppressive or subjugating power; it also curtails its *authoritative* power – a power that, in Mommsen's words, is 'more than advice and less than a command' and may not 'safely' be ignored. By contrast with freedom-enabling accounts of political institutions, my reciprocally transformative, co-constitutive perspective opens possibilities for profound, far-reaching, ongoing and open-ended social transformation through ethical-political action by humans whose self-determining agency is itself a process of self-transformation to which social institutions contribute constitutively. Viewed in this way, social change is a matter of self-transformation on the part of both institutional and human agency, or, as I have also put it, internal transformation or transformation from within.[28] I come back to this, too, in the final chapter.

Within contemporary Frankfurt School theory, Jürgen Habermas and Rainer Forst take a step in the direction I propose, developing a view of political freedom as dialectically constituted in processes of interaction between political agents and institutional agencies. They refer to this as the 'co-originality' thesis (Habermas 1996; Forst 2012). It is the thesis that personal autonomy and public autonomy are inseparable, of equal weight and mutually dependent.[29] However, both theorists restrict self-transformation to the *moral* domain, in the narrow Kantian sense of 'moral', thereby limiting possibilities for fundamental and far-reaching social transformation.[30]

Forst views his version of the co-originality thesis as a development of Habermas' position that overcomes some of its serious weaknesses (2012, 33n32). Since I agree that Forst's version is more convincing than that of Habermas (Cooke 2020b, 577; 2024), I focus on it in the following. Like Habermas, Forst construes political will-formation dynamically as a dialectical relationship between personal autonomy and political autonomy. This view of political will-formation fits well with the dynamic, co-constitutive relationship that I posit between ethical-political agency and institutional power. However, as both Forst and I agree, Habermas' account of the co-constitutive relationship is marred by an individualistic – 'privatistic' – element that creeps into his theory of law and democracy, leading him to articulate personal ('private') autonomy as a *retreat from* communicative relationships (Forst 2012, 114; Cooke 2020b; 2022). Forst's approach overcomes this shortcoming of Habermas' account, enabling an understanding of the relationship between the agency of citizens and institutional power that construes it as reciprocally transformative. However, the transformative potential of the co-constitutive relationship between ethical-political and institutional agency is restricted to *moral* norms and principles, which Forst defines as claims to reciprocity and generality. This holds both for individual and collective political agents and for institutionalized processes of law-making, political decision-making and public policy-making. On the one side, only arguments that are reciprocally binding for everyone can claim political legitimacy; accordingly, only objections based on arguments that meet these criteria have transformative force. On the other side, directives issued by governmental institutions are authoritative for political agents only when they express norms and principles that are reciprocally and generally binding. In consequence, the ethical identities of political agents, on the one side, and the ethical identities of institutional bodies, on the other, are protected from the pressure of critical contestation, together with reimaginings and rearticulations of conceptions of the good life and good society that may result from it. (Here I am adopting Habermas' and Forst's narrow use of 'ethical'.[31]) This significantly limits the transformative power of both political agency and institutional agency in Forst's account.[32] Put differently, Forst construes the transformative dimension of politics as a matter of improving the *moral* quality of the existing democratic institutions in the narrow sense, or, more generally, the existing 'basic structure' of society (Rawls 1996). Politics is not concerned with the 'revolutionary reconstitution of society at large' and cannot contribute to it directly. This is not to deny that politics may have the kind of *indirect* ethically transformative effects I acknowledged in Chapter 4 in the case of 'green' politics as well as earlier in this chapter in the case of 'rights of nature' legislation. However, the mode of political theorizing I envisage seeks to go further than this. It explores ways in which political institutions might contribute directly and continuously to changing society for the better in an ethical sense, at times in radically reconstituting ways.

In this chapter, I have sketched a picture of institutional self-transformation that is relevant for discussion of the broader question of the 'revolutionary reconstitution of society at large'. In the next and final chapter, I propose a perspective on fundamental social transformation in which it is a complex, multifaceted process of reconstitution from within.

8

Transformations, Futures

The early Frankfurt School critical theorists did not doubt the need for fundamental transformations in every dimension of the capitalist lifeform they inhabited. The devastating effects of anthropogenic planetary depredation, accelerated and intensified within capitalist modernity and expanded further in recent decades by the 'digital revolution', reinforce their call for radical social transformation, while compounding the challenges. Despite the multiple complex issues involved, one thing seems certain: humans must fundamentally alter the ways they relate to themselves, to other beings, human and other-than-human, and to the biospheres that sustain life on the planet. My book has sought to show that Frankfurt School critical theory can contribute to the required transformative processes on condition that it radically transforms itself. To this end, I develop a decentring, expansive and exploratory mode of critical social theorizing, motivated by a concern for better lives and better futures for every human on the planet, in relationships with others, humans and other-than-human. In the perspective I propose, critical theory's emancipatory explorations are oriented by a concern for human freedom, construed in broadly Hegelian terms as *Bildung*, the free development of ethical agency in interaction with others in public life. I envisage freedom in this sense as self-transforming, self-determining, ecologically entangled, ethically oriented human agency. Such agency is concerned to explore the ethical significance of its multiple complex entanglements with other-than-human agencies by way of communicative engagements with other humans, with a view to better understanding human and other-than-human relationality. I contend, furthermore, that these explorations of the ethical significance of human and other-than-human relationality must be mediated by the use of propositionally articulated languages, alongside non-propositional contributions to the communicative process, as necessary.

The critical theorizing I envisage is conscious that pernicious kinds of Eurocentrism and anthropocentrism, manifest in what I refer to as the 'exclusive humanist' worldview, are embedded in Western modern traditions of moral and political theorizing and have been reproduced within Frankfurt School critical theories.[1] For this reason, I am concerned with possibilities for expanding, enriching and, if necessary, reinventing their ethical vocabularies by encouraging communicative engagements with the inhabitants of worldviews and cosmologies whose epistemologies and ontologies are alien to, and perhaps even ultimately incompatible with, the Western modern worldview.

The communicative engagements I envisage are exploratory, potentially revitalizing of the ethical meanings prevailing in a given context and oriented towards better futures for everyone. What is meant here by 'future'? The discussions in the previous chapters have addressed this question indirectly. It is time to consider it more closely.

Past, present and future

For critical theories, the question about the meaning of 'future' is also a question about the past and about the present. In the Frankfurt School tradition, the interrelations between past, present and future have been viewed in different ways. As discussed in Chapter 1, the Hegelian-Marxist philosophy of history underwrites Horkheimer's emancipatory project in his 1930s research programme. Accordingly, the validity of critical theory's diagnoses of the past and present, together with its emancipatory projections of a better future, is secured by the thesis that there is a rationality immanent to the historical process. These rational potentials can be actualized through human agency, aided by the 'enlightening explanations' (Marx) and 'existential judgments' (Horkheimer) provided by critical philosophers. History is viewed as a necessary and progressive movement from the contradictions, conflicts and crises of past and present societies towards a future society of universal freedom and happiness. Progress towards this *telos* is enabled by theoretically guided human action in the present (*praxis*), whose rationality is likewise guaranteed. I pointed out, however, that even the early Horkheimer hesitated to endorse certain elements of this Hegelian-Marxist view; by the 1940s, he and his colleagues clearly regarded it suspiciously (though not all of them for the same reasons). The main objection, shared by virtually all subsequent theorists in this tradition, is to its closure of the historical process; this has led to various revisions and rearticulations of the Hegelian-Marxist perspective on the past, present and future. However, all theorists in this tradition, even those who distance themselves from Hegelian teleology, retain at least one key element of the Hegelian-Marxist perspective: the idea that the past harbours potentials, accessible to the theorist in the form of manifestations of discontent in the present, for a better future. The question, accordingly, is how to reconfigure the relationship between past, present and future while keeping open the historical process. In general, from the 1940s onwards, theorists in the Frankfurt School tradition have tended to be especially alert to the danger of one of two kinds of closure, pushing them in each case towards a different variant of critical theorizing. Critical theorizing that adopts the decentring, expansive, exploratory approach that I propose can learn from objections to both kinds of closure. I distinguish them schematically as a Habermasian objection, which maintains that the Hegelian-Marxist philosophy of history inhibits the creative, generative potentials of communicative action among human agents in the present, curtailing possibilities for the future; and a Benjaminian objection, which maintains that it suppresses the unsettling, disruptive, troubling moments of the past and deadens the demands they issue to human agents in the present to struggle for a better future.[2]

The philosophy of history: A Habermasian objection

The Habermasian objection is a reminder to critical theories that the substantive content of emancipatory ideas such as universal freedom and happiness can never be determined in advance of actual communicative activities between human agents in concrete social realities. Habermas himself expresses the nub of the objection succinctly. He remarks that the philosophy of history 'can only glean from historical processes the reason it has already put into them with the help of teleological concepts' (1996, 2). His remark, as I read it, contains two criticisms. On the one side, it criticizes the *metaphysical injection* of an idea of reason into human history that cannot be explained in terms of human agency within actual historical processes. On the other side, it criticizes the Hegelian-Marxist *predetermination* of the meaning of progress independently of human processes of intersubjective communication.

My discussions in previous chapters raise doubts about the first criticism. The metaphysical injection of an idea of reason into the historical process is not necessarily reprehensible, when reason is understood in a general sense to refer to a human-transcending (and other-than-human-transcending) normative power. Indeed, I have argued that decentring, expansive and exploratory critical theories *must*, in a sense, 'metaphysically inject' a human-transcending idea of 'the good' into human history in order to avoid ideological closures resulting from the exclusive humanist worldview. However, I have also argued for a dual perspective on normativity, in which it is at once socially constructed *in its reality* by humans within actual historical processes and has an inherent human-transcending moment. The immanent moment helps to mitigate the risks of epistemological and ethical authoritarianism as well as bad utopianism. The transcending moment opens the theory outwards, towards unfamiliar epistemologies and ontologies; backwards, towards emancipatory potentials that can be retrieved from the past; and onwards, towards better, possibly hitherto unimagined futures. My point could be rephrased in Habermasian language as a distinction between the human-transcending (and in this sense metaphysical) *source* of the normativity of communicative reason and the *actualization* of reason by human agents within human reality through normatively generative communicative activities.

The second part of the criticism, which targets the Hegelian-Marxist *predetermination* of the meaning of human emancipation independently of human processes of intersubjective communication, is more pertinent for present purposes. The discussions in the preceding chapters can be read as an extended response to this criticism. They highlight the importance of openness in critical theorizing, including openness to the findings of the empirically based natural and human sciences, openness to the subjective experiences of human agents in existing social realities, and openness to alien epistemologies and ontologies. They warn of the danger of ideological closures, to which critical theories are prone, and propose an argumentation-based model of philosophical criticism of society in order to mitigate the risk. This is a decisively Habermasian element in my proposal. However, moving beyond Habermas, I propose a decentring, expansive, exploratory model of argumentation concerned with the validity of matters that, in the final instance, are ethical-existential or ethical-political in character; as I explained, Habermas' account of context-transcending validity cannot accommodate argumentations concerned to evaluate ethical validity claims. Furthermore, again in contrast to Habermas, argumentation, as I construe it, is a continuous dialectical process of reciprocal ethical self-transformation between human agents, in which each agent may be changed for the better and, in being so changed, contribute to ethical transformations in other human agents. Despite my insistence that propositional language is indispensable in ethical argumentation,

I acknowledge the disclosive force of critical interventions that are not articulated in propositional language (I call them 'co-arguments'); connected with this, I emphasize the need for ongoing expansion and enrichment of the conceptual and methodological lexicon of Frankfurt School theory. Furthermore, rather than aiming at full intelligibility or complete understanding, argumentation as I construe it is a process of making partial epistemic connections between apparently incompatible worldviews and establishing ontological openings that could enable playful 'world-travelling'. Understood in this decentred, expansive and exploratory way, argumentation concerned with the good life for humans requires a view of ethical normativity ('the good') that is neither generated by any kind of human activity nor owned by the inhabitants of any specific normative context and, in this sense, has a human-transcending moment. I also point out that it cannot be generated or owned by any specific other-than-human entity either. For this reason, it is more accurately characterized as 'human-transcending and other-than-human-transcending'. However, since this formulation is cumbersome, I have tended to abbreviate it to 'human-transcending', for this is the key point in my critique of exclusive humanism, a central concern of the book.

The philosophy of history: a Benjaminian objection

Critical theories concerned with exploration of better futures can also learn from a Benjaminian version of the objection to Hegelian-Marxist closures of the historical process. By this I mean an objection to one-sided narratives of the past, which obscure or suppress parts of a particular historical legacy that could potentially revitalize the present and inspire thinking and action towards social change for the better. In his 1940 theses 'On the Concept of History' (2005), Benjamin criticizes the 'historicist' reading of the past by the bourgeois historian. As he describes it, historicism is concerned merely to establish a causal nexus of various moments of history, viewing its task as recording for posterity 'how it really was'. Benjamin's counter-historian contemplates the resulting record of past achievements with horror. He is appalled by the historicist narrative of a 'triumphal procession' of cultural spoils in which today's rulers 'tread over those who are sprawled underfoot' (ibid., Thesis VII). Benjamin's name for the counter-historian is 'the dialectical materialist', attesting to his self-understanding as a theorist who reads history along Marxist lines.[3] However, despite this apparent endorsement of Marx's Hegelian philosophy of history, his critique of historicism illuminates a danger for *any* account of history that leaves no room for counter-narratives – whether Marxist or historicist. Such hermetic accounts not only discount alternative perspectives on history from the outset; they also block attempts to unsettle the power of the narratives they offer. Benjamin himself emphasizes the danger of conformism posed for historians in every epoch (the danger, I add, also arises for critical theorists) and the need for historians to deliver the legacy of the past from this conformism. Accordingly, he calls for writers of history 'with the gift of setting alight the sparks of hope in the past' (ibid., Thesis VI). Such writers establish 'a concept of the present as that of the here-and-now [*Jetztzeit*], in which splinters of messianic time are shot through' (ibid., Addendum). In this Benjaminian perspective, critical theorists qua counter-historians perform several important tasks. They retrieve the disruptive, troubling moments in the past that have disappeared from memory in the dominant historical narratives. They enable those they address to hear their call for remembrance of past suffering.[4] They help them to experience these moments in the present – in the here-and-now – as vivid re-presentations of the horrors of the past and unsettling reminders of the evils of human history.[5] Experienced in this way, moments from the past provoke responses that demand fundamental social transformation of an emancipatory kind.

Recalling the discussion in Chapter 2, such disruptions of the dominant historical narratives may be described as *re*generative, preserving moments of the past that can be creatively rearticulated with emancipatory effect in the present. However, Benjaminian disruptions are not on their own sufficient to prevent ideological closures in critical theorizing. As I noted, Benjamin expresses allegiance to a Marxist version of dialectical materialism. Due to Marx's exclusive humanist perspective and celebration of human productive powers, discussed in previous chapters,[6] his dialectical materialism is vulnerable not only to objections of Eurocentrism and anthropocentrism; it is also open to the accusation that it insulates critical theories against pressures to change human thinking and behaviour that arise from their ecological entanglements and inhibits their imaginings of the future.

As I observed in Chapter 1, critical theories are inherently prone to ideological closures, no matter how energetically they strive to establish and maintain their openness, outwards, backwards and forwards. In my discussions in the preceding chapters I have suggested some ways in which the danger could be lessened. Édouard Glissant's idea of 'errantry' [*errance*], which provides the epigraph for my book, further helps to mitigate it.

Errant critical social theorizing

Errant persons, as described by Glissant, strive to know the totality of the world, yet they already know that they will never accom-
plish this: 'The thinking of errantry conceives of totality but willingly
renounces any claims to sum it up or possess it' (1997, 21). I read this
as encouragement to contemporary critical theories not to give up on
their utopian visions of a revolutionarily reconstituted, emancipated
society – to keep sight of what Glissant calls 'the totality' – while at
the same time resisting the temptation to hypostatize the envisaged
society as *the* good society and to keep open the horizons of critical
social thinking for ways of being, knowing and living with others,
human and other-than-human, that are unfamiliar, uncongenial or,
as things stand, even partly incomprehensible. Moreover, to do so
in communication with the past. Glissant writes of 'the unknown'
– which could also be called 'the future' – as the 'projection of a
reverse image of all that has been left behind, not to be regained for
generations except – more and more threadbare – in blue savannahs
of memory or imagination (ibid., 6–7).

Furthermore, for Glissant, conceiving of totality requires receptivity
to the poetic moments in even the darkest episodes of human history.
Evoking the ghosts of the slave ships from his birthplace Martinique
in the Caribbean, he writes of the abyss: 'At the bow [of the slave ship]
there is still something that we now share: this murmur, cloud, rain or
peaceful smoke. We cry our cry of poetry. Our boats are open and we
sail them for everyone' (1997, 9). This points towards a way of reading
Benjamin that helps to avoid certain ideological closures in his account
of history arising from his allegiance to Marxist dialectical materialism.
Indeed, Glissant's 'cry of poetry' chimes with much of what Benjamin
writes, for instance his famous words that the 'true picture of the past
whizzes by [*huscht vorbei*]. Only as a picture, which flashes its final
farewell in the moment of its recognizability, is the past to be held
fast' (2005, Thesis V).[7] Whereas Benjamin emphasizes the ephemeral
nature of the fleeting moment of recognition enabled by the counter-
historian, Glissant draws attention to its *pictorial* aspect. In my earlier
discussion of fictions and ciphers, I likewise drew attention to this
aspect. I suggested that the unrepresentable transcendent 'object of
desire' (what Jaspers calls 'Transcendence', Glissant calls 'the totality'
and I have called 'the good') may require mediation by way of vivid
and warmly coloured images in order to exert an affective pull or
allure. With his idea of errantry, Glissant adds something more to this
by drawing attention to the 'poetic cry' that emanates from certain

pictures, including Benjamin's pictures of the past. Furthermore, as poetry, they are inherently resistant to closure.

In these ways, thoughts extrapolated from the writings of Habermas, Benjamin and Glissant provide a resource for critical theories to think about the interrelationship between past, present and future in ways that mitigate the ever-present danger of ideological closures. The Habermasian objection I sketched calls upon decentring, expansive, exploratory critical theories likewise to adopt a decentring, expansive and exploratory argumentative approach in their critical diagnoses and emancipatory projections; the Benjaminian objection emphasizes the need for critical theories to disrupt and unsettle the dominant historical narratives; insofar as it appeals to a dogmatic version of dialectical materialism, it also reminds them of the difficulties of doing so without merely substituting one closure by another, thereby reproducing rather than overcoming what is wrong with the dominant narratives. Glissant augments the Habermasian and Benjaminian objections with the thought of errantry as a poetic venture – and adventure – that involves expanding and enriching the imagination in communication with the past.

The 'revolutionary reconstitution of society at large'

Thinking the interrelationship between past, present and future along the Habermasian-Benjaminian-Glissantian lines sketched above points towards a way of interpreting Marx and Engels' revolutionary summons congruent with the self-understandings and methodologies of decentring, expansive and exploratory critical theories. It invites such theories to interpret the 'revolutionary reconstitution of society at large' as a call for fundamental social transformation, understood as a regenerative communicative process, fraught with difficulties and dangers, in which those actively involved are aware that their efforts to change the prevailing order of things may instead reproduce the components of it they seek to overcome. It draws attention to the importance for this endeavour of receptive responsiveness to the poetry of the present, infused by the memories of the past, which ignites glimmerings of hope in the darkest times and amidst the deadening or crushing routines of everyday life.

Furthermore, it suggests that decentring, expansive and exploratory critical theories should interpret Marx and Engels' revolutionary call in an open way – as a demand for fundamental change that makes the structure and shape of the radically transformed society dependent on multiple reimaginings and rearticulations by those actively engaged in efforts to realize it. It suggests, likewise, that the 'how' of revolutionary change cannot be determined in advance by any theory. Finally, it urges attentiveness to practices of protest and resistance that so far have not been part of Frankfurt School critical theory's lexicon of revolutionary activities.

This general perspective, when interwoven with threads from discussions in my previous chapters, also points towards a specific understanding both of 'revolution' and 'reconstitution'. Concerning 'revolution', it suggests a broadly Arendtian interpretation, such as the one that Sofia Näsström adopts, in which the openness of the historical process, the radicality of the projected political change and the newness of its outcomes are foregrounded. Concerning 'reconstitution', it supports the picture of institutional change as *self*-transformation or transformation *from within* that I outlined in the preceding chapter. Social institutions, as I depicted them, are self-transforming agencies with an ethical dimension. The relationship between the ethical dimensions of self-determining human agency and institutional agency is reciprocally constitutive: institutions do not *enable* freedom; instead, they contribute to its constitution. Conversely, self-determining human agency contributes to the constitution of the ethical agency of institutions. This means, in turn, that even revolutionary institutional transformation is not imposed externally, but results from reciprocal learning processes that change human agents, on the one side, and institutional agency, on the other. Accordingly, fundamental social transformation is primarily a matter of restoring and revitalizing the ethically orienting authority of institutions by challenging its perversion into authoritarian power and only rarely calls for abolishing or dismantling the institution completely. As history attests, such institutional self-transformative processes are often set in train by social struggles by human agents who have been denied a sense of belonging to given institutions and effectively excluded from them, but who nonetheless strive to be part of them. My example in the last chapter was taken from W. E. B. Du Bois in *The Souls of Black Folk* (2007). As Du Bois tells his readers, in striving to be part of US institutions in the late nineteenth and early twentieth centuries, 'Black Folk' desire to fundamentally reconstitute these institutions so that they can live within them as 'American Negros'.

A similar position finds expression in *Manifesto for Now*, a series of essays published online between 2023 and 2025 by the artists Sarah Garton Stanley and Owais Lightwala in response to the multiple crises in the Arts Sector in Canada.[8] In the original essay, they write:

> Our institutions have an important role. They are our memory.
> Our yesterday is informing our present and they − government

institutions, funding institutions, educational institutions, civic institutions, big institutions, small institutions, community institutions, undocumented institutions – will be the things we look to when the dust settles ... And [institutions] will likely have to change and accept change in order to survive and in order that they can be of service.

The authors conclude, accordingly, that what is needed today is de-instituting, re-instituting and new instituting.

Their reference to 'de-instituting' is important. In Chapter 7, I acknowledged that, on occasion, even institutions premised on the normative aim of fostering human freedom may become so degenerate and corrupt that they must be 'de-instituted' before they can be 're-instituted'. However, I also drew attention to Garton Stanley and Lightwala's characterization of institutions as 'memory banks', as depositories of the ethical hopes and aspirations of the past that have made us who we now are. This enables a view of 're-instituting' following 'de-instituting' as likewise a process of institutional transformation from within – as I put it in Chapter 7, as an endeavour to rescue buried ethical hopes and aspirations from the institutional ruins.

My discussion of institutions in Chapter 7 was concerned primarily with the freedom-constituting role of institutional authority, coupled with its easy slide into authoritarianism. To this, it could be objected that my focus on the contestation of *authoritarian* power leads me to an interpretation of the demand for the 'revolutionary reconstitution of society at large' that is too narrow and misses the broader picture in which institutionalized authority is merely one element in an entire system of disciplinary power.

One of Michel Foucault's major contributions to contemporary critical theory (1995) is to show how in capitalist modernity 'discipline' becomes a new modality of power that infiltrates every part of the social order and constitutes the kinds of human agents required to sustain and reproduce it. Disciplinary power for Foucault is not instrumental. It is neither power as a means of enabling agents to achieve their goal (Hobbes 2017), nor power as a relationship in which one agent (or group) imposes their will on others (Weber 1921). It is also very different from power that is manifested through the magnificence of those who exercise it, such as the divinely appointed monarch.[9]

Disciplinary power comprises a whole set of instruments, techniques, procedures, levels of application and targets. It is not imposed from outside. In consequence, it operates insidiously and its effectiveness requires internalization. This explains why disciplinary power *neutralizes* counter-power: it does not supress rebellions, agitations, spontaneous protests and the like; it prevents them from happening in the first place.

One reason why Foucault's account of disciplinary power seems as relevant to the societies of contemporary capitalism as it was to the societies of the 1960s and 1970s is that it offers an explanation of how capitalism as a lifeform continues to be maintained and reproduced, despite major historical shifts in how it operates (for example, the 'digital revolution') and major economic crises (for example, the 'Great Recession' of the early twenty-first century, which precipitated the financial crash of 2008).[10] Indeed, as noted in Chapter 6, Albena Azmanova argues that the various crises that capitalism has undergone in recent decades have strengthened it, not weakened it: in her words, they have been crises not *of* capitalism, but *for* capitalism. But if this is so, the objection I anticipate to my focus on authoritarian power is even more forceful: is not disciplinary power the real problem that should be placed at the centre of critical theory's transformative concerns? Moreover, is it not a more challenging problem than authoritarian power, since disciplinary power, unlike authority, *neutralizes* counter-power, preventing the human agents it constitutes from challenging it through contestation?

I agree with Foucault that 'discipline' became a structuring, identity-forming principle for institutional and human agencies in capitalist modernity and continues to be one today. Nonetheless, I disagree with two interconnected elements in his account. One is the view of the social constitution of human agency that is implicit in his conceptualization of disciplinary power; the other, connected to the first, is his conceptual conflation of authority with authoritarianism.

In the previous chapter I offered an account of authoritarian power as a perversion of the authoritative, ethically transformative power of social institutions. My account posits a co-constitutive relationship between human ethical agency and institutional ethical agency. I characterize this as a dialectical relationship, in which each agency has relative independence of the other, even though they are permanently in process of mutual constitution. I attribute this relative independence to the *ethical* component of the agencies involved in these processes of reciprocal constitution. In the account I offer, ethical agency is not *entirely* socially constituted. Its constitution in social processes is animated by reflective recollection of unsettling, ethically significant experiences of a human-transcending force. Accordingly, ethical agency is not *entirely* the product of the co-constitutive process I describe; nor is it *entirely* the product of any other kind of social process. It is this gap between agential identity and the identity-determining power of social forces that permits ethical transformation for the better. By contrast, in his writings on disciplinary power, Foucault does not allow for any such gap. The internalization of disciplinary power is complete, resulting in configurations of agential identities that are entirely socially produced. In consequence, no resistance to disciplinary power is conceivable. Indeed, even passive refusal will inevitably reproduce the system and perhaps even strengthen it.[11]

For the same reason, Foucault's account of disciplinary societies cannot acknowledge the normative ambivalence of institutionalized power and, in consequence, conceptually collapses authority and authoritarianism. By contrast, in the co-constitutive perspective I propose, the radically transcending moment in ethical normativity makes possible in principle a distinction between authoritarian power, on the one hand, and authoritative but nonauthoritarian power, on the other. This means, in turn, that resistance to such power, and protest against it, is conceivable and always potentially possible.

If this is so, the key question arising from the challenge posed by disciplinary power is not whether it vitiates my account of combating authoritarian power. The question, instead, is how critical theories of the decentring, expansive, exploratory kind that I envisage should think about protest and resistance aimed at fundamental social transformation under contemporary conditions, in which the normalizing, depoliticizing effects of disciplinary power complicate efforts to address new manifestations of authoritarianism, new forms of ideological manipulation and new forms of ideological closure, for example ones enabled by the 'digital revolution'. In Chapter 1, I observed that, in contemporary societies, authoritarian regimes use new technologies, including new technologies of information dissemination, to manipulate everyday consciousness in identity-constituting ways and drew attention to the epistemically closed structures that they generate, such as echo bubbles and echo chambers. But I also referred to empirically based accounts of how resistance to such manipulation and escape from such structures takes place, typically following processes of self-transformation by the human agents affected. My account of ethical normativity adds a conceptual explanation to such empirically based accounts. The radically transcending moment I attribute to ethical normativity, which opens human agents intellectually and affectively to an ethically significant dimension beyond the social processes that form and shape them, means that human agents can in principle *always* fundamentally transform themselves for the better and can in principle *always* fundamentally change their societies for the better. As I observed in Chapter 4, this is also a strength of the dialectical-materialist approaches to the constitution of human agency adopted respectively by Horkheimer, Adorno and Menke. By attributing a material dimension to human agency that is not socially constituted, these theorists posit a gap between human agency and the ways in which it is shaped and formed through social structures, institutions and relations. In Horkheimer's account the gap is due to certain 'natural facts' about humans as a species, while, for Adorno and Menke, it is due to a pre-social drive [*Trieb*]. This gap explains how socially transformative human action is possible even in what Horkheimer and Adorno call a 'context of delusion' [*Verblendungszusammenhang*]. In *Dialectic of Enlightenment* (2002), in their critique of the 'culture industry', they strongly suggest that the inhabitants of advanced capitalism are trapped within a context of *total* delusion. But this would contradict their accounts elsewhere of the constitution of human subjectivity, in which it has a context-transcending moment; this means that delusion can never be complete and awareness by human agents of their ideological manipulation and epistemic entrapment is always possible in principle. However, the dialectical-materialist accounts offered by Horkheimer, Adorno and Menke also have a shortcoming. Since the transcending dimension in their respective accounts has no ethical quality, they cannot easily explain how ideologically manipulated, epistemically entrapped human agents could be motivated to *change themselves and the society they inhabit for the better*. By contrast, the ethical quality I attribute to the human-transcending dimension of socially constituted human agency helps to explain how this motivation is possible.

In sum, unlike Foucault's single-lens perspective, my dual perspective on ethical agency, as at once socially constituted and transcendent of its social constitution helps to explain both the possibility of active engagement in the 'revolutionary reconstitution of society at large' and the possibility of motivation for such engagement. Importantly, however, it links such active engagement to self-transformation. As I now show, this has implications for critical theories of protest and resistance. To begin with, it calls for a differentiated account of political activism. In this respect Adorno's criticisms of the student revolutionaries in the Federal Republic of Germany in the 1960s are instructive.

Political activism

In his writings on student revolutionary activism, Adorno takes his earlier critique of ideology a step further.[12] His claim now is not merely that capitalism generates the false perceptions of interests, needs and aspirations necessary for its own maintenance and reproduction; in addition he claims that it produces human agents whose protests against, and resistance to, the capitalist system maintain and reproduce it. He does not deny that protest and resistance are possible in principle (as I have just observed, this would contradict his own account of the constitution of subjectivity in terms of a transgressive drive). His view, rather, is that, under the given historical conditions, protest and resistance run a grave risk of reproducing the rationality of the contested social order; in consequence, human agents concerned with fundamental social transformation should instead practise theoretically informed, unsparing self-reflection on their own perhaps inadvertent complicity with the prevailing social order.

This led Adorno to a hard-hitting critique of the 'actionism' [*Aktionismus*] of the student protesters – a term he used pejoratively to describe an unreflective, theoretically uninformed form of activism in which protest and violence are performed ultimately for their own sake, and group-thinking determines its methods and targets.[13] For Adorno, actionists are concerned only with what 'has to be done' in the immediate situation, impervious to the need to comprehend theoretically what is wrong with the system they are fighting to transform; accordingly, the means of social transformation serve ends on which there has been no reflection and with which there has been no critical engagement, either with Marxist theory or with Adorno's own critical theory. As he puts it in one interview, the student revolutionaries use his critical theory like a 'Molotov cocktail' (2002, 15).

Above all, the student actionists lack theoretically informed insight into the *totalizing* tendencies of the system of capitalism; these tendencies make autonomous agency fully possible 'only for saints', who alone are able to escape the pressure to conform to the norms imposed by the all-pervasive instrumentalizing and objectifying rationality – and, Adorno adds, 'even a saint's existence is precarious today' (2000a, 168). For ordinary mortals, in the given historical conjuncture, autonomy is available at best only in compromised form. The same holds for resistance to the normativity of the prevailing capitalist order; it too is inevitably complicit with that very order, inadvertently reproducing it and strengthening its power. Indeed, Adorno takes the view that opting out, not joining in, not conforming [*nicht mitspielen*] has become impossible; failure to acknowledge this is self-delusion. What is required, accordingly, is a critical-theoretical perspective that highlights the impossibility in the given historical situation of active protest and recognizes that the only effective form of transformative action is withdrawal from society to as great an extent as is possible. He insists that withdrawal is transformative, since it allows for (as he admits, compromised) autonomous reflection on society that enables a theoretical critique of capitalism which, with the support of the empirically based social sciences, demonstrates how in each of its new permutations it prevents the realization of genuine freedom and happiness.

The call to action issued by The Invisible Committee's manifesto *Now*, published online in 2017, could be seen as a contemporary example of what Adorno calls 'actionism'.[14] The Committee writes:

> All the reasons for making a revolution are there. Not one is lacking. The shipwreck of politics, the arrogance of the powerful, the reign of falsehood, the vulgarity of the wealthy, the cataclysms of industry, galloping misery, naked exploitation, ecological apocalypse – we are spared nothing, not even being informed about it all.

The Committee continues:

> This world no longer needs explaining, critiquing, denouncing. We live enveloped in a fog of commentaries and commentaries on commentaries, of critiques and critiques of critiques of critiques, of revelations that don't trigger anything, other than revelations about the revelations. And this fog is taking away any purchase we might have on the world . . . We live in a world that has established itself *beyond any justification*. Here, criticism doesn't work.

The conclusion they draw is expressed in the manifesto's poetic epigraph:

> No more waiting.
> No more hoping.
> No more letting ourselves be distracted, unnerved.
> Break and enter.
> Put untruth back in its place.
> Believe in what we feel.
> Act accordingly.
> Force our way into the present.
> Try. Fail this time. Try again. Fail better.
> Persist. Attack. Build.
> Go down one's road.
> Win perhaps.

In any case, overcome.
Live, therefore.
Now . . .

In a similar vein, Andreas Malm (2018; 2020) argues that the urgency of the need to arrest and alter ecological devastation, coupled with the planetary scale of the task, means that time is past for democratic processes and widespread democratic participation. He too proclaims that what is needed is action *now*.[15]

In the context of contemporary calls for 'action now', Adorno's criticisms of 'actionism' are a timely reminder that activism without autonomous reflection and theoretical guidance is not only ineffective (and often self-serving); it is likely to contribute to the reproduction of the society it attacks. Nonetheless, his insistence that withdrawal is the only genuine kind of transformative action possible under the given social conditions is discouraging (Cooke 2019c). By linking transformation of society with *self*-transformation, my approach opens a path contrary to the one taken by Adorno. It also draws attention to a shortcoming of his critique of actionism. While acknowledging that transformation of society is possible, Adorno appears to ignore possibilities for self-transformations on the part of activists that would be conducive to the required fundamental social change. The biography of Malcolm X illustrates what I mean.

Self-transforming activism

Around the same time in the United States, faced with the same problem of a totalizing system, Malcom X's response was very different from that of Adorno.

In his co-authored autobiography, Malcolm X provides an account of his own fundamental ethical-existential self-transformation, which started in 1946 with a prison sentence of ten years for burglary and larceny (Malcolm X and Haley 1999). While in prison, he was captivated by the writings of Elijah Muhammad, the spiritual leader of the Nation of Islam, leading to a complete reorientation of his thinking and behaviour. Later on, he underwent a second profound self-transformation following a visit to Mecca, which led, among other things, to a break with Muhammad. Malcolm X's transformative leadership of movements of resistance to US racism in the twelve years between his release from prison and his assassination in 1965 can be attributed to these ethical-existential self-transformations

(Cooke 2019d). While concerned above all with ethical-existential transformations on the side of black Americans, Malcolm X came to see the need for self-transformations on the side of white Americans as well. However, he saw little prospect of achieving transformation on this other side, holding that the seeds of racism were too deeply rooted in white people collectively.[16]

Ethical-existential self-transformations are a matter of work by the self on the self that aims in part to *release* the self from ways of thinking and patterns of behaviour that trap it in a condition of unfreedom (Sadek 2023). In his later, unfinished writings on the history of sexuality, Foucault develops an idea of 'care for the self' that points in this direction (1986; 1988). He describes care of the self as 'those intentional and voluntary actions by which men not only set themselves rules of conduct, but also seek to transform themselves, to change themselves in their singular being, and to make their life into an oeuvre' (Foucault 1986, 10). It involves a lifelong commitment to ascetic daily practices and exercises. Combining Foucault's idea of care for the self with his emphasis on *parrhesia* (truth-telling) in these same writings, Barbara Nascimento offers an intersubjective understanding of such care. On the one side, parrhesiastic care of the self is a practice that links truth to ethical self-care. Here, Foucault draws on lines of thinking in ancient philosophy, from Plato through Stoicism, Epicureanism and Cynicism, in which human individuals cannot attain truth without first transforming themselves through rigorous self-practice. On the other side, parrhesia adds an ethical-political dimension to care of the self, showing that it is not simply an isolated activity but one that involves engaging with others and the broader ethical-political context (Nascimento 2024). Nascimento's intersubjectivist approach to care of the self adds a dimension missing in Foucault's account that is important for the perspective I adopt on fundamental social transformation. Her approach understands care of the self not just as a practice of releasing the self from ways of thinking and behaving that trap it in a condition of unfreedom; it construes it, in addition, as a process of *reconstituting* the self through communicative engagements with other humans (to which I add: also encounters with other-than-human agencies).

The 'who' of revolution

I have proposed an understanding of Marx and Engels' call for the 'revolutionary reconstitution of society at large', in which its revolutionary character consists in its potential radicality and its openness to the new, and its reconstituting character involves fundamental institutional change 'from within'. Who are the agents of revolutionary change in my account?

In Marxist theory, there traditionally have been two opposing views on the agents of the 'revolutionary reconstitution of society at large'. One position holds that the agents of transformation are those most oppressed by the capitalist social order, who have 'nothing to lose but their chains' (Marx and Engels 1967, 121). But, as discussed in Chapter 1, even Max Horkheimer, who in important respects endorsed Marx's dialectical materialism and philosophy of history, no longer found this position credible when developing his research programme in Germany in the 1930s.[17] The second position holds that *everyone* is a potential agent of social transformation. This is because, under conditions of capitalist exploitation and subjugation, *everyone* is oppressed. Since this violates the fundamental human interest in living a life of free development in association with all others, everyone has an interest in revolutionary action. The discussions in the previous chapters lend support to the second position. Indeed, they take it further by arguing that every human agent potentially has an ethical-existential *motivation* to engage in action that would fundamentally transform society, and that – contrary to what Foucault suggests[18] – it is always *possible in principle* for them to do so. This possibility is supported empirically by Jennifer Todd's sociological study, discussed in Chapter 1, which analyses the ethical dimension of social transformation and the ways in which changes in ethical identity can foster or impede it. While also emphasizing the importance of political interventions and innovations on a formal level, Todd highlights the importance for social transformation of everyday agency, showing how it can magnify with successive iterations, feeding into ongoing institutional change and creating a new sense of ethical agency that eventually cascades, leading to the collapse of authoritarian group authority.

When the answer to the 'who' question is *everyone*, when fundamental institutional transformation is understood as change *from within* and when the importance of *everyday agency* is acknowledged, Marx and Engels' call for the 'revolutionary reconstitution of society at large' invites consideration of practices that take place on the micro level, on the margins or in the interstices of the existing capitalist social orders.

Practising revolutionary agency

Anna Tsing offers an example. In *The Mushroom at the End of the World* (2015), her ethnographic study of practices of matsutake mushroom foraging, Tsing explores barely noticed, social practices in micro spaces within the capitalist social order. She claims that such practices open possibilities for 'life in capitalist ruins', by which she means primarily the contemporary planetary situation of ecological depredation, social precarity and existential alienation. She maintains that micro practices such as mushroom-foraging or working the landscape, by changing both the human agents and the ecologies involved, may contribute to far-reaching change on a social level. As observed in Chapter 4, her ethnographic musings highlight ecological entanglements, drawing attention to the ways in which matsutake mushrooms, humans and pines together shape the trajectories of human landscapes and how human histories are made in concert by humans, plants and fungi (ibid., 171–2). Tsing's study relates a story of complexes of interaction among foragers and woodland revitalization groups, opening a vista in which small-scale disturbances have effects that could, in her view, overcome the alienating effects of capitalism and build a world of overlapping lifeways in which 'mutualistic transformation' might be possible (ibid., 258). She concludes that matsutake-forest revitalization, though it does not offer redemption, picks through the heap of capitalism's ruins to open possibilities for new ways of living together with multispecies others 'without knowing where the world-in-process is going' (ibid., 264).

Prefigurative politics offers a related but different example of revolutionary practices on a micro level, on the margins or in the interstices of the existing capitalist social orders. The socially transformative, political concerns of prefigurative politics are readily apparent, for example, in Daniel Loick's sketch of a new 'politics of forms of life' (2018), which suggestively hints at the radically transformative potential of prefigurations of 'good societies' within existing (capitalist) social reality. Or again, in a detailed study of micro-level prefigurative practices within a capitalist context, Eva Von Redecker (2021) highlights their revolutionary potential. Offering a host of illuminating examples and a wealth of theoretical reflections on the dynamics of incremental and piecemeal social change, she argues that fundamental social transformation takes place in the interstices of the existing social order.

Transformative prefigurative politics of these kinds share a feature with the regenerative refusal that defines the politics of the undercommons, as discussed in Chapter 2. Common to both is a refusal to be part of the established social order of recognition, which is one of domination and subjugation and which marginalizes and excludes. The marginalized and excluded human agents refuse invitations to be part of this social order. By contrast with Adorno, however, who simply refuses to 'join in' [*mitspielen*], they combine their refusal with an invitation to those included within the socially recognized groups to join them in their spaces of refusal and resistance.[19]

The undercommons and prefigurative politics are similar, too, in their *(re)generative* practices of refusal. Both seek to create experimental spaces for establishing new social norms, structures and relationships, providing tangible examples of what a transformed society might look like. Both involve practices of resistance and refusal within current practices in the present that embody the modes of sociality and habits of living of a projected future society. However, advocates of prefigurative politics seem more explicitly and directly concerned with fundamental transformation of 'society at large'.

Critical theory as a revolutionary agent

If everyone is an agent of revolutionary social reconstitution, critical theories are agents too. As discussed in Chapter 1, the early Frankfurt School theorists followed Marx (and not Hegel) in viewing critical theory as an active revolutionary agent – in Horkheimer's words, cited in that chapter, critical theory is a 'critical, promotive factor in the development of the masses' (1972, 214). As also discussed, Horkheimer retreated from this position when confronted with the propaganda machines deployed by authoritarian political regimes in Europe and its environs in the 1930s. However, it is an open question whether he abandoned his view of critical theory as an agent of revolutionary change or simply perceived no possibility for critical theory to exercise its social transformative agency in the historical conditions of his time.

There is little doubt, however, that a view of critical theorizing as itself an agent of revolutionary change fell out of favour in Frankfurt School critical theory from the 1980s onwards following Habermas' communicative turn. A concern to avoid (what I call) epistemological and ethical authoritarianism may explain why Habermas distanced himself from the 'promotive' role that Horkheimer ascribed to critical theory (Habermas 1991b; 2003a). My discussions throughout this book have provided ample reasons why critical theories must be alert to the risk of authoritarianism in their own theorizing. However, they have also emphasized the ethical-existential-political dimension of critical theorizing. Furthermore, they have explored various ways in which critical theories could contribute directly towards social change for the better through their ethically disclosive interventions and ethically oriented arguments, without falling prey either to epistemological and ethical authoritarianism or to pernicious kinds of Eurocentricism, anthropocentrism and other manifestations of ideological closure. I conclude, accordingly, with an invitation to critical theorists, in the broadest sense, to build on the lines of argument opened in my discussions, reimagining themselves as authoritative but nonauthoritarian agents of the 'revolutionary reconstitution of society at large'.

Notes

Introduction

1 For example, Marx's 1844 *Economic and Philosophical Manuscripts* were first published only in 1932.
2 Freedom in this sense may be described as a variant of Hegel's idea of *Bildung*. See Stojanov (2017).
3 In a book published in 1951, Hannah Arendt (2017) introduced the term 'totalitarian' to characterize this type of regime. The term is not used by Horkheimer and his colleagues at this time, but they clearly view Stalinism as totalitarian in Arendt's sense.

Chapter 1: Frankfurt School Critical Theory: Openings and Closures

1 In my discussions throughout the book I use the term 'ethical' interchangeably with the term 'moral'. In this I diverge from contemporary Frankfurt School theorists such as Habermas (1993) and Forst (2012). However, I adopt Habermas' and Forst's terminological distinction between ethics and morality when considering specific elements of their work.
2 The early Frankfurt School theorists often use the terms 'freedom' and 'happiness' interchangeably. Hauke Brunkhorst (1985) points out, for example, that Horkheimer tends to refer to happiness rather than freedom as the aim of human emancipation from enslaving circumstances. However, Brunkhorst acknowledges that he usually employs the terms synonymously and that, in any case, no tension between the two is discernible in his writings. Contemporary theorists in this tradition, such as Habermas and Forst, tend to favour freedom as an emancipatory goal. My ethical-existential approach to freedom destabilizes any sharp distinction between freedom and happiness. Thus, like the early theorists, I view them as intimately entwined.
3 Usually translated as: *The Journal for Social Research.*
4 When referring to the alternative mode of social theory he advocates, Horkheimer does not initially use the term 'critical theory'. In his 1931 inaugural address as director of the Frankfurt Institute, he describes his proposed alternative as a mode of 'social philosophy' (2018). In his 'Notes on Science

and the Crisis' (1972, 3–9) he refers to 'the Marxist theory of society' and to a 'correct theory of the present social situation'. Indeed, in many of these early writings, the alternative mode of theorizing is referred to simply as 'materialism' (1993; see also Brunkhorst 1985, 368).

5 Amended translation. The original is: 'die Emanzipation des Menschen aus versklavenden Verhältnissen' (1992b, 263).

6 I discuss the fruitfulness for contemporary critical theory of Horkheimer's idea of social critique in Cooke 2023b and 2025c. I do not deny that there are many inconsistencies, even contradictions, in the programme for social research set out by Horkheimer in the 1930s. In Hauke Brunkhorst's apt phrase, Horkheimer is an 'anti-philosopher' in a double sense: both because he seeks to bring about a 'social scientific transformation of philosophy' and because his research programme is not philosophically stringent (Brunkhorst 1985, 354).

7 Cf. Horkheimer 1988, 20.

8 In earlier writings I argue that 'bad utopianism', which I distinguish from 'good utopianism', can either take the form of projections of a better society that are too far removed from people's real concerns to have motivating power; or it can take the form of blueprints for a better society that deny the essential historicity of such imaginative projections (2006a, 161–5).

9 Brunkhorst draws a contrast between Horkheimer's research programme and György Lukács' theoretical writings, whose book *History and Class Consciousness* played a *substantive* role in the development of the undogmatic Marxist paradigm developed by Frankfurt School critical theorists (Brunkhorst 1985, 353; Lukács 1972).

10 Horkheimer gives as an example 'the fact that under certain conditions the lowest strata of society have the most children plays an important role in explaining how a society built on exchange necessarily leads to capitalism' (1972, 226).

11 Horkheimer pays less attention to this side of the feedback loop.

12 As discussed above, Horkheimer's feedback loop allows for learning on both sides. Although he has little to say about the ways in which empirical-scientific praxis learns from philosophical theory, this question certainly merits closer consideration. However, while acknowledging the importance of the mutuality of the learning process, my concern is mainly with learning on the side of critical theorizing (and blockages to it).

13 Indeed, in Chapter 4, I point out that Horkheimer's appeal to 'natural facts' is a strength of his perspective on the constitution of human agency, for it allows him to attribute to human agency a material dimension that has some independence of human history and the social processes that constitute it, thus taking account of human 'naturalness' [*Naturwüchsigkeit*].

14 By contrast, Horkheimer insists that the suffering of past generations can never be vindicated: 'even after the new society shall have come into existence, the happiness of its members will not make up for the wretchedness of those who are being destroyed in our contemporary society (1972, 251).

15 The Hegelian philosophy of history effects a further closure through its explicit Eurocentrism. Uma Narayan draws attention, for example, to Hegel's view that Africa is not a 'historical part of the world', having no 'movement of development to exhibit'. Marx says something similar about India, claiming that it has no history at all, or at least no known history (Narayan 1997).

16 'Ideologie [ist] objektiv notwendiges und zugleich falsches Bewusstsein' (Adorno 1972, 465).

17 The early Frankfurt School theorists stand accused of a lack of awareness of other reasons for silence in the face of oppression. One important reason they fail to consider is the violence imposed by colonial regimes through slavery, (mis)education and militarized coercion; it has been argued that what these theorists perceive as lack of awareness is often fear of the consequences of deviating from the structures and norms imposed by the oppressive regime (Baum 2015; Bhambra 2021).

18 A further characteristic of ideologies is that they satisfy some deep-seated need, interest or desire on the part of the human agents concerned (Cooke 2006b).

19 Aletta Norval (2000) offers a helpful review of the first post-Habermasian return of ideology critique, to which I later made a minor contribution (Cooke 2006a; 2006b).

20 See note 17 above.

21 A less totalizing view also lessens the risk of 'bad utopianism', arising when the theory's critical perspective on subjectively experienced needs, interests and aspirations is too far removed from the perspectives of the human agents concerned.

22 Todd notes that the social movement literature gives many examples of how groupness subverts or even colonizes seemingly transformative processes: it reverses some of the achievements of pro-democracy movements; it crystallizes and at times generates group division and it informs counter movements (2024, 577).

23 Todd points out that this goes against a widely held view that attributes such changes to the impersonal process of 'secularization'.

24 Todd also emphasizes the importance of political interventions and innovations on a formal level.

25 In my critical discussion of Ernesto Laclau's writings on radical politics and the simultaneous 'necessity and impossibility of the universal' (Laclau 1996), I distinguish between what I call (harmless) 'metaphysical closure and (pernicious) ideological closure' (Cooke 2006a, 99–118).

26 I take issue with Ernesto Laclau's account of ideological closure for this reason (Cooke 2006a, 99–118; 2006b).

27 I am assuming that Honneth means here that critical theorizing should be based on empirical studies that document such interests or experiences.

28 I explain why they are unreliable in my discussion of 'fictions' in Chapter 3.

Chapter 2: Philosophical Criticism of Society: Closures and Openings

1 'A new categorical imperative has been imposed by Hitler upon unfree mankind: to arrange their thoughts and actions so that Auschwitz will not repeat itself ... When we want to find reasons for it, this imperative is as refractory as the given one of Kant was once upon a time. Dealing discursively with it would be an outrage, for the new imperative gives us a bodily sensation of the moral addendum – bodily, because it is now the practical abhorrence of the unbearable physical agony to which individuals are exposed (Adorno 1973, 364–5).

2 Overall, Adorno's stance towards philosophical argumentation is ambivalent. In an extended conversation between Adorno and Horkheimer in 1956, the two critical theorists appear to agree that 'if you find yourself in the situation of having to explain why something is bad, you are already lost'. On the other hand, they caution against philosophical thinking that renounces argument – in their view exemplified at the time by 'the Husserls and Heideggers' (Adorno and Horkheimer 2011, 72–3; Jay 2012).

3 Unlike Habermas, I take the view that this epistemic objective is inherently human-transcending and, as such, can never finally be reached by humans. However, I also hold that argumentation can help us to move closer to the epistemic 'object of desire'. I clarify my position in Chapter 3. See also Cooke 2006a, 148–52.

4 In contrast to his previous writings, since the 1990s Habermas distinguishes between truth claims and moral claims (2003a). In the case of truth claims, he now posits a gap between the truth of a claim and its justification in intersubjective processes of argumentation. In the case of moral claims, he denies any such gap.

5 For example, Joshua Cohen (1997) takes a purely procedural position when he writes that democratic procedures are the source of legitimacy. A more recent example is Boss 2023. See Cooke 2000.

6 See Chapter 3.

7 Habermas distinguishes categorially between moral and ethical validity claims (1993; Cooke 1994). Moral claims are universalizable and can be accepted as such by all participants in moral 'discourses', a form of argumentation that satisfies certain demanding procedural conditions. Ethical claims, by contrast, are claims about 'the good life' for humans and are not univeralizable; their validity is limited to local communities or groups bound together by shared conceptions of 'the good'.

8 Habermas (1993) allows for the hermeneutic explication and clarification of ethical validity claims in argumentation ('ethical discourses').

9 I am grateful to Ruth Sonderegger for suggesting the German verb '*mitargumentieren*' to me.

10 For a detailed discussion of Adorno's use of thinking in constellations as a practice of social critique, see Buck-Morss 1977, 90–121.

11 In the same vein, María Pía Lara analyses how feminist films contribute to reconfiguring the concept of the public sphere (see Chapter 1).

12 Joe McPhee, born 1939, is an African American saxophonist/multi-instrumentalist and composer, whose reputation has been built mainly on free jazz music. His musical performance of a poem by LeRoi Jones (then Amiri Baraka), 'nation time', was recorded in Chicago at the Vassar College Urban Center for Black Studies, where McPhee lectured in late 1970, and was released on a live album in 1971. Baraka wrote the poem in the 1960s, performed it publicly himself on several occasions and recorded it in 1970. For historical context, see Iton 2008, 81–101. For an analysis of the poem, see Jones 2003.

13 For example, the artist Adrian Piper, cited in Moten 2003, 241.

14 I say more about this in Chapter 5.

15 Oonagh Fitzgerald and Risa Schwartz explain: 'A braid is a single object consisting of many fibres and separate strands; it does not gain its strength from any single fibre that runs its entire length, but from the many fibres woven together' (2017, 3).

Chapter 3: Immanence and Transcendence: Decentrings, Openings

1 'The good', 'the just' and 'the true' are some familiar names for the transcendent ethical object of critical theorizing, the source of the momentous, emphatic or unsettling experiences described in this chapter. For the most part, in the following I refer to 'the good'. However, nothing important depends on my selection of this term rather than either of the others or, indeed, some other one.

2 As I explain later in this chapter, for convenience I frequently use 'human-transcending' as shorthand for 'human-transcending and other-than-human-transcending'.

3 McNay (2022) devotes a chapter each to criticizing what she calls the formalist approaches of Rainer Forst, Nancy Fraser, Axel Honneth, Alessandro Ferrara and Rahel Jaeggi.

4 I reference Davis' critical study of the US prison system briefly in Chapter 1.

5 As discussed in Chapter 6, Fraser's critique of capitalism has a context-transcending moment. Her critique appeals to the normative promise of modernity – universal freedom, equality and solidarity – arguing that capitalist societies, for structural and systemic rreasons, make it impossible to realize these values. The context-transcending moment resides in the gap between this promise and the possibilities for freedom, equality and solidarity actually available within advanced capitalist societies.

6 To this I add interactions between human agencies and other-than-human agencies.

7 Following a suggestion by Kelly Agra, this could be called 'anthropocendence' (Agra, personal communication).

8 I refer here to my discussion of 're-presentation' in Cooke 2006a. Later in this chapter, I offer a brief explanation of my use of the 'hyphen'.

9 Wellmer writes: 'in ihr, der Metaphysik, sieht er [Adorno], wenngleich in verkehrter Form, die Idee des Absoluten, die Idee der Versöhnung bewahrt, gerettet aus den Trümmern der Theologie. Aber dies Absolute ist schwarz verhüllt' (1985b, 155).

10 As noted in Chapter 2, Auschwitz for Adorno is emblematic of twentieth-century evil in the world.

11 Menke also rejects the view that it is an anthropological fact, as is implied by Hannah Arendt's view of human natality (2022, 605n.140; see also Chapter 7 below).

12 My dual perspective on normativity is a variant of the dual perspective on human nature I attributed to the early Marx in Chapter 1. There, to recall, I ascribed to Marx the view that the human 'essence' is a fact of nature, but *in its reality* an ensemble of the prevailing social relations. Menke, to the best of my knowledge, does not use the term 'dual perspective'.

13 This is also how I understand Adorno's concepts of 'naturalness' and 'drive'. See Chapter 4.

14 Moses is Menke's example of the religious model of liberation; Walter White is his example of the economic model of liberation.

15 Menke (correctly in my view) describes his conception as 'aesthetic materialism'. It is materialist, he claims, since it defines the subject as an effect of something that precedes it, that is prior to or outside it, and forever remains so (2022, 14). This also holds for the ethical version of materialism I propose.

16 Menke suggests a link between the ethical and the aesthetic that invites further exploration. It invites, in particular, further consideration of the role of the imagination in critical social theorizing. By 'imagination' in this context, I mean attempts to articulate the unthinkable and ineffable and efforts to navigate the tensions between them.

17 Karl Jaspers, whom I bring into the discussion later in the chapter, likewise describes 'the freedom to make myself' as a *gift* of transcendence (1967, 65–8).

18 In Lutheran theology, 'grace' ('the gift') is transformative for the recipient as it empowers them to be themselves, liberating them from obligation towards the prevailing normative orders and towards others. The transformed person then seeks to share their experience of liberation with others; the call to action arises out of that concern. Thus, in the Lutheran perspective, too, the gift puts an end to obligation. However, in this perspective there is an intersubjective moment lacking in Menke's account. I am grateful to Martin Sauter for helping me with this point.

19 'At these moments an insignificant creature, a dog, a rat, a beetle, a stunted apple tree, a cart path winding over the hill, a moss-covered stone, mean more to me than the most beautiful, most abandoned lover ever did on the happiest night' (Hofmannsthal 2005, 125).

20 Chandos' ability to convey his experiences to Bacon in the linguistic vocabulary available to him may be attributed to residual poetic skills he had acquired as a youthful Wunderkind. It is also of course due to Hofmannsthal's poetic gifts.

21 This is an additional reason why contemporary critical theories should look warily at Habermas' discourse theory of moral validity, which makes argumentatively achieved consensus constitutive of truth in the moral domain (see Chapter 2 above and Cooke 2025c).

22 I discuss this further in Chapter 5.

23 Adopting the terminology of Ernesto Laclau (2000), I describe fictions as incarnations of a transcendent object that occupy the 'empty place' of truth a space vacated by Truth and its equivalents such as God, Progress, Reason, or History (Cooke 2006a, 115). However, I dispute that the 'place of truth' is completely empty. I suggest, instead, that the vacated space of normativity is better thought of as indeterminate.

24 I understand Laclau's use of the term 'object' as along the same lines.

25 I compare and contrast the use of imaginary constructions in the work of Laclau and Habermas – specifically, Laclau's idea of political representation and Habermas ideal-speech situation (Cooke 2006a, 97–127).

26 In his *Critique of Pure Reason*, Kant writes: 'The ideas of God and immortality . . . [are] only conditions of the necessary object of a will determined by this [moral] law, that is, of the mere practical use of our pure reason; hence with respect to those ideas we cannot affirm that we cognise and have insight into [*erkennen* und *einzusehen*] . . . even the possibility of them . . . [T]heir possibility in this practical relation can and must be assumed . . . [B]y means of the concept of freedom objective reality is given to the ideas of God and immortality and a warrant, indeed a subjective necessity (a need of pure reason) is provided to assume them . . . [A]ll that is given is that their possibility, which was hitherto only a problem, here becomes an assertion' (1998, 5:3–5, quoted in Gardner (2011, 187).

27 'Fullness' is a concept frequently employed by Charles Taylor (2007) to convey the experiential dimension of transcending experiences. I find it appropriate here.

Chapter 4: Self-Determining Agency: Decentrings, Openings

1 As explained in Chapter 3, for convenience I frequently refer simply to a 'human-transcending' idea of the good, although I mean 'human-transcending and other-than-human transcending'.

2 In this section, I draw on my argument in Cooke 2025a.

3 I discuss the social moment of human need in Cooke 2025a.

4 As noted in the previous chapter, Menke also refers to 'force' or 'energy' [*Kraft*] (2017).

5 Unlike Habermas, as discussed in Chapters 2 and 3, Taylor does not distinguish sharply between ethical and moral concerns and for the most part uses the terms 'ethical' and 'moral' interchangeably (2007, 543).

6 By contrast, my focus in earlier writings is on the trope of the sovereign human will more generally (Cooke 2020a; 2023a; 2023b).

7 In the following, I refer to 'worldviews' when I consider perspectives on human existence in which there is either a clear distinction between the human and other-than-human world or in which the very idea of an other-than-human world is meaningless. I reserve the term 'cosmologies' for perspectives in which there is no sharp divide between the human and the other-than-human world and in which human existence is open, porous and vulnerable to a world of spirits and powers.

8 For Menke, every historical institutionalization of the form of law generates particular forms of society and subjectivity.

9 Menke's focus in his Critique of Rights is on the modern liberal understanding of human naturalness as a drive for self-preservation, not on the transgressive drive to become something other than what one is (2020).

10 Elsewhere, I address the question of the universality of what Habermas calls ethical validity claims in the context of a critical discussion of Axel Honneth's theory of recognition (Cooke 2009).

11 Freyenhagen argues for a negativist reading of Adorno's practical philosophy, maintaining that it is based on a conception of the bad rather than the good and offers only a 'guide for living less wrongly'. Furthermore, he endorses his negativist ethics, according to which we can only know the bad and not the good in our modern social world, claiming that this knowledge is enough to underpin a critical theory of society including an ethics of resistance (2013, 11).

12 Clearly, therefore, contrary to Gordon, I applaud Habermas' shift towards a weaker version of postmetaphysical thinking (Cooke 2023c).

13 See Chapter 2.

14 As noted in Chapter 1, note 4, Horkheimer initially refers to the new mode of social philosophy he advocates simply as 'materialism', only later giving it the name 'critical theory'.

15 In Chapter 1, I drew attention to Marx's sixth thesis on Feuerbach: 'the human essence [is] in its reality . . . the ensemble of the social relations' (2000e, Thesis VI, 172).

16 In my discussions of the power of social institutions in Chapters 7 and 8, the ethical dimension of human 'naturalness', alongside its material dimension, is crucial for the possibility of ethical self-transformation by both political and institutional agencies.

Chapter 5: Freedom as Ethical Agency: Explorations

1 'Negative' conceptions of freedom, too, can be relational. For example, Philip Pettit's conception of political freedom as nondomination (1999). Pettit defines freedom negatively, as the absence of a certain kind of external control. At the same time, he emphasizes that it is a form of freedom available only in a social context through relationships with other persons; it is not freedom *from* others, but freedom *in relation to* others (2012, 91).

2 Contemporary Frankfurt School political theories often build a space of 'negative' liberty into their 'positive' conceptualizations of collective self-authorship. This is most obvious in Habermas' theory (1996), but it is also a feature of Axel Honneth's (2014) and Rainer Forst's (2012) accounts of political freedom. In other writings, I argue against this (Cooke 2022; 2024).

3 Michiel Meijer (2019), discussing Taylor's writings between 1959 and 2015, underscores the persistent gap between his phenomenological approach and his claims about ontology.

4 See my discussion of Menke's book in Chapter 4.

5 Rosa's short book, *Unverfügbarkeit* (2019b), is translated into English by J. C. Wagner as *The Uncontrollability of the World* (2020a). In his translation of *Resonance* (2019a), Wagner mainly translates *Unverfügbarkeit* as 'inaccessibility' (ibid., 249n81). In an article on Rosa, Simon Susen (2020), translates *Unverfügbarkeit* as 'unavailability'; however, in his book on Rosa, Susen (2024) mainly uses the word 'uncontrollability'. As Susen acknowledges, the German term is not well expressed by either 'unavailability' or 'uncontrollability' (or indeed, 'inaccessibility'): it has connotations of all three. The inadequacy of these English terms should be borne in mind in what follows.

6 See note 5.

7 See also Rosa's reply to my critique of his notion of resonant self-efficacious agency (Rosa 2020b; Cooke 2020c))

8 Rather than thinking of transcendence as going beyond the ordinary, Zigon suggests that we think of it as an essential constituent of the ordinary and, therefore, as constitutive not only of the ethical subject but of social existence as such. He describes transcendence as 'ecstatic relationality', the 'open space between us' where ethical subjects become possible (2024, 7–8). Accordingly, I understand the 'between' as a space of transcendence in a horizontal sense (this is my terminology, not Zigon's).

9 Truth is the 'relational attunement – the between – that allows an existent to show itself as itself and allows other existents to let that showing as unfolding happen' (2024, 35). The Heideggerian conception of freedom corresponds to the 'essence of truth', which for Zigon is the 'between', letting unconcealment unfold (ibid.).

10 I owe this vignette to Carmen Dege, who drew my attention to Nastassja Martin's book and has herself written about it (Dege and Keum, 2025).

11 Martin's therapist friend tells her that the bear is a mirror, an expression of something other than himself, of something to do with her. Something about this rings false to Martin; she is troubled by the reduction of 'all the other souls around us' to mere reflections of our own states of mind (2021, 46). She asks: 'Who can say what [the bear] carries with him; what he feels; who can explain the reasons that prompt his movements, beyond the basic functionalist

explanation? There are things I will never know, this much is obvious. Which does not mean I should give up, renounce the obligation to understand further' (ibid., 47).

12 *Medka* is an Even word, 'marked by the bear', referring to someone who has survived an encounter with a bear and now lives between the worlds (Martin 2021, 21).

13 In light of the discussion in previous chapters, it is noteworthy that Martin reflects on her indigenous friend's statement, 'the bears give us a gift'; moreover, that she describes the gift she receives as 'uncertainty'; also, that she discerns within this statement that dialogue with animals is possible, even if rarely in any controllable form (2021, 59–60).

14 Referring to her indigenous friend, Martin writes: 'People like Daria know that they are not alone as they live, feel, think, and listen in the forest, that other forces are at work around them. There is a potency here that is external to people, an intention unrelated to humanity' (2021, 59).

15 Borrowing a term used by the anthropologist Marilyn Strathern (2020), de la Cadena calls this 'displacement'.

16 Accordingly, 'excess' too is a key term for de la Cadena, designating a second ethnographic mode alongside, and complementary to, co-labouring (de la Cadena 2021, 248).

17 de la Cadena tells her readers that she does not speak Quechua.

18 *Ayllu* is usually translated as family or clan, the institution formed by a group of people who collectively own land, the basic socioeconomic unit of Inca society in Peru. (Cf. de la Cadena 2021, 247.)

19 The title of de la Cadena's major ethnographic study, *Earth Beings* (2015), seeks to convey this lack of separation.

20 I acknowledge the importance of, but leave aside, the question of whether humans can learn ethically from other-than-human artefacts (such as the 'machinery' that is part of Martin's new hybrid identity and, more generally, AI. My discussion of institutions (Chapter 7) moves in this direction.).

Chapter 6: Critiques of Capitalism: Decentrings, Openings, Explorations

1 In the German original, 'eine revolutionäre Umgestaltung der ganzen Gesellschaft'. I consider the question of a '*revolutionäre Umgestaltung*' (revolutionary reconstitution) more carefully in Chapter 8.

2 In 'On the Jewish Question', Marx's criticism is different. He characterizes bourgeois freedom as the right to do everything that harms no one else; it is the freedom of man as a 'self-sufficient monad' (2000a, 60–1).

3 In Chapter 1, I drew attention to Marx's view of the human animal as distinct from other animals due to the human interest in free creative activity and ability to produce 'according to the laws of beauty' (Marx 2000c, 90).

4 See Chapter 4. In his account of freedom as 'self-will' Menke draws on Marx's characterization of bourgeois freedom as the right to do everything that harms no one else (see note 2 above).

5 As quoted previously, both in the Introduction and in Chapter 1, Marx and Engels call for 'an association, beyond the antagonisms of class society, in which the free development of each is the condition for the free development of all' (1967, 105).

6 Thus, the German title of Nancy Fraser's book *Cannibal Capitalism* (2022) as *Der Allesfresser* (2023) is apt.

7 Marx and Engels make clear that they use the terms 'bourgeoisie' and 'capital' more or less interchangeably, e.g. when they write: '. . . as the bourgeoisie, i.e., capital, is developed' (1967, 87).

8 In *Minima Moralia*, Adorno described critical theory's interventions as 'messages in a bottle on a flood of barbarism' (1974, 209).

9 Pierre Charbonnier draws attention to the productivist paradigm characteristic of nineteenth-century socialism. See Chapter 4.

10 See note 9.

11 Marx (2000f, 615) writes: 'In a higher phase of communist society . . . after labour has become not only a means of life but life's prime want; after the productive forces have also increased with the all-round development of the individual, and all the springs of co-operative wealth flow more abundantly – only then can . . . society inscribe on its banners: from each according to his ability, to each according to his needs!'

12 In Chapter 4, I argued that Charbonnier's proposed reconfiguration of socialism, although anti-productivist, is open to the objection that it is exclusively humanist.

13 Recall Horkheimer's insistence that critical theory is concerned with 'the social life-process in its totality', as discussed in Chapter 1.

14 Anthropogenic planetary depredation would be an example of such a problem.

15 Marisol de la Cadena calls epistemism 'the hierarchy-making twin of racism that, unlike the latter, remains uncontested and legitimate (2021, 251).

16 In Chapter 5, I sought to make sense of earth-beings (*tirakuna*), *runakuna* and *ayllu* with the help of de la Cadena.

17 In 2020, Ausangate was officially declared a Regional Conservation Area. However, this is unlikely to be the end of extractivist practices in the area.

18 This fits with the insights of Western deep ecologists, although the vocabulary they use is different.

19 The ouroboros is an ancient symbol which entered the Western tradition by way of Egyptian iconography; it depicts a dragon or snake eating its own tail. It is the cover picture for Fraser's book *Cannibal Capitalism*. For an alternative interpretation of the symbol to Fraser's, see Assmann (2017).

20 Fraser is careful to distinguish between crisis *tendencies* and full-blown crises. In her 2018 conversation with Jaeggi, she did not think the crisis tendencies had become overt and acute. Four years later she took a different view. Her most recently articulated position is that humans everywhere are experiencing an epochal crisis of capitalism. It is a general crisis, 'a crisis of ecology, economy, society, politics, public health and more' (2022, 58). However, she emphasizes that to speak of an epochal crisis is not to proclaim imminent breakdown. Nor does it rule out the advent of a new regime of accumulation that could provisionally manage or temporarily defer the current crisis (ibid, 75).

21 For Fraser. these include livelihood insecurity, the denial of labour rights, public disinvestment from social reproduction, the chronic undervaluation of care work, ethno-racial-imperial oppression, gender and sex domination, dispossession, expulsion and exclusion of migrants, militarization, political authoritarianism and police brutality.

22 See Chapter 4.

23 Fraser claims that pre-capitalist eco-crises occurred largely thanks to igno-rance – for example, the failure to anticipate the consequences of deforesta-tion and overplanting. The remedy was social learning that prompted shifts in social practice. Likewise, in the case of self-proclaimed post-capitalist societies (paradigmatically the former Soviet Union), the problem was contingent not structural, explicable by the external constraints and internal deformations that shaped their ecologically destructive practices.

24 Fraser insists that socialism does not mean 'that we must institutionalize degrowth as a hardwired counter-imperative. It means, rather, that we must make the question of growth . . . a political question, to be decided via multi-dimensional reflection informed by climate science' (2022, 101–2; cf. ibid., 78).

25 Jaeggi presses Fraser on the question of ethical critique, but Fraser is evidently reluctant to embrace the concept, worrying that it too readily becomes essen-tialist and conservative (Fraser and Jaeggi 2018, 126–30). In the end Fraser, concedes that there is a sense in which her own critique of capitalism has an ethical dimension, while stressing that it is a non-essentialist approach that is perhaps better described as structural-ethical (ibid., 130).

26 Azmanova pursues a comparable critical strategy in her 2012 book *The Scandal of Reason* (see Cooke 2014b).

27 See Chapter 1.

28 See Chapter 3.

Chapter 7: Critiques of Politics: Decentrings, Openings, Explorations

1 For reasons explained in Chapter 3, this power is more accurately character-ized as 'human-transcending and other-than-human-transcending'. However, since this formulation is cumbersome, I usually abbreviate it to 'human-transcending', since this is the key point for my critique of the perniciously anthropocentric and Eurocentric 'exclusive humanist' perspective on human agency.

2 See Chapter 3, note 1.

3 As quoted repeatedly in the preceding chapters, the authors envisage com-munism as an 'association, beyond the antagonisms of class society, in which the free development of each would be the condition for the free development of all' (Marx and Engels 1967, 105). Admittedly, neither Marx and Engels nor Marx in his subsequent writings offer their thoughts on the institutional framework required for such an association (Maguire 2009).

4 It is likely that Marx's remark on 'the real ground' of the constitution expresses his exclusive humanist worldview, to which I referred in Chapter 6. However, if read as a stand-alone remark, the quoted passage is compatible with my own dual perspective on normativity, introduced in Chapter 3.

5 Well-known examples are the 2008 Ecuadorian Constitution and the 2017 Whanganui River settlement in New Zealand/Aotearoa.

6 I propose a differentiated account of anthropocentrism in Chapter 4, in which I distinguish between relatively benign and pernicious kinds.

7 A similar line of argument is found in Landemore 2020.

8 In this sense, supreme court judges, too, are 'citizens in robes'.

9 Theorists of constituent power normally focus on legal-political-administrative institutions. However, I see no reason in principle why they cannot adopt

the more encompassing view of social institutions that I develop later in this chapter.

10 See Chapter 1.

11 The work of Patrick Nitzschner (2024; 2025), although it does not explicitly embrace a constituent power perspective, pursues a similar but somewhat different path.

12 See Chapter 4.

13 See Chapter 4

14 As observed in Chapter 4.

15 My critique of the exclusive humanist idea of normative self-sufficiency does not imply rejection of all aspects of the idea of sovereignty, for example, its connection with mastery and control, as discussed in Chapter 4. (see Cooke 2023a).

16 In this, too, Näsström follows Arendt (2006a), as she readily acknowledges.

17 Näsström's argument supports my emphasis on the importance of 'a space of one's own' for the development of ethical agency. See Chapter 5.

18 Näsström also shows how democratic corruption plays out in relation to elections and democratic citizenship.

19 See Chapter 4.

20 Unlike Arendt, Näsström does not make an anthropological distinction between action, work and labour. Furthermore, she does not follow Arendt in her strict demarcations between the public and private realms, and between politics, the household and the economy.

21 As discussed in Chapter 5.

22 A caveat: discussions in the preceding chapters have shown that ontological divisions should be mobile and fluid – for example, humans and mountains may also be earth-beings. Insisting on clearly demarcated ontological categories limits the emancipatory imaginations of decentring, expansive, exploratory critical theories, inhibiting their explorations of alternative, better modes of being in the world. This should be borne in mind in what follows.

23 In my account, 'things' that are not humanly fabricated have their own normativity, in part distinct from their generic agency (e.g. the corn plant's rather than the bean's or the squash's) and in part shared with 'family members', as is the case for these 'three sisters' (see Chapter 4). Humanly fabricated 'things' likewise have their own normativity, in part distinctive of their particular agency and in part shared with 'family members'. These are avenues for further exploration, which I do not pursue here.

24 Rahel Jaeggi (2009) makes a similar point.

25 Mommsen (1888) writes: 'In diesem Sinne ist auctoritas mehr als ein Ratschlag und weniger als ein Befehl, ein Ratschlag, dessen Befolgung man sich nicht füglich entziehen kann.'

26 Durkheim conceives of the moral being in secular terms as 'society', but grants that it could equally well be described in religious terms as 'God' or 'the divine'.

27 I do not deny that a system of checks and controls may be important from a *pragmatic* point of view. For example, it may serve as an 'advance warning system' that flags the need for 'institutional repair' to certain institutions (Alexander 2006).

28 Patrick Nitzschner (2024) makes a similar point. In his case, he looks to Adorno's *Negative Dialectics* (1973) to make his case for internal rather than external institutional change.

29 Habermas refers to the co-originality of *private* and *public* autonomy. For present purposes, nothing turns on the difference in terminology in Habermas' and Forst's respective versions of the thesis.
30 As observed in Chapter 2, note 7, Habermas uses 'moral' in this narrower sense, distinguishing categorially between moral validity and ethical validity.
31 See Chapter 1, note 1 and Chapter 2, note 7.
32 It has the further disadvantage that it leads to an ethically abstinent critical theory of politics based on a model of political will-formation in which the *ethical-existential* quality of laws, political decisions and public policies is a matter of public indifference (Cooke 2024).

Chapter 8: Transformations, Futures

1 As I have explained, I borrow the term 'exclusive humanist' from Charles Taylor (2007). See Chapter 4.
2 To be clear: I do not attribute the two objections directly to Habermas and Benjamin – I refer to two kinds of objections, relevant for present purposes, that can be *extrapolated* from their respective writings. This is why the writings of other theorists in the Frankfurt School tradition, for example Adorno, may display elements of both the Habermasian and the Benjaminian positions.
3 It is clear from the text that, by 'dialectical materialism', Benjamin means Marxist versions of it.
4 See also Ricoeur 1996.
5 I use the term 're-presentation' here in the sense explained in Chapter 3.
6 I discuss these troubling features of Marx's vision of socialism in most detail in Chapter 6.
7 The German original reads: 'Nur als Bild, das auf Nimmerwiedersehen im Augenblick seiner Erkennbarkeit eben aufblitzt, ist die Vergangenheit festzuhalten.'
8 I previously drew attention to their view of institutions in Chapter 7.
9 Foucault (1995) writes that disciplinary power substitutes for the magnificence of the sovereign a power that *objectifies* those on whom it is exercised.
10 In depicting capitalism as a 'lifeform', I refer back to Nässström's view of democracy as a lifeform (Chapter 7), to Fraser's account of capitalism as a type of society rather than just an economy and to Jaeggi's characterization of it as a form of life (Chapter 6).
11 In his later writings Foucault appears to take a different view of subjectification, allowing for subjective resistance to the prevailing social system. However, the *ethical* dimension in resistant subjectivity is absent even in his later account.
12 See Chapter 1.
13 I discuss this in more detail in Cooke 2019c.
14 In using The Invisible Committee's *Now* as a possible example of 'actionism', I may seem to deny its aesthetic brilliance and its potential effectiveness as an agent of fundamental social transformation. I do not. To the contrary, I consider it to exemplify the power of disclosive philosophical criticism of society, as discussed extensively in Chapter 2. However, I repeat my proviso, elaborated in that chapter, concerning the importance of combining disclosive criticism with argumentation.

15 Malm acknowledges the risk that his call for 'action now' that bypasses demo-cratic processes opens the door for political authoritarianism and eco-fascism.
16 An emphasis on the importance of ethical-existential self-transformations on the side of both the dominated and the dominating is also evident in Gandhi's writings.
17 Furthermore, there is a wealth of literature showing that the main agents of change in most anticolonial struggles have not been those most oppressed but rather those motivated by an ethical-existential-political concern for universal freedom and happiness.
18 I refer here to Foucault's writings on disciplinary power in the early 1970s. The later Foucault, in his writings on care of the self, evidently takes a different position.
19 I am grateful to Ruth Sonderegger for helping me to understand this.

References

Abromeit, J. (2012). *Horkheimer and the Foundations of the Frankfurt School*. Cambridge: Cambridge University Press.

Adorno, T. W. (1972). *Soziologische Schriften*. Frankfurt/Main: Suhrkamp.

Adorno, T. W. (1973 [1966]). *Negative Dialectics*, trans. E. B. Ashton. London: Routledge.

Adorno, T. W. (1974 [1951]). *Minima Moralia. Reflections on a Damaged Life*, trans. E. Jephcott. London: Verso.

Adorno, T. W. (1977 [1962]). 'Commitment'. In Adorno et al., *Aesthetics and Politics: Debates between Bloch, Lukács, Brecht, Benjamin Adorno*, Afterword by F. Jameson. London: New Left Books, pp. 177–95.

Adorno, T. W. (1982 [1967]). 'Notes on Kafka'. In Adorno, *Prisms*, trans. S. Weber and S. Weber. Cambridge, MA: MIT Press, pp. 243–71.

Adorno, T. W. (1983 [1955]). *Prisms*, trans. S. Weber Nicholsen and S. Weber. Cambridge, MA: MIT Press.

Adorno, T. W. (1997). *Aesthetic Theory*, trans. R. Hullot-Kentor. Minneapolis: University of Minnesota Press.

Adorno, T. W. (2000a). *Problems of Moral Philosophy*, trans. R. Livingstone. Stanford, CA: Stanford University Press.

Adorno, T. W. (2000b). 'The Actuality of Philosophy'. In B. O'Connor (ed.), *The Adorno Reader*. Oxford: Blackwell, pp. 23–39.

Adorno, T. W. (2002 [1969]). 'Who's Afraid of the Ivory Tower? A Conversation with Th. W. Adorno', trans. G. Richter. *Monatshefte* 94 (1): 10–23.

Adorno, T. W. (2005). *Critical Models: Interventions and Catchwords*, trans. H. Pickford. New York: Columbia University Press.

Adorno, T. W. (2017a [1942]). 'Theses on Need', trans. M. Schuster and I. Macdonald. *Adorno Studies* 1 (1): 101–4.

Adorno, T. W. (2017b). *An Introduction to Dialectics*, ed. C. Ziermann, trans. N. Walker. Cambridge: Polity.

Adorno, T. W. and Horkheimer, M. (2011). *Towards a New Manifesto. Conversations between Adorno and Horkheimer (1956)*, trans. R. Livingstone. London: Verso.

Agra, K. (2023). 'Epistemic Paralysis and Non-Recognition: The Case of (Mis-) education'. Unpublished dissertation, School of Philosophy, University College Dublin.

Alexander, J. (2006). *The Civil Sphere*. Oxford: Oxford University Press.

Allard-Tremblay, Y. (2022). 'Braiding Liberation Discourses: Dialectical, Civic and Disjunctive Views about Resistance and Violence'. *Canadian Journal of Political Science* 55: 259–78.

Álvarez, S. E. (1999). 'Advocating Feminism: The Latin American Feminist NGO "Boom"'. *International Feminist Journal of Politics* 1 (2): 181–209.

Améry, J. (1994). *On Aging. Revolt and Resignation*, trans. J. D. Barlow. Bloomington: Indiana University Press.

Andreev, P. D. (2023). *Outwitting Enlightenment: Philosophical Style, Critique, and History in Adorno and Horkheimer's Dialectic of Enlightenment*. https://reposi tory.essex.ac.uk/36660/.

Arendt, H. (1998 [1958]). *The Human Condition*, 2nd edn. Introduction by M. Canavan. Chicago, IL: Chicago University Press.

Arendt, H. (2006a [1963]). *On Revolution*. London: Penguin Classics.

Arendt, H. (2006b [1954]). 'What Is Authority'? In Arendt, *Between Past and Future: Eight Exercises in Political Thought*. London: Penguin Books, pp. 91–141.

Arendt, H. (2006c [1960]). 'What Is Freedom?' in Arendt, *Between Past and Future. Eight Exercises in Political Thought*. London: Penguin Books, pp. 143–71.

Arendt, H. (2017 [1951]). *The Origins of Totalitarianism*. London: Penguin Classics.

Assmann, J. (2017). 'Das altägyptische Mythos vom Sonnenlauf'. In R. Beil (ed.), *Never-Ending Stories: Der Loop in Kunst, Film, Architektur, Musik, Literatur und Kulturgeschichte*. Berlin: Hatje Cantz Verlag, pp. 58–63.

Austin, J. L. (1962). *How to Do Things with Words*. Oxford: Blackwell.

Azmanova, A. (2012). *The Scandal of Reason. A Critical Theory of Political Judgment*. New York: Columbia University Press.

Azmanova, A. (2020). *Capitalism on Edge: How Fighting Precarity Can Achieve Radical Change Without Crisis or Utopia*. New York: Columbia University Press.

Baum, B. (2015). 'Decolonizing Critical Theory'. *Constellations* 22 (3): 420–43.

Benhabib, S. (1992). *Situating the Self*. New York: Columbia University Press.

Benhabib, S. (2004). *The Rights of Others: Aliens, Residents, and Citizens*. Cambridge: Cambridge University Press.

Benjamin, W. (1968). *Illuminations*, trans. H. Zohn, ed. and with an Introduction by H. Arendt. New York: Schocken Books.

Benjamin, W. (1999 [written 1927–40, unfinished]). *The Arcades Project*, trans. H. Eiland and G. McLaughlin. Cambridge, MA: Belknap Press.

Benjamin, W. (2005 [written *c.* 1940]). 'On the Concept of History'. https://www. marxists.org/reference/archive/benjamin/1940/history.htm.

Bennett, J. (2020). *Influx and Efflux: Writing Up with Walt Whitman*. Durham, NC: Duke University Press.

Berger, P. and Luckmann, T. (1967). *The Social Construction of Reality: A Treatise in the Sociology of Knowledge*. New York: Knopf Doubleday.

Berlin, I. (1969). 'Two Concepts of Liberty'. In Berlin, *Four Essays on Liberty*. Oxford: Oxford University Press, pp. 118–72.

Bhabha, H. (1996). *The Location of Culture*. New York: Routledge.

Bhambra, G. K. (2021). 'Decolonizing Critical Theory? Epistemological Justice, Progress, Reparations'. *Critical Times* 4 (1): 73–89.

Boltanski. L. (2011). *On Critique*, trans. G. Elliott. Cambridge: Polity.

Borrows, J. et al. (eds.) (2019). *Braiding Legal Orders. Implementing the United Nations Declaration on the Rights of Indigenous Peoples*. Waterloo, ON: Centre for International Governance Innovation.

Boss, G. (2023). 'Political Theory and the Politics of Need. *European Journal of Political Theory* 24 (3): 357–80.

Boulot, E. and Sterlin, J. (2022). 'Steps Towards a Legal Ontological Turn: Proposals for Law's Place beyond the Human'. *Transnational Environmental Law* 11 (1): 13–38.

Brunkhorst, H. (1985). 'Dialektischer Positivismus des Glücks. Max Horkheimers materialistische Dekonstruktion der Philosophie'. *Zeitschrift für Philosophische Forschung* 39 (3): 353–81.

Buck-Morss, S. (1977). *The Origin of Negative Dialectics. Theodor W. Adorno, Walter Benjamin, and the Frankfurt Institute.* Hassocks, Sussex: Harvester Press.

Butler, J. (2000a). 'Restaging the Universal. Hegemony and the Limits of Formalism'. In J. Butler, E. Laclau and S. Žižek, *Contingency, Hegemony, Universality*. London: Verso, pp. 11–43.

Butler, J. (2000b). 'Competing Universalities'. In J. Butler, E. Laclau and S. Žižek, *Contingency, Hegemony, Universality*. London: Verso, pp. 136–81.

Butler, J. (2000c). 'Dynamic Conclusions'. In J. Butler, E. Laclau and S. Žižek, *Contingency, Hegemony, Universality*. London: Verso, pp. 263–80.

Butler, J. (2003). 'What Is Critique? An Essay on Foucault's Virtue'. In S. Salih with J. Butler (eds.), *The Judith Butler Reader*. Oxford: Blackwell, pp. 302–21.

Celikates, R. (2019). 'Constituent Power beyond Exceptionalism: Irregular Migration, Disobedience, and (Re-)Constitution', *Journal of International Political Theory* 15 (1): 67–81.

Celikates, R., Jaeggi, R., Loick, D. and Schmidt, C. (2023). '11 Theses on Needs'. https://criticaltheoryinberlin.de/en/interventions/11-theses-on-needs/.

Charbonnier, P. (2021). *Affluence and Freedom: An Environmental History of Political Ideas*, trans. A. Brown. Cambridge: Polity.

Cohen, J. (1997). 'Deliberation and Democratic Legitimacy'. In J. Bohman and W. Rehg (eds.), *Deliberative Democracy*. Cambridge, MA: MIT Press.

Cooke, M. (1992). 'Habermas, Autonomy, and the Identity of the Self'. *Philosophy and Social Criticism* 18 (3–4): 269–91.

Cooke, M. (1994). *Language and Reason. A Study of Habermas's Pragmatics.* Cambridge, MA: MIT Press.

Cooke, M. (1997). 'Authenticity and Autonomy: Taylor, Habermas, and the Politics of Recognition'. *Political Theory* 25 (2): 258–88.

Cooke, M. (1999a). 'Questioning Autonomy: The Feminist Challenge and the Challenge for Feminism'. In R. Kearney and M. Dooley (eds.), *Questioning Ethics: Contemporary Debates in Philosophy*. New York: Routledge, pp. 258–82.

Cooke, M. (1999b). 'Habermas, Feminism and the Question of Autonomy'. In P. Dews (ed.), *Habermas: A Critical Reader*. Oxford: Blackwell, pp. 178–210.

Cooke. M. (1999c). 'A Space of One's Own: Autonomy, Privacy, Liberty'. *Philosophy and Social Criticism* 25 (1): 23–53.

Cooke, M. (2000). 'Five Arguments for Deliberative Democracy'. *Political Studies* 48 (5): 947–69.

Cooke, M. (2005). 'Avoiding Authoritarianism: On the Problem of Justification in Contemporary Critical Social Theory'. *International Journal of Philosophical Studies* 13 (3): 379–404.

Cooke, M. (2006a). *Re-Presenting the Good Society*. Cambridge, MA: MIT Press.

Cooke, M. (2006b). 'Resurrecting the Rationality of Ideology Critique: Reflections on Laclau on Ideology'. *Constellations* 13 (1): 4–20.

Cooke, M. (2009). 'Beyond Dignity and Difference: Revisiting the Politics of Recognition'. *European Journal of Political Theory* 8 (1): 76–95.

Cooke, M. (2014a). 'Truth in Narrative Fiction, Kafka, Adorno and Beyond'. *Philosophy and Social Criticism* 40 (7): 629–43.

Cooke M. (2014b). '*The Scandal of Reason. A Critical Theory of Political Judgment*, by Albena Azmanova'. *Perspectives on Politics* 12 (2): 517–18.

Cooke, M. (2017). 'Contingency and Objectivity in Critical Social Theory: Horkheimer and Habermas'. In G. Marchetti and S. Marchetti (eds.), *Facts and Values: The Ethics and Metaphysics of Normativity*. London: Routledge, pp. 60–79.

Cooke, M. (2019a). 'Discourse Ethics'. In P. Gordon, E. Hammer and A. Honneth, *The Routledge Companion to the Frankfurt School*. London: Routledge, pp. 65–81.

Cooke, M. (2019b). 'Linguistification'. In A. Allen and E. Mendieta (eds.), *The Cambridge Habermas Lexicon*. Cambridge: Cambridge University Press, pp. 254–6.

Cooke, M. (2019c). 'Forever Resistant? Adorno and Radical Transformation of Society'. In P. Gordon et al., *Blackwell Companion to Adorno*. Oxford: Blackwell, pp. 583–600.

Cooke, M. (2019d). 'Disobedience in Civil Regeneration: Radical Transformations in the Civil Sphere'. In J. Alexander et al., *Breaching the Civil Order. Radicalism and the Civil Sphere*. Cambridge: Cambridge University Press, pp. 235–60.

Cooke, M. (2020a). 'The Ethics and Politics of the Anthropocene'. *Philosophy and Social Criticism* 46 (10): 1167–81.

Cooke, M. (2020b). 'Private Autonomy and Public Autonomy: Tensions in Habermas' Discourse Theory of Law and Politics'. *Kantian Review* 25 (4): 559–82.

Cooke, M. (2020c). 'Self-Efficacious Subjects. Rosa on Alienation and Its Antithesis'. *International Journal of Political Power* 13 (3): 366–81.

Cooke, M. (2020d). 'A Pluralist Model of Politics'. In V. Kaul and I. Salvatore (eds.), *What Is Pluralism?* Delhi: Routledge, pp. 139–54.

Cooke, M. (2021a). 'Immanent Critique of the Immanent Frame: The Critical Potential of *A Secular Age*'. *International Journal of Philosophical Studies* 29 (5): 738–58.

Cooke, M. (2021b). 'Existentially Lived Truth or Communicative Reason? Habermas' Critique of Kierkegaard'. *Constellations* 28 (1) 51–9.

Cooke, M. (2022). 'Beyond Positive and Negative Liberty. Habermas and Honneth on Political Freedom'. In J. Christman (ed.), *Positive Freedom*. Cambridge: Cambridge University Press, pp. 194–216.

Cooke, M. (2023a). 'Reenvisioning Freedom: Human Agency in Times of Ecological Disaster'. *Constellations* 30 (2): 119–27.

Cooke, M. (2023b). 'Social Theory as Critical Theory. Horkheimer's Program and its Relevance Today'. *Constellations* 30 (4): 384–9.

Cooke, M. (2023c). 'Detranszendentalisierte Religion oder dezentrierte Vernunft? Zum gesellschaftskritischen Potential der Religion im Zeitalter der ökologischen Katastrophe: über die Übersetzung hinaus'. In M. Breul and K. Viertbauer (eds.), *Über das Unverfügbare*. Freiburg: Herder.

Cooke, M. (2024). 'Ethische Orientierung statt ethischer Enthaltsamkeit. Zur Repolitisierung der demokratischen Willensbildung'. In M. Bassiouni et al. (eds.), *Die Macht der Rechtfertigung. Perspektiven einer kritischen Theorie der Gerechtigkeit*. Berlin: Suhrkamp, pp. 597–614.

Cooke, M. (2025a). 'Decentring and Opening the Politics of Need'. *Critical Review of International Social and Political Philosophy*, 1–22. https://doi.org/10.1080/13698230.2025.2535865.

Cooke, M. (2025b). 'Reflexive Resonanz. Dezentrierungen in der kritischen Gesellschaftstheorie'. In J. Oberthür and B. Hollstein (eds.), *Resonanz und Kritik*. Berlin: Suhrkamp.

Cooke, M. (2025c). 'Decentring Critical Theory with the Help of Critical Theory: Ecocide and the Challenge of Anthropocentricism'. *Philosophy & Social Criticism* 51 (7): 1029–43.

Damasio, A. (2005 [1994]). *Descartes' Error. Emotion, Reason and the Human Brain*. London: Penguin.

Davis, A. (2003). *Are Prisons Obsolete?* New York: Seven Stories Press.

de la Boétie, É. (2012 [1577]). *Discourse on Voluntary Servitude*, trans. J. Atkinson and D. Sices. Indianapolis, IN: Hackett Publishing.

de la Cadena, M. (2015). *Earth Beings. Ecologies of Practice across Andean Worlds*. Durham, NC: Duke University Press.

de la Cadena. M. (2017). 'Matters of Method; Or, why Method Matters: Toward a *Not Only* Colonial Anthropology'. *HAU: Journal of Ethnographic Theory* 7 (2): 1–10.

de la Cadena, M. (2021). 'Not Knowing. In the Presence of . . .'. In A. Ballestero (ed.), *Experimenting with Ethnography: A Companion to Analysis*. Durham, NC: Duke University Press, pp. 246–56.

Dege, C. (2023). 'Myth, Modernity, and the Legacy of the Axial Age: Taylor, Habermas, Assmann, and Jaspers'. *Journal of the History of Ideas* 84 (4): 743–73.

Dege, C. and Keum, T.-Y. (2025). 'Toward a Theory of Myth Critique: Ideology, Learned Ignorance, and the Conditions of Imaginative Success'. *Constellations* 32: 286–97.

Descola, P. (2013 [2005]). *Beyond Nature and Culture*, trans. J. Lloyd. Chicago, IL: University of Chicago Press.

Diamond, C. (2003). 'The Difficulty of Reality and the Difficulty of Philosophy'. *Journal of Literature and the History of Ideas* 1 (2): 1–26.

Dotson, K. (2012). 'A Cautionary Tale: On Limiting Epistemic Oppression'. *Frontiers: A Journal of Women Studies* 33 (1): 24–47

Du Bois, W. E. B. (2007 [1903]). *The Souls of Black Folk*. Oxford: Oxford University Press.

Durkheim, É. (1965). *Sociology and Philosophy*. trans. D. F. Pocock, with an introduction by J. G. Peristiany. London: Cohen and West.

Finlayson, G. (2002). 'Adorno on the Ethical and Ineffable'. *European Journal of Philosophy* 10 (1): 1–25.

Fitzgerald, O. and Schwartz, R. (2017). 'Introduction'. In *UNDRIP Implementation: Braiding International, Domestic and Indigenous Laws*. Special Report. Waterloo, ON: Centre for International Governance Innovation.

Forst, R. (2012 [2007]). *The Right to Justification. Elements of a Constructivist Theory of Justice*, trans. J. Flynn. New York: Columbia University Press.

Fraser, N. (1985). 'What's Critical about Critical Theory? The Case of Habermas and Gender'. *New German Critique* 35: 87–131.

Fraser, N. (1990). 'Rethinking the Public Sphere. A Contribution to the Critique of Actually Existing Democracy'. *Social Text* 25/26: 56–80.

Fraser, N. (2022). *Cannibal Capitalism: How our System is Devouring Democracy, Care and the Planet – and What We Can Do About it*. London: Verso.

Fraser, N. (2023). *Der Allesfresser. Wie der Kapitalismus seine eigenen Grundlagen verschlingt*, trans A. Wirthensohn. Berlin: Suhrkamp.

Fraser, N. and Jaeggi, R. (2018). *Capitalism. A Conversation in Critical Theory*. Cambridge: Polity.

Freyenhagen, F. (2013). *Adorno's Practical Philosophy: Living Less Wrongly*. Cambridge: Cambridge University Press.

Foucault, M. (1986). *The Use of Pleasure*, trans. R. Hurley. New York: Vintage.

Foucault, M. (1988). *The Care of the Self*, trans. R. Hurley. New York: Vintage.

Foucault, M. (1995 [1975]). *Discipline and Punish: The Birth of the Prison*, 2nd edn., trans. A. Sheridan. New York: Vintage.

Foucault, M. (1997). 'What Is Critique?' In S. Lotringer and L. Hochroth (eds.), *The Politics of Truth*. New York: Semiotext(e). This is a revised, translated version of a 1978 lecture given at the French Society of Philosophy.

Gardner, S. (2011). 'Kant's Practical Postulates and the Limits of the Critical System'. *Bulletin of the Hegel Society of Great Britain* 63: 187–215.

Glissant, É. (1997 [1990]). *Poetics of Relation*, trans. Betsy Wing. Ann Arbor: The University of Michigan Press.

Gordon, P. E. (2005). 'Self-Authorizing Modernity: Problems of Interpretation in the History of German Idealism' (review essay). *History and Theory* 44: 121–37.

Gordon, P. E. (2016). 'Critical Theory between the Sacred and the Profane'. *Constellations* 23 (4): 466–80.

Gordon, P. E. (2020). *Migrants in the Profane. Critical Theory and the Question of Secularization*. New Haven, CT: Yale University Press.

Gordon, P. E. (2023). *A Precarious Happiness. Adorno and the Sources of Normativity*. Chicago, IL: Chicago University Press.

Guenther, L. (2021). 'Six Senses of Critique for Critical Phenomenology'. *Puncta* 2 (2): 5–23.

Habermas, J. (1984/1987 [1981]). *Theory of Communicative Action*, 2 vols., trans. T. McCarthy. Boston, MA: Beacon Books.

Habermas, J. (1990 [1988]). *The Philosophical Discourse of Modernity: 12 Lectures*, trans. F. Lawrence. Cambridge, MA: MIT Press.

Habermas, J. (1991a [1988]). 'Excurs: Transzendenz von innen. Transzendenz ins Diesseits'. In Habermas, *Texte und Kontexte*. Frankfurt/Main: Suhrkamp, pp. 127–56. (Available in English as 'Transcendence from Within, Transcendence in this World', in E. Mendieta (ed.) (2002). *Religion and Rationality. Essays on Reason, God, and Modernity*. Cambridge: Polity, pp. 67–94.)

Habermas, J. (1991b [1982]). *Moral Consciousness and Communicative Action*, trans. C. Lenhardt and S. Shierry Nicholson. Cambridge, MA: MIT Press.

Habermas, J. (1992 [1988]). *Postmetaphysical Thinking*, trans. W. M. Hohengarten. Cambridge, MA: MIT Press.

Habermas, J. (1993 [1991]). *Justification and Application: Remarks on Discourse Ethics*, trans. C. Cronin. Cambridge, MA: MIT Press.

Habermas, J. (1996 [1992]). *Between Facts and Norms*, trans. W. Rehg. Cambridge, MA: MIT Press.

Habermas, J. (1998). *On the Pragmatics of Communication*, ed. M. Cooke. Cambridge, MA: MIT Press.

Habermas, J. (2003a [1999]). *Truth and Justification*, trans. C. Cronin. Cambridge, MA: MIT Press.

Habermas, J. (2003b [2001]). *The Future of Human Nature*, trans. W. Rehg et al. Cambridge: Polity.

Habermas, J. (2017 [2012]). *Postmetaphysical Thinking ll,* trans. C. Cronin. Cambridge: Polity.

Habermas, J. (2019). *Auch eine Geschichte der Philosophie,* vols. 1 & 2. Berlin: Suhrkamp.

Haraway, D. (2016). *Staying with the Trouble. Making Kin in the Chthulucene.* Durham, NC: Duke University Press.

Harney, S. and Moten, F. (2013). *The Undercommons. Fugitive Planning and Black Study.* New York: Minor Compositions.

Hartmann, S. (2019). *Wayward Lives, Beautiful Experiments: Intimate Histories of Social Upheaval.* New York: W. W. Norton.

Hartog, F. (2015 [2003]). *Regimes of Historicity: Presentism and Experiences of Time,* trans. S. Brown. New York: Columbia University Press.

Hegel, G. W. F. (2005 [1831]). *Philosophy of Right,* trans. S. W. Dyde. New York: Dover Philosophical Classics.

Hegel, G. W. F. (2018 [1807]). *The Phenomenology of Spirit,* trans. T. Pinkard and M. Baur. Cambridge: Cambridge University Press.

Heidegger, M. (1962 [1927]). *Being and Time,* trans. J. Macquarrie and E. Robinson. Oxford: Blackwell.

Hobbes, T. (2017 [1652]). *Leviathan.* London: Penguin Books.

Hofmannsthal, H. von (2005 [1902]). 'A Letter'. In *The Lord Chandos Letter: And Other Writings by Hugo Von Hofmannsthal,* trans. J. Rotenberg. New York: New York Review of Books Classics.

Honig, B. (2017). *Public Things. Democracy in Disrepair.* New York: Fordham University Press.

Honneth, A. (1994). 'The Social Dynamics of Disrespect: On the Location of Critical Theory Today', trans. J. Farrell. *Constellations* 1 (1): 255–69.

Honneth, A. (1995 [1992]). *The Struggle for Recognition. A Moral Grammar of Social Conflict,* trans. J. Anderson. Cambridge, MA: MIT Press.

Honneth, A. (2014 [2011]). *Freedom's Right. The Social Foundations of Democratic Life,* trans. J. Ganahl. New York: Columbia University Press.

Horkheimer, M. (1972). *Critical Theory. Selected Essays,* trans. M. O'Connell and others. New York: Continuum.

Horkheimer, M. (1988). 'Die gegenwärtige Lage der Sozialphilosophie und die Aufgaben eines Instituts für Sozialforschung'. *Gesammelte Schriften, Vol. 3: 1931–1936.* Frankfurt/Main: Fischer Verlag.

Horkheimer, M. (1992a). 'Traditionelle und kritische Theorie'. In Horkheimer, *Traditionelle und kritische Theorie. Fünf Aufsätze.* Frankfurt/Main: Fischer Verlag, pp. 205–59.

Horkheimer, M. (1992b). 'Nachtrag'. In Horkheimer, *Traditionelle und kritische Theorie. Fünf Aufsätze.* Frankfurt/Main: Fischer Verlag, pp. 261–9.

Horkheimer, M. (1993 [1931]). 'Materialism and Morality'. In Horkheimer, *Between Philosophy and Social Science: Selected Early Writings,* trans. G. F. Hunter, M. Kramer and J. Torpey. Cambridge: MA: MIT Press, pp. 85–117.

Horkheimer, M. (2018 [1931]). 'The State of Contemporary Social Philosophy and the Tasks of an Institute for Social Research', trans. J. C. Wagner. *Journal for Cultural Research* 22 (2): 113–21.

Horkheimer, M., and Adorno, T. W. (2002). *Dialectic of Enlightenment: Philosophical Fragments,* trans. E. Jephcott. Stanford, CA: Stanford University Press.

Imbert, C. (2009). 'On Anthropological Knowledge'. In B. Wiseman (ed.), *Cambridge Companion to Lévi-Strauss*. Cambridge: Cambridge University Press, pp. 118–38.

Iton, R. (2008). *In Search of the Black Fantastic: Politics and Popular Culture in the Post-Civil Rights Era*. Oxford: Oxford University Press.

Jaeggi, R. (2009). 'Was ist eine (gute) Institution?'. In R. Forst et al. (eds.), *Sozialphilosophie und Kritik*. Frankfurt/Main: Suhrkamp, pp. 528–44.

Jaeggi, R. (2014 [2005]). *Alienation*, trans. F. Neuhouser and A. E. Smith. New York: Columbia University Press.

Jaeggi, R. (2018 [2014]). *Critique of Forms of Life*, trans. C. Cronin. Cambridge, MA: Harvard University Press.

James, W. (1935 [1901–2]). *The Varieties of Human Experience. A Study of Human Nature*. London: Longman, Green and Co.

Jaspers, K. (1967 [1962]). *Philosophical Faith and Revelation*, trans. E. B. Ashton. London: Collins.

Jaspers, K. and R. Bultmann (2005 [1954]). *Myth and Christianity. An Inquiry into the Possibility of Religion without Myth*, trans. N. Gutermann. Introduction by R. J. Hoffman. New York: Prometheus Books.

Jay, M. (2012). Review of T. W. Adorno and M. Horkheimer, *Towards a New Manifesto*. *Notre Dame Philosophical Reviews*. https://ndpr.nd.edu/reviews/towards-a-new-manifesto/.

Jay, M. (2020). *Splinters in Your Eye. Frankfurt School Provocations: Essays on the Frankfurt School*. London: Verso.

Jones, M. D. (2003). 'Politics, Process & (Jazz) Performance: Amiri Baraka's "It's Nation Time"'. *African American Review* 37 (2–3): 245–52.

Jullien, F. (1999 [1995]). *The Propensity of Things: Towards a History of Efficacy in China*, trans. J. Lloyd. Princeton, NJ: Princeton University Press.

Kant, I. (1798 [1784]). 'An Answer to the Question: What is Enlightenment?' https://www.marxists.org/reference/subject/ethics/kant/enlightenment.htm.

Kant, I. (1998 [1781/1787]). *Critique of Pure Reason*, trans. and ed. P. Guyer and A. W. Wood. Cambridge: Cambridge University Press.

Kimmerer, R. W. (2013). *Braiding Sweetgrass. Indigenous Wisdom, Scientific Knowledge and the Teaching of Plants*. Minneapolis, MN: Milkweed Editions.

Koselleck, R. (2004 [1979]). *Futures Past: On the Semantics of Historical Time*, trans. K. Tribe. New York: Columbia University Press.

Krause, S. (2020). 'Environmental Domination'. *Political Theory* 48 (4): 443–68.

Krause, S. (2023). *Eco-Emancipation: An Earthly Politics of Freedom*. Princeton, NJ: Princeton University Press.

Laclau, E. (1996). 'The Death and Resurrection of the Theory of Ideology', *Journal of Political Ideologies* 1 (3): 202–20.

Laclau, E. (2000). 'Identity and Hegemony: The Role of Universality in the Constitution of Political Logics'. In J. Butler, E. Laclau and S. Žižek, *Contingency, Hegemony, Universality*. London: Verso, pp. 44–89.

Lafont, C. (2017). 'Citizens in Robes: The Place of Religion in Constitutional Democracies'. *Philosophy & Social Criticism* 43 (4–5): 453–64.

Lafont, C. (2019). *Democracy without Shortcuts: A Participatory Conception of Deliberative Democracy*. Oxford: Oxford University Press.

Lafont, C. (2023). 'The Return of the Critique of Ideologies'. *Constellations* 30: 390–4.

Landemore, H. (2020). *Open Democracy: Reinventing Popular Rule for the Twenty-First Century*. Princeton, NJ: Princeton University Press.

Lang, A. F. (2017). 'Global Constituent Power Protests and Human Rights'. In A. Hehir and R. W. Murray (eds.), *Protecting Human Rights in the 21st Century*. London: Rowman & Littlefield, pp. 19–33.

Lara, M. P. (2020). *Beyond the Public Sphere: Film and the Feminist Imaginary*. Evanston, IL: Northwestern University Press.

Latour, B. (2004). 'Whose Cosmos, Which Cosmopolitics? Comments on the Peace Terms of Ulrich Beck'. *Common Knowledge* 10 (3): 450–62.

Latour, B. (2018 [2017]). *Down to Earth. Politics in the New Climatic Regime*, trans. C. Porter. Cambridge: Polity.

Lefort, C. (1988 [1986]). *Democracy and Political Theory*, trans. D. Macey. Cambridge: Polity.

Lightwala O. and Garton Stanley, S. (2023). *Manifesto for Now*. https://manifestofornow.com/.

Loewenstein, K. (1937). 'Militant Democracy and Fundamental Rights'. *The American Political Science Review* 31 (3): 417–32.

Loick, D. (2018). 'On the Politics of Forms of Life'. In A. Allen and E. Mendieta (eds.), *From Alienation to Forms of Life. The Critical Theory of Rahel Jaeggi*. University Park, PA: Penn State University Press, pp. 119–36.

Lugones, M. (1987). 'Playfulness, "World"-Travelling, and Loving Perception'. *Hypatia* 2 (2): 3–19.

Lukács, G. (1972 [1923]). *History and Class Consciousness*, trans. R. Livingstone. Cambridge, MA: MIT Press.

Maguire, J. (2009 [1978]). *Marx's Theory of Politics*. Cambridge: Cambridge University Press.

Malcolm X and Haley, A. (1999 [1965]). *The Autobiography of Malcolm X as Told to Alex Haley*. New York: Random House.

Malm, A. (2018). 'Revolutionary Strategy in a Warming World'. *Climate & Capitalism*. https://climateandcapitalism.com/2018/03/17/malm-revolutionary-strategy/.

Malm, A. (2020). *Corona, Climate, Chronic Emergency: War Communism in the Twenty-First Century*. London: Verso.

Marcuse, H. (1968 [1937]). 'The Affirmative Character of Culture'. In Marcuse *Negations: Essays in Critical Theory*, trans. J. Shapiro. Boston, MA: Beacon Press, 88–113.

Marcuse, H. (1979 [1977]). *The Aesthetic Dimension: Toward a Critique of Marxist Aesthetics*. Boston, MA: Beacon Press.

Marcuse, H. (1991 [1964]). *One Dimensional Man: Studies in the Ideology of Advanced Industrial Society*, 2nd edn. Boston, MA: Beacon Press.

Marcuse, H. (2008 [1936]). *A Study on Authority*, trans. Joris de Bres. London: Verso.

Martin, N. (2021 [2019]). *In the Eye of the Wild*, trans. S. R. Lewis. New York: New York Review of Books.

Martín Alcoff, L. (2022). 'Extractivist Epistemologies'. *Tapuya: Latin American Science, Technology and Society* 5 (1). https://doi.org/10.1080/25729861.2022.2127231.

Marx, K. (1975 [1843]). 'Letters to Ruge'. In *Karl Marx: Early Writings*, trans. T. Nairn with an Introduction by L. Colletti. London: Penguin Books, pp. 109–209.

Marx, K. (2000a [1843]). 'On the Jewish Question'. In *Karl Marx: Selected Writings*, ed. D. McLellan. Oxford: Oxford University Press, pp. 46–70.

Marx, K. (2000b [1843]). 'Critique of Hegel's Philosophy of Right'. In *Karl Marx: Selected Writings*, ed. D. McLellan. Oxford: Oxford University Press, pp. 32–42.

Marx, K. (2000c [1844]). 'Alienated Labour'. In *Karl Marx: Selected Writings*, ed. D. McLellan. Oxford: Oxford University Press, pp. 85–95.

Marx, K. (2000d [1844]). 'Towards a Critique of Hegel's *Philosophy of Right*. Introduction'. In *Karl Marx: Selected Writings*, ed. D. McLellan. Oxford: Oxford University Press, pp. 71–82.

Marx, K. (2000e [1845]). 'Theses on Feuerbach'. In *Karl Marx: Selected Writings*, ed. D. McLellan. Oxford: Oxford University Press, pp. 171–74.

Marx, K. (2000f [1875]). 'Critique of the Gotha Program'. In *Karl Marx: Selected Writings*, ed. D. McLellan. Oxford: Oxford University Press, pp. 610–16.

Marx, K. and Engels, F. (1967 [1848]). *The Communist Manifesto*. Introduction and notes by A. J. P. Taylor. Harmondsworth: Penguin.

Mattingly, C. (2025). 'Identity Perplexity, Stigma, and Social Critique: Critical Phenomenology with an Errant Twist'. *Anthropological Theory* 25 (3): 338–64.

Maus, I. (2011). *Über Volkssouveränität. Elemente einer Demokratietheorie*. Berlin: Suhrkamp.

Mauss, M. (2016). *The Gift: Expanded Edition*, trans. J. Guyer. Chicago, IL: Hau Books.

McCarthy, T. (1994 [1990]). 'The Critique of Impure Reason: Foucault and the Frankfurt School'. In M. Kelly (ed.), *Critique and Power: Recasting the Foucault/Habermas Debate*. Cambridge, MA: MIT Press, pp. 243–82.

McNay, L. (2022). *The Gender of Critical Theory: On the Experiential Grounds of Critique*. Oxford: Oxford University Press.

Medina, J. (2012), The *Epistemology of Resistance: Gender and Racial Oppression, Epistemic Injustice and the Social Imagination*. Oxford: Oxford University Press.

Meijer, M. (2017). 'Does Charles Taylor Have a Nietzsche Problem?' *Constellations* 24: 372–86.

Meijer, M. (2019). 'Ontological Gaps: Retrieving Charles Taylor's Realism'. *Philosophy Today* 63 (1): 155–73.

Mendieta, E. (ed.) (2002). *Religion and Rationality. Essays on Reason, God, and Modernity*. Cambridge: Polity.

Menke, C. (2017). *Kraft. Ein Grundbegriff ästhetischer Anthropologie*. Berlin: Suhrkamp.

Menke, C. (2020 [2015]). *Critique of Rights*, trans. C. Turner. Cambridge: Polity.

Menke, C. (2022). *Theorie der Befreiung*. Berlin: Suhrkamp.

Mommsen, T. (1888). *Römisches Staatsrecht*, Vol. 3, Part 2. Leipzig.

Montesquieu, Baron de (1989 [1748]). *The Spirit of the Laws*, trans. and ed. A. M. Cohler, B. C. Miller and H. S. Stone. Cambridge: Cambridge University Press.

Moten, F. (2003). *In the Break: The Aesthetics of the Black Radical Tradition*. Minneapolis: University of Minnesota Press.

Moten, F. (2018). *Stolen Life*. Durham, NC: Duke University Press.

Narayan, U. (1997). *Dislocating Cultures: Identities, Traditions and Third World Feminism*. London: Routledge.

Nascimento, B. (2024). 'Dissent beyond the Rule of Law: Civil Disobedience as a Political Praxis'. PhD thesis, Belo Horizonte.

Näsström, S. (2021). *The Spirit of Democracy: Corruption, Disintegration, Renewal.* Oxford: Oxford University Press.

Neuhouser, F. (2003). *Foundations of Hegel's Social Theory: Actualizing Freedom.* Cambridge, MA: Harvard University Press.

Nguyen, C. Thi (2020). 'Echo Chambers and Epistemic Bubbles'. *Episteme* 17 (2): 141–61.

Niesen, P. (2017). 'Constituent Power in Global Constitutionalism'. In A. Lang and A. Wiener (eds.), *Handbook on Global Constitutionalism.* Cheltenham: Edward Elgar, pp. 222–33.

Niesen, P. (2019). 'Reframing Civil Disobedience: Constituent power as a Language of Transnational Protest'. *Journal of International Political Theory* 15 (1): 31–48.

Nitzschner, P. (2024). 'Defending What Is Yet to Come: Towards a Critical Theory of Democratic Defense'. Dissertation, Department of Political Science, Lund University.

Nitzschner, P. (2025). 'On Militant Democracy's Institutional Conservatism'. *Philosophy and Social Criticism* 51 (1): 29–49.

Norval, A. (2000). 'The Things We Do with Words: Contemporary Approaches to the Analysis of Ideology' (review essay). *British Journal of Political Science* 30: 313–46.

Okiji, F. (2018). *Jazz as Critique: Adorno and Black Experience Revisited.* Stanford, CA: Stanford University Press.

Pensky, M. (2004). 'Method and Time: Benjamin's Dialectical Images'. In D. S. Ferris (ed.), *The Cambridge Companion to Walter Benjamin.* Cambridge: Cambridge University Press, pp. 177–98.

Pettit, P. (1999). *Republicanism: A Theory of Freedom and Government.* Oxford: Oxford University Press.

Pettit, P. (2012). *On the People's Terms: A Republican Theory and Model of Democracy.* New York: Cambridge University Press.

Pettit, P. (2019). 'The General Will, the Common Good, and a Democracy of Standards'. In Y. Elazar and G. Rousselière (eds.), *Republicanism and the Future of Democracy.* New York: Cambridge University Press, pp. 13–36.

Popova, M. (2019). *Figuring.* New York: Pantheon Books

Rawls, J. (1996 [1993]). *Political Liberalism.* New York. Columbia University Press.

Ricoeur, P. (1996). 'Memory, Forgetfulness, and History'. *Iyyun: The Jerusalem Philosophical Quarterly* 45: 13–24.

Robbins, J. (2020). *Theology and the Anthropology of Christian Life.* Oxford: Oxford University Press.

Rorty, R. (1992 [1967]). *The Linguistic Turn. Essays in Philosophical Method.* Chicago, IL: Chicago University Press.

Rosa, H. (2019a [2016]). *Resonance: A Sociology of our Relationship to the World,* trans. J. C. Wagner. Cambridge: Polity.

Rosa, H. (2019b). *Unverfügbarkeit. Eine Soziologie der Weltbeziehungen.* Berlin: Suhrkamp.

Rosa, H. (2020a [2019]). *The Uncontrollability of the World,* trans. J. C. Wagner. Cambridge: Polity.

Rosa, H. (2020b). 'Beethoven, the Sailor, the Boy and the Nazi: A Reply to My Critics'. *Journal of Political Power* 13 (3): 397–413.

Rosen, M. (1996). *On Voluntary Servitude: False Consciousness and the Theory of Ideology.* Cambridge: Polity.

Saar, M. (2007). *Genealogie als Kritik. Geschichte und Theorie des Subjekts nach Nietzsche und Foucault*. Frankfurt/Main: Campus Verlag.

Sadek, K. (2023). 'Self-transformation in the Anthropocene'. *Constellations* 30 (2): 141–52.

Schupmann, B. (2024). *Democracy Despite Itself: Liberal Constitutionalism and Militant Democracy*. Oxford: Oxford University Press.

Sieyès, E. (2003 [1789]). *Political Writings: Including the Debates between Sieyes and Tom Paine in 1791*, ed. M. Sonenscher. Indianapolis, IN: Hackett Publishing.

Sorel, G. (1975 [1906]). *Reflections on Violence*, trans. T. E. Hulme. New York: AMS Press.

Spivak, G. C. (1996 [1994]). 'Translator's Preface and Afterword to Mahasweta Devi, *Imaginary Maps*'. In D. Landry and G. MacLean (eds.), *The Spivak Reader. Selected Works of Gayatri Chakravorty Spivak*. New York: Routledge, pp. 267–86.

Stengers, I. (2005a). 'The Cosmopolitical Proposal'. In B. Latour and P. Weibel (eds.), *Making Things Public: Atmospheres of Democracy*. Cambridge, MA: MIT Press, pp. 994–1003.

Stengers, I. (2018). *Is Another Science Possible? Manifesto for a Slow Science*. Oxford: Wiley.

Stojanov, K. (2017). *Education, Self-Consciousness and Social Action: Bildung as a Neo-Hegelian Concept*. New York: Routledge.

Strathern, M. (2020). *Relations. An Anthropological Account*. Durham, NC: Duke University Press.

Susen, S. (2020). 'The Resonance of Resonance: Critical Theory as a Sociology of World-Relations?'. *International Journal of Politics, Culture, and Society* 33 (3): 309–44.

Susen, S. (2024). *Humanity and Uncontrollability: Reflections on Hartmut Rosa's Critical Theory*. Switzerland: Springer Nature.

Taylor, C. (1989). *Sources of the Self: The Making of Modern Identity*. Cambridge: Cambridge University Press.

Taylor, C. (2007). *A Secular Age*. Cambridge, MA: Belknap Press.

Taylor, C. (2011). 'Disenchantment–Reenchantment'. In Taylor, *Dilemmas and Connections*. Cambridge, MA: Harvard University Press, pp. 287–302.

The Invisible Committee (2017). *Now*. Cambridge, MA: MIT Press.

Todd, J. (2024). 'Does Identity Change Matter? Everyday Agency, Moral Authority and Generational Cascades in the Transformation of Groupness after Conflict'. *Theory and Society* 53: 571–96.

Tsing, A. (2015). *The Mushroom at the End of the World: On the Possibility of Life in Capitalist Ruins*. Princeton, NJ: Princeton University Press.

Vetlesen, A. (2023). 'Ethics in the Anthropocene: the Case for Questioning Anthropocentrism'. *Constellations* 30 (2): 153–61.

Von Redecker, E. (2021). *Praxis and Revolution: A Theory of Social Transformation*, trans. L. Duggan. New York: Columbia University Press.

Walser, M. (1987 [1978]). *A Runaway Horse*, trans. L. Vennewitz. New York: Henry Holt.

Weber, M. (1921). *Economy and Society*. https://archive.org/details/MaxWeber EconomyAndSociety.

Wellmer, A. (1985b). 'Adorno, Anwalt des Nicht-Identischen. Eine Einführung'. In *Zur Dialektik von Moderne und Postmoderne*. Frankfurt/Main: Suhrkamp, pp. 135–66.

Wesche, T. (2023). *Die Rechte der Natur*. Berlin: Suhrkamp.

Young, I. M. (1990). *Justice and the Politics of Difference*. Princeton, NJ: Princeton University Press.

Zigon, J. (2024). *How Is It Between Us? Relational Ethics and Care of the World*. Chicago, IL: University of Chicago Press.

Index